THE WORLD'S WORST AIRCRAFT

James Gilbert

M & J HOBBS
in association with
MICHAEL JOSEPH

Also by James Gilbert

THE GREAT PLANES

First published in Great Britain
by M. & J. Hobbs Ltd
25 Bridge Street, Walton-on-Thames, Surrey
and
Michael Joseph Ltd
52 Bedford Square, London W.C.1.
1975

ISBN 0 7181 1269 5

Filmset and printed by
BAS Printers Limited, Wallop, Hampshire
and bound by Dorstel Press, Harlow

THE WORLD'S WORST AIRCRAFT

William Henson, a Somerset lace maker, designed and patented this aerial steam carriage in the 1840s. He made a 20-foot model of it, but it wouldn't leave the ground.

'There is a march of science;
but who shall beat the drums for its retreat?'

Charles Lamb, 1830

Contents

Acknowledgements

My gratitude to these authors, publishers and literary agents for permission to quote from their works in my book: *Aviation: an historical survey* by Charles H. Gibbs-Smith, published by HMSO; *Aircraft Annual 1973*, edited by John W. R. Taylor, published by Ian Allan Ltd; *The Challenging Skies* by C. R. Roseberry, published by Doubleday & Co. Inc; *The Old Flying Days* by Major C. C. Turner, published by Sampson (Curtis Brown Ltd, literary agents); *Skyhooks* by Kurt R. Stehling and William Beller, published by Doubleday & Co. Inc; *The German Giants* by G. W. Haddow and Peter M. Grosz, published by Putnam & Co; *The World of Wings and Things* by A. V. Roe, published by Hurst and Blackett; *Slide Rule* by Nevil Shute, published by William Heinemann Ltd (acknowledging also A. P. Watt & Son, literary agents, and William Morrow & Co. Inc); *My Zeppelins* by Hugo Eckener, published by Putnam; *The Story of the British Light Aeroplane* by Terence Boughton, published by John Murray (Publishers) Ltd; *The Flying Flea* by Henri Mignet, published by the Air League; *Baa Baa Blacksheep* by Pappy Boyington, published by Putnam & Co; *Zero Fighter* by Martin Caidin, published by E. P. Dutton and Co. Inc (Laurence Pollinger Ltd, author's agents); *Fighter over Finland* by Eino Luukkanen, published by Macdonald; *One of Our Pilots is Safe* by William Simpson, published by Hamish Hamilton, copyright William Simpson 1942; *Duel of Eagles* by Peter Townsend, published by George Weidenfeld & Nicolson Ltd; *Test Pilot at War* by H. A. Taylor, published by Ian Allan Ltd; *Strike Hard, Strike Sure* by Ralph Barker, published by Chatto & Windus Ltd; *Warplanes of the Third Reich* by William Green, *Rocket Fighter* by Mano Ziegler and *Sent Flying* by Bill Pegg, all published by Macdonald; *Airlines of the United States* by R. E. G. Davies and *British Flying Boats and Amphibians* by G. R. Duval, both published by Putnam & Co; an article, *How a Great Corporation Got out of Control* by Richard Austen Smith, in *Fortune* magazine (Time/Life); and an article by Dr Wilkie in the *New Scientist* magazine.

I'd also like to acknowledge that the chapter on man-powered flight first appeared in *Air Progress* magazine, and that on the Gee Bee racers in *Air Progress World's Great Aircraft*, both published by Petersen Publishing Co.

Particularly generous help in preparing this book was received from John Blake, librarian of the Royal Aero Club, and John W. R. Taylor, editor of *Jane's All the World's Aircraft*.

The author acknowledges these sources of illustrations:

Plates 2, 12, 13 from the Radio Times Hulton Picture Library; plates 5, 47, 48, 59, 61 from *Flight International*; plates 11, 12, 19, 20, 44, 45, 46 from Musée de l'Air; plates 14, 15, 16, 17, 18 from *Aircraft 73* ed. J. W. R. Taylor. Published by Ian Allen Limited. Three-view by Peter Lewis; plates 19, 21, 22, 23, 25, 29, 30, 31, 32, 33, 34, 35, 55, 66, 67, 68, 70, 71, 74 from the Imperial War Museum; plate 9 from National Motor Museum; plate 24 from *The German Giants*, published by Putnam & Co.; plates 26, 27, 28 from *Air Enthusiast Magazine*; plate 36 from Royal Aeronautical Society; plates 37, 39, 40, 42, 43, 65 from the Smithsonian Institution; plates 38, 41 from Pratt and Whitney; plate 40 from *Air Progress—World's Great Aircraft*—Peterson; plates 49, 50, 51, 52 from Novosti Press Agency; plates 54, 56, 57, 58 from Dornier-werke; plate 60 from *Aeroplane Monthly*; plate 63 from Harold Best-Devereux; plate 64 from Keystone Press Agency; plates 72, 73, 76, 77 Heinkel Zwilling, Messerchmitt archives; plates 79, 80 from The Bristol Aeroplane Company; plate 81 from Vickers Ltd.; plates 82, 84 from British Hovercraft Corporation; plates 85, 86 from Maurice Brennan; plates 87, 88 from General Dynamics Corporation; plate 89, 93 John W. R. Taylor; plate 90 from the *Man Powered Flight* by Keith Sherwin, Model and Allied Publications Ltd.

Introduction

This book was conceived one day in America when I flew the first really bad aircraft I'd ever encountered. A real beast of an aeroplane is a rarity nowadays, since all civil aircraft must be 'certificated' by government airworthiness authorities before they can be offered for sale, and this certification effectively weeds out most of the rubbish. But amateur-designed, home-built aircraft still escape the full measure of this official control, and it was one of these home-brewed contraptions that first showed me just how bad an aeroplane might be. This one was exceedingly noisy and uncomfortable, and seemed to be trying to roll on to its back if only you would let it; it was unstable in pitch, and it weaved from left to right in yaw. When you lowered the flaps for landing, it grew worse still. But what an *interesting* machine, I thought, from the handling point-of-view. And why not a whole book—the world's very first—devoted just to thoroughly bad aircraft?

There is, of course, no shortage of books about the famous, the successful, the great aircraft (I've even written one myself). But there is as much to be learned from the rotten ones. So here is a selection of interesting aeronautical failures. Not all of them, let me quickly say, were disastrous purely as flying machines: some were simply military types that flew all right, but in combat caused more havoc to their own crews than to the enemy. Some were management rather than engineering failures, among them some commercial transports that proved ludicrously uncommercial. Some were the extravagant fantasies of genuine nut-cases; or of politicians secure in the certainty that their own term of office would run out before the public purse did. Not all my 'worst aircraft' came to tragic ends, either; some were more farcical than tragic. A few, such as the Zeppelins, the Komet rocket fighter, and the Convair jetliners, were technological near-misses that came close to real success.

Above all, this book shows that pilots as a breed are brave men; there's no aircraft so unlikely that someone cannot be found to try and fly it. The English aeronautical experimenter Sir George Cayley prophesied in 1846 that 'a hundred necks have to be broken before all the sources of accident can be ascertained and guarded against'. Prophetic, but a sad under-estimate.

1. *Above, left:* Thomas Moy, a patent agent, built this steam-powered model aircraft, a fine piece of Victorian ironmongery, in 1875. Running tethered around a fountain at the Crystal Palace, it is supposed to have lifted a few inches. *Above, right:* an early example of the bedstead approach to flying was this French 'auto aviator' of 1900. It never lifted an inch. *Below:* Clement Ader, a French electrical engineer, built this steam-powered bat-winged monstrosity in 1890. Unstable and uncontrollable, it may still have been the first manned aircraft to take off under its own power.

1

The Fore-runners

'The idea of human flight has engaged the waking and sleeping thoughts of men from the time when they developed visual imagination and began to regard the birds with envy,' says Charles Gibbs-Smith, in *Aviation*. 'With the envy came the ambition to emulate. For flying has never appeared to its devotees as a mere method of transportation, faster or more convenient than travel by land or sea; nor was it finally achieved by any pressure of economic need. Aviation has drawn its strength from an appeal to the emotions, an appeal to the longing for escape, or to the desire for exhilaration and power . . . "O that I had wings like a dove" wrote the Psalmist, "for then I would fly away and be at rest."'

The first dreams of flight imagined winged men, angels, *divine* beings of necessity since no merely *mortal* man ever showed any signs of being able to grow wings. Perhaps the Jewish seraphim were the first to be reported: 'I saw the Lord sitting upon a throne, high and lifted up and his train filled the temple,' wrote the Prophet Isaiah. 'Above it stood the seraphim; each one had six wings; with twain he covered his face, and with twain he covered his feet, and with twain he did fly.' The prophet Ezekiel managed to get the number of wings per seraph down to four in his visions; opinion soon crystalised that two would be enough, probably extensions of the shoulderblades—pretty wing-like bones in themselves:

> Fearless, I direct my flight
> To the vast Olympian height;
> Thence at random, I repair,
> Wafted in the whirling air;
> With an eddy wild, and strong,
> Over all the field of song.
> Let me live and let me sing,
> Like a bird upon the wing.
> (Aristophanes, *The Birds*.)

The dream of becoming an angel had its limitations; you had to be already dead and to have led a largely blameless (or maybe supremely evil) life before you died. Even clerics were prepared to consider a wider range of possibilities. John Wilkins, Bishop of Chester, and a founder member of the Royal Society, writing in 1648 said:

'There are four severall ways whereby this flying in the air, hath been or may be attempted. Two of them by the strength of other things, and two of them by our owne strength.

1. By Spirits or Angels.
2. By the help of Fowls.
3. By Wings fastened immediately to the body.
4. By a flying Chariot

'1. For the first, we read of divers that have passed swiftly in the air, by the help of Spirits and Angels, whether good Angels, as Elias was carried into Heaven in a fiery Chariot: as Philip was conveyed to Azotus and Habbacuck from Jewry to Babylon and back again immediately: Or by evill Angels, as our Saviour was carried by the Devill to the top of a high mountain, and to the pinnacle of the Temple. Thus witches are commonly related to passe unto their usual meetings in some remote places; and as they doe fell windes unto Mariners, so likewise are they sometimes hired to carry men speedily through the open air. Acosta affirms that such kind of passages are usuall amongst divers Sorcerers with the Indians at this day.

'2. There are others who have conjectured a possibility of being conveyed through the air by the help of Fowls; to which purpose that fiction of the Ganzas is the most pleasant and probable. They are supposed to be great fowl of a strong and lasting flight, and easily tamable. Divers of which may be so brought up as to join together in carrying the weight of a man, so as each of them shall partake his proportionable share of the burden; and the person that is carried may be certain reins direct and steer them in their courses. However this may seem a strange proposall, yet it is not certainly more improbable than many other arts, wherein the industry of ingenious men hath instructed these brute creatures.

'3. 'Tis the more obvious and common opinion that this (flying) may be effected by wings fastened immediately to the body, this coming nearest to the imitation of nature, which should be observed in such attempts as these. This is that way which Fredericus Hermannus in his little discourse *de Arte volandi* doth onely mention and insist upon. And if we may trust credible story, it hathe been frequently attempted not without some successe.

''Tis related of a certaine English Munk called Elmerus, about the Confessor's time, that he did by such wings fly from a Tower above a furlong; and so another from S. Mark's steeple in Venice; and another at Norinberge; and Busbequins speaks of a Turk in Constantinople, who attempted something this way. M. Burton mentioning this quotation, doth beleeve that some new-fangled wit ('tis his cynical phrase) will sometime or other find out this art. Though the truth is most of these Artists did unfortunately miscarry by falling down and breaking their arms or legs, yet that may be imputed to their want of experience, and too much fear, which must needs possesse men in such dangerous and strange attempts.

'4. But the fourth and last way seems unto me altogether as probable and much more useful than any of the rest. And that is by a flying Chariot, which may be so contrived as to carry a man within it; and though the strength of a spring might be serviceable for the motion of this engine, yet it were better to have it assisted by the labour of some intelligent mover as the heavenly orbs are supposed to be turned. And therefore if it were made big enough to carry sundry persons together then each of them in their severall turns might successively labour in the causing of this motion.

2. An early tower jumper was 'the flying tailor of Ulm', here being fished (with ridicule) from the river. At least his broken wings kept him afloat.

'The uses of such a Chariot may be various; besides the discoveries which might thereby be made in the lunary world; It would be serviceable also for the conveyance of a man to any remote place of this earth: as suppose to the Indies or Antipodes. For when once it was elevated for some few miles, so as to be above that orb of magnetick virtue, which is carried about by the earth's diurnall revolution, it might then be very easily and speedily directed to any particular place of this great globe.

'It would be one great advantage in this kind of travelling, that one should be perfectly freed from all inconveniences of ways or weather, not having any extremity of heat or cold, or tempests to molest him, this aethereall air being perpetually in an equal temper and calmnesse. The upper parts of the world are always quiet and serene, no winds and blustring there, they are these lower cloudy regions that are so full of tempests and combustion.'

Anyone who has ever flown through a thunderstorm, or blundered into clear air turbulence, will appreciate the error of the last statement but, by and large, Bishop Wilkins did some sturdy thinking there. The good bishop, being a man of peace, could only see serenity in aerial travel by means of flying chariots, but there were plenty of others able to envisage its military uses, notably a Jesuit father named Francesco Lana Terzi, writing in 1670:

'For who sees not, that no City can be secure against attack since our Ship may at any time be placed directly over it, and descending down may discharge Souldiers; the same would happen to private Houses, and Ships on the Sea; for our Ship descending out of the Air to the sails of Sea Ships, it may cut their ropes, yea without descending by casting Grapples, it may over-set them, till their men burn their Ships by artificial Fireworks and Fire-balls. And this they may do, not only to Ships but to great Buildings, Castles, Cities, with such security that they which caste these things down from a height out of Gunshot, cannot on the other side be offended by those from below.'

Strange that he didn't imagine the range of gunshot, or the power of firework rockets, being extended to reach up to such aerial bomber ships; or indeed that aerial fighter ships be developed for defence—but the remainder of his imagining was remarkably prescient of the horrors of strategic bombing, circa 1940.

But let's go back to Bishop Wilkins and his four methods. First, 'Spirits or Angels'. Says Charles Gibbs-Smith:

'Thus Egypt came to have her winged deities; Assyria her winged bulls; and Arabia her flying carpet, of mysterious origin. The Far East had not only many levitated beings and bird-gods, but flying chariots. . . . Classical Greece and Rome produced such familiar figures as the winged god Mercury, the winged horse Pegasus, and the flying chariot of Triptolemos. Then came the angels and *putti* of Christianity, the former—through countless thousands of pictures—providing a constant stimulus to airmindedness throughout the centuries, for cleric and layman alike.'

No one, so far as I know has ever made it aloft 'by the help of Fowls', notably due to the difficulty of co-ordinating the activities of the requisite number of tethered and presumably terrified birds. One supposed to have tried it was Kai Koos, an ancient King of Persia:

'To the King, it became a matter of great concern how he might be enabled to ascend the heavens, without wings; and for that purpose he consulted the astrologers, who presently suggested a way in which his desires might be successfully accomplished.

'They contrived to rob an Eagle's nest of its young, which they reared with great care, supplying them with invigorating food.

'A Frame of Aloes-wood was then prepared and at each of the four corners was fixed perpendicularly a javelin, surmounted on the point with the flesh of a goat. At each corner again one of the eagles was bound, and in the middle the king was seated with a goblet of wine before him. As soon as the eagles became hungry they endeavoured to get at the goat's flesh upon the javelins, and by flapping their wings, and flying upwards they quickly raised the throne from the ground. Hunger still pressing on them, and still being distant from their prey, they ascended higher and higher in the clouds, conveying the astonished king far beyond his own country. But after a long and fruitless exertion their strength failed them, and unable to keep their way the whole fabric came tumbling down from the sky, and fell upon a dreary solitude in the Kingdom of Chin:—where Kai Kaoos was left a prey to hunger, alone, and in utter despair.'

From the Shah-Nameh, the King's Name-book, written in the tenth century.

'A dreary solitude in the Kingdom of Chin' is the nicest description of the scene of an aircraft accident yet.

Another bishop, Francis Godwin, in 1718, imagined that twenty-five large geese might do the trick.

Bishop Wilkins' third approach, 'By Wings fastened immediately to the body', was a hoary old favourite, and one that has enjoyed a contemporary revival in the astonishing growth of the sport of hang-gliding. The old Latin legend of Daedalus and Icarus is its best-known manifestation, too well-known for me to want to give it here. But there was even an ancient Brit who tried this approach: Bladud, supposedly King of Britain from 883 to 863 BC. Geoffrey of Monmouth remembered him in AD 1147:

Bathe was by Bladud to Perfection brought,
By Necromanticke Artes, to flye he sought:
As from a Towre he thought to scale the Sky,
He brake his necke, because he soared too high.

Percy Enderbie, writing in 1661, thought Bladud's structural failure had the same cause as Icarus's, or else he was simply confusing the two legends:

'He poised his body on the twin wings he had made, and hung suspended in the quivering air. Anon, smitten by a longing to gain the sky, he urged his course higher: the nearness

3. King Kai Koos of Persia tried to fly with tethered eagles. Legend says he crashed.

of the sun's swift rays softened the perfumed wax that served to bind the wings upon him. An instant, and the wax melted, the arms he moved were now bare of wings: there was nothing to help him, and he had no longer any leverage upon the air. And so, destitute of help, he falls headlong, a just reward for his temerity, and breaks his neck.'

At least it was quick. And isn't 'quivering air' a nice description of gusty turbulence?

Wise tower-jumpers worked up to their actual tower by degrees, as did Sieur Bernier in this 1679 account by Robert Hooke:

'He began his Tryals first by springing out himself from a Stool, then from the top of a Table, then from a pretty high Window, a second story, and at last from a Garret, whence' (says Hooke, and I don't believe a bit of it) 'he flew over the houses of the Neighbours; practising thus with it little by little, till he had brought it to the perfection it now hath.'

The satirist Joseph Addison in 1713 envisaged the eventual success of aviation ushering in an era of permissiveness and sexual freedom and, while it is true that the two have somehow occurred together, it didn't quite happen as he imagined. He proclaimed it to be his intention 'to prevent any person from flying in my time, chiefly by reason of the evil influence it would have on love affairs. It would fill the world with innumerable immoralities, and give such occasions for intrigues as people cannot meet with who have nothing but legs to carry them. You should have a couple of lovers make a midnight assignation upon the top of the Monument, and see the cupola of St. Paul's covered with both sexes like the outside of a pigeon house. Nothing would be more frequent than to see a beau flying in at a garret window, or a gallant giving chase to his mistress, like a hawk after a lark.' Your modern hang-gliding enthusiast (in Britain at least) tends to be too chilled and weary and bruised after a day above the slopes to harbour strange licentious thoughts: a large scotch is more likely to be his dream.

The first successful hang-glides were not made until the 1890s—astonishingly late, when you consider how far advanced mankind was in other aspects of science. Even the Wright Brothers, when they made their first powered flights in 1903, allowed that this had been theoretically possible at least fifty years earlier, using a light steam engine or perhaps one of the first gas engines. But surely hang-gliding was possible *centuries* earlier? Look at a modern Rogallo hang-glider: it consists of three thin beams spread like a fan and held apart by a fourth as cross-bracing, the whole loosely covered with a nylon sail. True, they didn't have aluminium alloy tubes and nylon in earlier times, but they had bamboo, or spruce, and silk. Surely an effective hang-glider on this pattern was well within the constructional skills of, say, Columbus's shipwright in 1492? Or the ancient Chinese, centuries even before that? Why *did* it take so long? Perhaps because almost every experimenter slavishly copied the layout of a bird in building his device.

A bird, even when gliding, is highly unstable, using its eye and brain to make constant minute corrections to the set of its pinions and tail; a man-made copy of a bird could

4. The Wright Brothers began with gliders, with which they worked out how to make an aircraft controllable.

be made to fly, but would surely need gyros and a computer to give it artificial stability. And as for flapping wing propulsion, modern high-speed cameras have shown this to be not the simple motion it may look, but a complicated figure-of-eight pattern at the tips and something else again inboard.

Even if those early experimenters had mastered the motion, something called 'scale effect' meant they were wasting their time. Scale effect says that the power needed to drive a flying device increases hugely with its size. The power of animal muscle, however, does not even increase in proportion to the animal's size. Scale effect is the reason why a tiny humming-bird can hover, while an eagle can only soar. Poor man is really too feeble to fly at all by his own exertion—though he has lately just managed to (as you will see in the last chapter of this book). Flapping wing propulsion, however, is so inefficient that no man has yet flown this way by his own efforts.

Francis Rogallo is a NASA engineer who invented his Rogallo wing only recently, as a folding lift source that could be deployed from returning spacecraft to enable them to make steerable glide landings. It is true that nothing quite like it exists in nature; but there are some flying forms not too dissimilar, such as the wings of bats and the membranes of flying squirrels and lizards. The wheel does not exist in nature either, but man managed to work that out very early on. It is, I think, profoundly odd that no tower-jumping monk or sage managed to puzzle out a stable configuration for a hang-glider until less than a hundred years ago. A scaled-up paper dart would have been enough.

The tower-jumper, by the way, is still with us, even in this age of supersonics. It must be a psychological quirk, the overwhelming fantasy that overtakes these characters, for suddenly it seems they know how to fly, can fly, and without more ado must fly. So they fashion a crude set of bird-like wings (some acid-freaks even omit that precaution), ascend to some high place, face into the wind, and jump. (You see them occasionally still, in the centre pages of newspapers or on television news on quiet evenings.) One such man I knew had made a crude set of wings and attached them to his Raleigh three-speed bicycle. He cycled madly over the Sussex downs for months without rising so much as an inch above the turf.

Every library has books on the theory of aerodynamics and structures; every aviation magazine carries advertisements for sensible and proven hang-gliding kits, but no, these people prefer to toil away in blissful ignorance, down in the potting shed in a mess of glue and feathers.

But back, for the last time, to Bishop Wilkins. His fourth and last and 'as probable and much more useful way' was 'By a flying Chariot'. Another monk, Roger Bacon, had noted in 1250: 'It's possible to make Engines for flying, a man sitting in the midst whereof, by turning onely about an instrument, which moves artificial Wings made to beat the Aire, much after the fashion of a Bird's flight.' Bacon admitted, 'I never saw or know any who hath seen it, though I am exceedingly acquainted with a very prudent man, who hath invented the whole Artifice . . .' He never did say who! That was the trouble with those medieval sages: they stuck in their ivory towers, thinking and writing

5. Wings on your bicycle—every schoolboy's dream.

6. *Above, right:* Lilienthal made many flights with hang-gliders in the 1890s.

7. *Below:* modern Rogallo kites use weight-shifting for control—as did Lilienthal.

but never considering coming down and going into the workshop and getting their hands dirty and maybe learning something.

Even Leonardo da Vinci was the same: 'A bird is an instrument . . . which it is within the capacity of man to reproduce with all its movements', he wrote. And he filled his sketch books with drawings of ingenious, but quite impractical, ornithopters and helicopters. If only he had deigned to experiment, and learn from his errors, and experiment again. I suppose it was beneath the dignity of a sage to be in error.

There were philosophers, and there were artisans, but they belonged to different unions. Even Cayley, the Victorian country squire who *did* experiment and who came close to discovering the secrets of flight long before the Wrights, persuaded his coachman make the actual test runs. 'I was hired to drive, not to fly,' said the coachman, tendering his notice. The coachman's name is not recorded, but it is high time he received formal recognition from the Society of Experimental Test Pilots as the first of their kind. Perhaps it might take the form of an award in his name to their oldest and least bold member?

When the Wrights finally made man's first successful powered flights in 1903, it was

8. At the end of its fourth flight the original Wright *Flyer* dove into the sand, breaking its front booms.

by using propellers for propulsion, driven by a light-but-powerful gasoline engine; big light wings—far bigger in proportion than a bird's; and employing three-axis aerodynamic control through tilting elevators and rudders and twistable wing tips moved by levers through wires. They arrived at this format for an aeroplane through years of careful testing and experiment, even building their own wind tunnel along the way. None of their predecessors had so much as a fraction of their persistence and patience and intellectual humility. The Wrights were careful and excellent scientists, keeping voluminous notebooks and correspondence and taking photographs of their progress at every step. 'We saw,' they later wrote, 'that the calculations upon which all flying machines had been based were unreliable. . . . Truth and error were everywhere so intimately mixed as to be indistinguishable.' And if light engines were a fairly recent development, much of what they discovered to be necessary was not as new. There had been man-made propellers for six hundred years; there is a drawing of a windmill in a psalter written about 1290, and a sketch of a pull-string helicopter toy, clear in every detail, in a Flemish manuscript of about 1325.

'By a flying Chariot' said the Bishop: Lord knows, enough chariots were planned, drawn, proposed, and even built to fill a book—in fact they fill several books. All these chariots, prior to 1903, have just one thing in common: they couldn't fly. Perhaps the grandest, most magnificent of them all was William Henson's 'aerial steam carriage', named *Ariel*, designed in 1842. It was to have a cab a little like the prow of a ship, set on three iron wheels, a big 150-foot span wing of 4,500 square feet in area, a stabilising tail, but without control surfaces, and a 30 hp steam engine mounted in the cab driving two pusher propellers at the rear of the wings. Not too far off the mark.

Henson, a Somerset lace maker, had wild dreams of founding the world's first airline, with a fleet of his steam carriages flying to every outpost of the far-flung British empire. He filed patents for *Ariel*, and tried to promote an 'Aerial Transit Company'. He found, or maybe was found by, an ambitious publicity agent named Frederick Marriot who commissioned marvellous coloured engravings and other souvenirs showing an aerial steam carriage airline in full and glorious operation. He had these published all around the world, and they were a wild success. Then Henson built a little 20-foot span model of his *Ariel*, and took it up on the downs and tried to make it fly—but it wouldn't. He tried for two whole years, and still it wouldn't fly, so he abandoned it, took a wife, left Somerset and England and emigrated to America, an early forerunner of the 'brain drain'.

Mind you, even the Wrights' first *Flyer* was a most marginal aircraft. It had only just enough power to fly at all: its nominally 16 hp motor quickly came back to about 12 hp as it began to overheat. The booms holding its elevators and rudders were far too short, giving insufficient moment arm. Its front elevator format made it wildly unstable in pitch. The drive train to its twin contra-rotating propellers was complex and gave endless trouble; and its control system was a nightmare of confused thinking. But it flew—the first successful bad aircraft.

9. An Edwardian ascent by two gentlemen and a lady. For victuals, champagne and chicken sandwiches.

2

Balloonatics

Balloons are very silly aircraft: I mean, they can only go where the wind takes them. True you can make a balloon go up a bit or come down, but even in that one dimension your control is imperfect.

Yet balloons were the first aerial vehicles and, for more than a century, the only ones. The first balloon builders were two French papermakers, the Montgolfier brothers of Avignon. We today are used to the march of science being a headlong rush; but they proceeded curiously slowly with their marvellous invention—it was fully a decade after they began experimenting before a free manned flight was made. They used hot air for lift; indeed any hot air balloon was a 'Montgolfier' for the next century. Their success came at the time when the relationships between density, pressure, temperature and buoyancy in gases were first being worked out, and no doubt some other experimenter would soon have stumbled on the trick if they hadn't.

I suspect the hot air balloon might well have been discovered centuries before, were it not that there is a kind of reverse scale effect at work here: the lift developed by any balloon is proportional to its volume, which varies as something like the square of its surface area or the cube of its dimensions. As you make a balloon bigger, so the lift it develops increases far faster than the empty weight of the balloon's structure. But with a small balloon, such as an experimenter might start with, the lift is unlikely to be sufficient for the thing to fly at all. I have just spent all morning constructing small hot air balloons from that feather-light plastic film that dry cleaners return garments draped in—a modern material of a lightness unknown to earlier experimenters, yet it was not until lunchtime that I had any success and got a balloon to lift.

To make them, I first sealed with a smear of glue the hole in the film envelope through which the clothes hanger had projected. I then formed a neck at the bottom with Scotch tape, and inflated the balloon with hot air from an aerosol blow lamp. The first two balloons thus constructed wouldn't lift at all: it was only when the third caught fire around the neck—so that the paper neck I'd made burned and fell away, lightening the little balloon by some tiny fraction of an ounce—that it finally lifted off. The slowly-burning plastic provided a continued hot air supply as it climbed to a hundred feet, now burning merrily, and astonishing the neighbourhood cats—not to mention the neighbours who happily have been too polite to mention my hazardous experiments even in garden fence conversation unless I raised the subject first. (One of these neighbours teaches architecture, and admitted he'd had similar problems: he once set his class of students to making little hot air balloons of balsa and tissue paper, but even the lightest one they constructed was still too heavy to fly.)

This leads me to suspect that the Montgolfiers must have been supremely fine paper-makers, for it is on record that their first balloon was only 40 cubic feet in capacity—not much bigger than mine—yet it lifted clear to the ceiling. They quickly discovered the trick of making the thing as big as they could, for their second envelope had a capacity of 600 cubic feet. After ten years of experimenting, they had progressed as far as giving public exhibitions of unmanned hot air balloons. They had attracted the curiosity of the Paris Royal Academy of Sciences, to whom they showed that their balloons could lift nearly 500 pounds. When Louis XVI wanted a demonstration they added, hanging under the huge spherical envelope, a little wicker basket in which they placed a sheep, a rooster and a duck, who came to no harm. By now their balloons were rising as high as 7,000 feet and cover a couple of miles before descending to earth. One, tethered, had briefly raised eight men from the ground.

Their balloons were not the simple functional constructions that our plastic age might prefer, but were elaborately decorated. The one they finished on October 10th, 1783, was 'oval, its height 70 feet, its diameter 46 feet, and its capacity 60,000 feet. The upper part, embroidered with *fleur-de-lis*, was further ornamented with the twelve signs of the zodiac, worked in gold. The middle part bore the monogram of the King of France, alternating with figures of the sun, while the lower part was garnished with masks, garlands and spread-eagles. A circular gallery, made of osiers and festooned with draperies and other ornaments, was attached by a set of cords to the bottom of the structure.'

This was the first balloon planned to carry a man, albeit firmly tethered to the ground, for the Montgolfiers approached the concept of men actually flying with a good deal of 'if-God-had-intended' type timidity. Flying in the face of the Scriptures, they knew they were, and that was an age when if you were wicked, you *knew* you were going to hell. And as if to take their minds off the truly awful fires that might wait 'down below', the Montgolfiers had provided a wire grating under the balloon's mouth on to which its pilots could shovel and burn straw to maintain its lift once aloft.

The Montgolfiers' balloon experiments were proving of enormous interest to the idle public, but this time they announced in the newspapers that the approaching experiments were to be 'of a strictly scientific character, and as they would be only interesting to *savants*, would not afford amusement to the merely curious'. The explanation of this measure was that 'the firmness of nerve of those engaged in the work might have suffered from the enthusiastic cries of excited spectators'—which is not a problem that bothers most public entertainers.

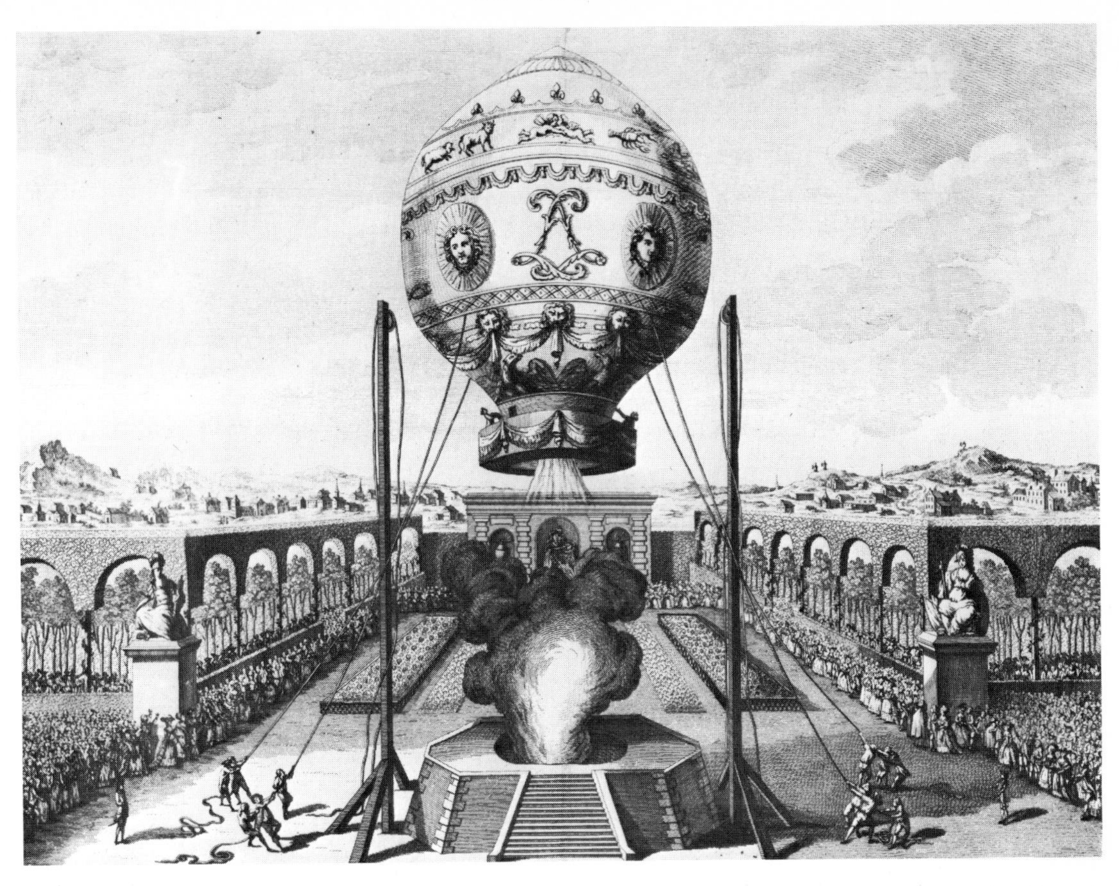

10. The first ascents were with the balloon well tethered. When asked if a free flight might not be allowed, Louis XVI suggested that this might be a novel way of disposing of convicted and worthless felons.

Nevertheless, or perhaps, inevitably, *tout Paris* came to gawp. A medical man named Pilâtre de Rozier made the first (tethered) ascents; for reasons unexplained the Montgolfiers themselves did not care to. Pilâtre de Rozier took, on various occasions, passengers. One of them was an infantry major and another was a nobleman named the Marquis d'Arlandes. This gentleman seems to have been chosen because of his social connections; he was able to ask the king if a free flight might not be allowed. 'Take two criminals who are under the death sentence and tie them to the balloon basket,' said His Majesty. 'That will be a novel way of disposing of worthless men.' D'Arlandes was acutely shocked and insisted that the glory of being the first to fly free should not be wasted on vile murderers. The king relented and d'Arlandes and de Rozier made the first free flight on November 21st, 1783.

In the manner of aircraft captains to this day de Rozier seems to have had a poor opinion of his co-pilot's attention to his duties. As they floated over Paris, the Marquis was overwhelmed with awe at the view. 'You are doing nothing, and the balloon is scarcely rising' rebuked de Rozier. D'Arlandes described it all most frankly in a letter to a friend afterwards: '"Pardon me", I answered, as I placed a bundle of straw upon the fire and slightly stirred it.' Then his attention wandered again to the spectacular view. '"If you look at the river in that fashion you will be likely to bathe in it soon" cried de Rozier. "Some fire, my dear friend, some fire!"' A little later: '"That river is very difficult to cross" I remarked to my companion. "So it seems" he answered, "but you are doing nothing. I suppose that is because you are braver than I and don't fear a tumble."'

D'Arlandes later justified himself by using a thoughtfully-provided damp sponge to extinguish several little fires that had started in the fabric of the balloon. They made a safe landing after sailing across most of Paris.

Soon after this, balloons filled with hydrogen became popular, the gas being easily generated by pouring oil of vitriol on to iron filings, and the controversy as to which was a better lifting medium, 'inflammable air' (hydrogen) or 'elastic air' (hot air) became a keen one. De Rozier thought the answer was simple—combine the two. He cobbled up a compound balloon, a 40-foot hydrogen balloon with a 10-foot hot air balloon attached underneath it. Now you and I may know that hydrogen is terrifyingly easily ignited, and explosive in any mixture with air of between 2% and 80%, but de Rozier seemingly didn't.

11. Pilâtre de Rozier (*left*) was the first balloonist to die, in a combination hydrogen and hot air balloon, while trying to cross the English Channel. 12. Madame Blanchard (*right*) was the second; her hydrogen balloon blew up during a night ascent with fireworks.

In 1785 he and a companion set off to cross the English Channel in this bomb: 'Scarcely a quarter of an hour had elapsed when, at a height of about 3,000 feet, the whole apparatus was discovered to be on fire. Its scattered fragments, with the unfortunate bodies of the aeronauts, fell to the ground near the sea-shore, about four miles from Boulogne. The aerial voyagers were instantly killed by the tremendous crash, and their bodies were of course awfully mangled.' So the world's first aerial voyager was also the first man to die while aerially voyaging.

The second was a lady: the widow of François Jean-Pierre Blanchard, an intrepid balloonatic who had appointed himself a kind of international ambassador of balloonacy, making the first ascents in Germany, Poland, Vienna, and the USA—where George Washington came to see him fly, and allowed him a 15-gun salute. But this ascent had cost Blanchard $2,000 expenses, and he had only been able to collect $400 from selling tickets to view the ascent, plus another $263 by passing his hat around the crowd outside. So he returned to Europe, disgruntled. Blanchard died naturally at sixty, in such poverty and depression that his last suggestion to his wife was that she had only the choice of hanging herself or drowning herself, since he had nothing to leave her.

Madame Blanchard, once widowed, found 'that she was not inclined to accept either alternative, instead of this she resolved to adopt her husband's profession, which she did with great success.' She made half a hundred ascensions, the last being a night extravaganza with fireworks, which predictably blew up the hydrogen-filled balloon. 'Madame Blanchard was thrown out and fell upon the roofs, from the roofs to the ground, and was instantly killed.'

So were many others down the years, for there were no airworthiness certificates required on balloons, nor any test in pilot skills and hydrogen handling demanded of balloonists. Any nut could try it, and many did, for although the costs were staggering, so were the profits that could be made from charging spectators, and besides, what food for the ego! Typical in an extreme way was a circus high-wire artiste named Washington H. Donaldson who made a spectacular ascent over Reading, Pennsylvania, in 1871 in a balloon bearing a circus trapeze. Once aloft, and suitably dressed in tights, he 'suddenly threw himself backward and fell, catching with his toes on the bar. That sent a thrill through the crowd, but with another spring he was standing up on the bar; and then followed one feat after another, hanging by one hand, one foot, by the back of his head, etc., until the blood ceased to curdle in the veins of the awestruck crowd, and they gave vent to their feelings in cheer after cheer. His glittering dress sparkled in the sun long after his outline was lost to the naked eye, and the shower of pamphlets he circulated, falling, gleamed like mirrors dazzling in the strong light.'

Donaldson was quickly hired by P. T. Barnum, who, though ignorant of ballooning, certainly appreciated showmanship. Donaldson was 'searching constantly for something new to spice up his act', but who it was that hit on the idea of the world's first aerial wedding I know not. Bride and groom were both members of Barnum's circus, and the wedding took place at dusk one warm evening in October. 'Both moon and sun were visible; the latter sinking round and lurid, to the west; the former rising pale, crescent-shaped, from the eastern hills. A lovelier wedding hour never dawned on a happy bride, and such a bonnier bride never welcomed it . . .' Donaldson was 'ready promptly, dressed to kill, and with bridal favors'; no mere bride was going to upstage *him*, and certainly not in his own balloon.

The balloon itself was also extravagantly decorated, the band played Mendelssohn's wedding march, and five thousand watched from below while the wedding party of seven went aloft. 'The richly decorated aerial ship rose as gently, as gracefully, as beautiful as a child's soap bubble, and ascended in a direct perpendicular line, while tens of thousands of throats shot up their plaudits.' After ten minutes, a small parachute was thrown out to announce that 'the nuptial ceremony had been completed', and the preacher proclaimed that as marriage was not an earthly but a heavenly institution, it was most fitting that its solemnization should be celebrated far above earth.

Hot air ballooning fell quickly out of favour, but hydrogen ballooning enjoyed a long popularity, either as a showman's stunt or as a thrilling pastime for the rich and bold. It was always very expensive, or no doubt would have been more popular still. Those who couldn't afford to do it could always watch, or read accounts of the joys of ballooning, such as the vivid description which follows—the work of Major C. C. Turner, an Edwardian Englishman who was perhaps the world's first modern 'air correspondent'. This account dates not long before the First World War:

'I am alone in a very small balloon over Surrey on the last day of a beautiful May. Light is the wind . . . There is scarcely a cloud in the sky. The sun is hot and the balloon, being one of gold-beater's skin inflated with hydrogen, is "lively" . . . The basket is quite tiny; two men in it would be a crowd . . . I am alone, and as the hours pass the loneliness becomes rather oppressive . . . Very slowly I approach a big wood. It would better express the situation were I to say that very slowly a big wood comes nearer to the balloon, for there is no sense of movement, and the earth below seems to be moving slowly past a stationary balloon . . .

'Fifteen hundred feet up and almost absolute silence, broken occasionally by the barking of a dog heard very faintly, or by a voice hailing the balloon, and by an occasional friendly creak of the basket and rigging if I move ever so slightly. Then quite suddenly I am aware of something new. My attention . . . is arrested by this new sound which I hear, surely the most wonderful and the sweetest sound heard by mortal ears. It is the combined singing of thousands of birds, of half the kinds which make the English spring so lovely. I do not hear one above the others; all are blended together in a wonderful harmony without change of pitch or tone, yet never wearying the ear. By very close attention I seem to be able at times to pick out an individual song. No doubt at all there are wrens, and chaffinches, and blackbirds, and thrushes, hedge sparrows, warblers, greenfinches and bullfinches and a score of others, by the hundred; and their singing comes up to me from that ten-acre wood in one sweet volume of heavenly music.'

Turner had a grand time ballooning, and enjoyed other near-mystical moments in several creaking baskets. Once he rode along as a journalist-passenger on an attempt on the world's distance record, making a night take-off from London's Crystal Palace, a popular balloonoport.

'Within a few minutes of leaving the ground we were rewarded with one of the finest spectacles ever seen by the airman. London's 150 square miles were spread before our eyes as we crossed the Thames . . . and gazed at the vast panorama. A crescent moon was not powerful enough to dim the stars, and we seemed to be poised in the centre of a vast illuminated globe whose dark sides were frosted with silver and gold, the roof glittering with the constellations seen, at our height of 2,000 feet, as they never appear to the eyes of the Londoner. Below us lay the millions of lamps patterning the great city, the wide, well-lit highways, such as Oxford Street, conspicuous, and the dark band of the river braceleted by the lights of the bridges. The roar of the traffic came up to us, an endless murmuring, and the whistling of trains and the barking of dogs came clearly to our ears.'

They drifted slowly out over the North Sea, and the balloon's captain decided to hang coloured flares at a safe distance below the balloon, and ignite them electrically, 'so that first green, then red and then white flares burst out below us, wasted their rays in the emptiness around, but lit up the balloon itself so that the great globe above us and every rope was dazzlingly illuminated. Then, as the fires died out the glorious stars were seen in multitudes and brilliance . . . complete silence reigned save for the occasional friendly creak.' Then they had some cold supper with hot drinks from thermos flasks. What they did in answer to the calls of nature on such a long journey Turner was too delicate to tell.

Such a voyage became very long, profoundly idle and rather lonely as the hours floated by. Turner found clouds absorbing to watch: since (unlike in an aeroplane) you were travelling exactly with them, you could enjoy their metamorphoses:

'The stars seemed friendly and close; Orion and the Great Bear majestic groups, the Pleiades a heavenly cluster, the Milky Way a celestial highway. But about one o'clock a sudden change occurred. At a great distance from us, but at about the same level, a great number of small fluffy clouds formed, and we were poised in the middle of the circle. Another ring formed nearer to us, and another. And we moved on, but with no perceptible sense of movement, with this weird escort.'

At five a.m., when they were about a mile above the ocean

'the cloud scenery now began to bestir itself. As if for our sole benefit it began a long series of wonderful groupings. Across the north-east sky a straight row of fantastic shapes appeared black as ink against the lightening sky. They resembled gigantic trees rearing themselves from a flat land covered with white mist . . . The dawn grew nearer, and a red tinge appeared behind the row of cloud trees, which became blacker and more sharply defined. A lovely green hue suffused the sky above the red. To the south the clouds bluish grey. The stars were still very brilliant.

'Almost suddenly the row of strange tree shapes lifted to a higher level, or we sank; then imperceptibly they dispersed and a series of mysterious and ever changing cloud forms took their place . . . In the far south a limitless stretch of cloud peaks looked like Switzerland moulded in snow.'

The breaking dawn seen from a balloon seems to have been Turner's favourite moment, perhaps because at that time tiredness could play tricks with his imagination. Here he is on another fantastic journey that began in England and ended far away in Russia:

'Across the light in the east regiments of vapoury figures slowly stalked. It was easy to imagine that these grotesque shapes were inhabited by spirits akin to their weird forms. There was strange commotion in the field of grey fog. Wisps of the cloud would suddenly rise here and there . . . Woolly hillocks passed and repassed each other, rose and fell before each other, and against the background of the lightening sky they appeared . . . like small moving pasteboard targets in a shooting gallery, only white and soft-edged like frisking lambs.'

A vision you could never get from any moving aeroplane.

Though the air you first climb up into in a balloon is the same air around you when you land (unless you have found an altered wind at altitude), it can by then be in a very different condition. The influence of distant pressure patterns and change of latitude can surround you with falling snow though you began in mild dryness, or have you rushing over the ground at sixty miles an hour though when you launched the air might have been so still you despaired of progress. Balloon landings are crash landings. Such indeed was their touchdown that stormy night in Russia:

'with a shrieking of wind in our ears and the flapping of the almost demented balloon, while we held on for our lives by the safety lines inside the basket, hanging with our limbs as relaxed as possible, waiting for the crash.

'It came like the crack of doom, and I thought every bone in my body must be broken. Everything in the basket was in wild confusion, but there was, or seemed to be, utter silence until the wind seized the balloon and lifted us again, so that there was a second crash almost as bad as the first . . . Pandemonium again outside; and then we began to move, the basket dragging along over ice and snow, through bushes, and seeming to gather speed until we were sweeping along like an express train in the darkness and with only our tough basket saving us from having our limbs broken . . . We finished up at last, and the basket turned over so that we were imprisoned underneath it . . . the basket was full of snow and grit, and our faces and necks were wet and muddy . . . It took us a good ten minutes to extricate ourselves.'

They found a cottage, full of 'good peasants . . . scared almost out of their wits by our

13. Coxwell and Glaisher are thought to have reached about 29,000 feet during an epic ascent in 1862; Coxwell had to climb the rigging and free the valve cord with his teeth to bring them down.

appearance' who cheered them with hot tea from a samovar and 'comfortable and perfectly clean, although rough, beds': and then they slept, like babies.

A special hazard of ballooning was that it enabled enormous altitudes to be reached, higher than the unprotected human body can adjust to. Three Italians got to about 20,000 feet in 1804; two became unconscious from hypoxia while the third remained conscious but later had to have several fingers amputated due to frostbite. James Glaisher and Henry Coxwell had a wild ride in 1862 in which they claimed to have reached 35,000 feet; from what is now known about the effects of high altitudes on the human body it seems impossible they could have survived so high, and 29,000 feet is thought to be more like it, with the imaginary 35,000 feet figure being simply one of the effects of their hypoxia.

They began boldly enough by climbing into a cu-nim.

'A torrent of rain splashed on the aerostat and poured into the basket. Violent gusts of wind hammered the balloon. It spun dizzily around its axis, twisting the riggings holding the basket. As though in agony, the ropes squealed with the strain. The balloon and basket unwound, throwing the passengers hard against the basket's side. Lightning darted through the sky while thunder clapped in apparent glee.'*

At the top of their climb Glaisher passed out, leaving a barely conscious and half-frozen Coxwell to climb the balloon's rigging to try to free the valve cord, tangled in the shrouds. 'He paused for breath and to swallow the blood in his mouth. Incipient nausea, which had been with him since the storm, suddenly matured. His lunch spilled out of his partly open mouth and through his broken tooth. When he could retch no more, he pushed himself forward while laboriously edging his mouth along the rope, using his lips for traction. He bit into the sisal fibers, already frozen by drops of saliva and blood.'

Success: on the descent Coxwell came to, and Glaisher poured brandy over his frost-bitten hands.

'I can show you where the barometer hand was while you were in a faint.' said Glaisher. Seven inches of mercury—35,000 feet. 'No man has ever gone so high before,' said Glaisher wonderingly. 'Nor ever will,' added Coxwell. Well, he was wrong there; a USAF captain in a pressurized capsule under a helium balloon got to 100,000 feet in 1961.

Hydrogen ballooning today is the sport practised by only a few rich old eccentrics, but hot air ballooning is enjoying enormous popularity, its resurgence due to the development of extremely efficient yet inexpensive propane burners. Balloonatics today have most of the ancient hazards plus some new ones: controlled airspace and airways that they must somehow stay out of, and modern man-made hazards such as power lines when they are trying to land. They have every bit as thrilling a time as their forefathers did.

* *Skyhooks* (Doubleday) by Kurt R. Stehling and William Beller.

3

Lilian Bland's Mayfly

Lilian Bland was born in Kent in 1878. Her father was an artist, and her grandfather was the Dean of Belfast. Her mother had died, so her father set up house (near Belfast) with his sister, who was the widow of General W. J. Smythe, RA, FRS. The widow was a grumpy lady whom Lilian couldn't abide, so she set about being what was then called 'independent'. She strode around in breeches instead of skirts, and sat astride her horse instead of riding it decently, side-saddle. She was the first woman to apply for a jockey's licence, which was, of course, refused. So she took up sportswriting, contributing articles on huntin', shootin' and fishin' for the Irish papers and the London magazines. (She was not above a bit of sport herself; she'd lie in wait with a shotgun in her hated aunt's fields, waiting for poachers and their lurchers, loosing off a precautionary burst at the feet of any who dared appear.) She bought a camera, and began illustrating her own reporting with photographs, 'receiving', says one biographer, 'quick acclaim for the brilliance and quality of her work with the camera'. Miss Bland was so damned independent she even smoked *cigarettes.*

Miss Bland turned thirty and still no husband: was it the breeches, the shotgun, or the fierce aunt that put off her suitors? Maybe she was simply happy with her own company; for when she was staying with friends in Scotland in 1908 she'd row herself across the Loch to an island at dawn, and stay there all day taking colour plates of birds. Watching seabirds by the hour induces a strange hypnosis in anyone with imagination, and Lilian Bland found herself becoming increasingly jealous of the gulls' abilities at soaring.

The next summer Louis Bleriot flew across the English Channel, the world went wild, and Lilian Bland's Uncle Robert (much nicer than the aunt), who was in France at the time, sent her a picture postcard of the machine, which included its dimensions. Lilian Bland was now 'hooked on aviation'—a long and expensive malady which must be deliciously familiar to quite a few readers of *this* book.

Then in October 1909 there was a flying meeting at Blackpool to which Miss Bland went, and saw real aeroplanes for the first time. She wasn't too impressed. To her father she wrote:

'I have seen them fly, and looked over all the flying machines; they are all made very much the same way and they looked smaller than I expected, but none of them are ready to fly. After hours of waiting Latham brought out his machine, and it started running along the field and then gradually rose and flew half a circuit, when its wings or skid caught in a ditch, and broke the skid and bent the propeller.

'Paulhan flew in a Farman machine several rounds of the course and alighted quite gracefully . . . in flying they keep their heads to the wind and turn a corner by drifting round tail-first . . . The few English machines are, I imagine, no good—much too small and fitted with motor-bike engines . . . most of them are covered with tyre fabric, lashed on like lace boots sewn or tacked . . . the wheels are on castors with small springs.'

Miss Bland omitted to explain that it had been blowing rather more than half a gale, and Latham had been extremely courageous in flying at all. He only did it because the crowd was getting restive, and got a bent machine for his pains. The weather stayed bad throughout the week-long meeting, but Lilian Bland busied herself measuring and examining all the machines—which was how even the best aircraft designers worked in those days; a little science and plenty of cribbing.

The Wright Brothers had begun by building reduced scale models which they flew as gliders and as kites. Miss Bland must have read of their long labours, for she too, back in Belfast, set-to in the workshop on a 6-foot span biplane glider. She was handy with tools, got it finished in no time and soon had it flying.

Next, a full-size, woman-carrying glider. She must have worked hard, for this 28-foot span contraption was ready less than three months after she'd gone round the Blackpool meet filling her notebooks with ideas and information. She called it Mayfly, with encouraging irony.

Mayfly was in style very like any other aeroplane of its day. Pirated. There was a lot of the Wright Flyer in it; something of Glenn Curtiss's June Bug; maybe some Paulhan too. But in truth, so little was known of aerodynamics in 1910 that about all even the 'experts' did was to tinker and experiment with, and frankly steal blind, every previous design that had shown the remotest signs of leaving the ground.

Mayfly embodied some fine carpentry. Its spars and leading-edge were ash, steamed to form the curved tips; trailing-edge was a wire; the ribs were 'sugar pine', also steamed to a nice curve—one based on the wing section of those Scottish gulls. The struts were spruce, mounted in metal sockets and braced conventionally with piano wire and turnbuckles which Miss Bland 'bought in'. The fabric, unbleached calico, was treated with a patent concoction of Miss Bland's own invention, a mixture of formalin and gelatine, to make it rain-resistant.

Mayfly weighed 200 lbs, but flew strongly as a glider under tow. Lilian Bland had a launching crew of three stalwart men, one of them her aunt's gardener's boy, who must

14. Mayfly was first flown as a tethered kite—a technique the Wright Brothers had also used.

have had a whale of a time, for he stayed on to assist her throughout her aviation experiments. Later on, Miss Bland enlisted four burly policemen of the Royal Ulster Constabulary to help her, and one breezy day *they* let go and the gardener's boy didn't, so I suppose he was the *second* person to fly in Northern Ireland.

She tinkered and experimented, trying half a dozen different undercarriages and types of fore- and tailplane. Ailerons were found necessary, and added. Soon Mayfly was deemed proven as a glider, and it was time for Stage Two: power.

An engine was ordered from Mr A. V. Roe in England, for delivery in May; by July Miss Bland was fuming with impatience and went over on the ferry to chase things up for herself. Roe staged a test run for her benefit, using one of his own 'Avro' propellers. This shattered to splinters, happily missing everyone. Another propeller was found to replace it, £100 was handed over, and Lilian Bland took herself back to Ireland, the precious engine resting, all 100 lbs of it, on its wooden bearers, on the carriage seat beside her.

It was the middle of the night before the engine was installed in Mayfly. Lilian Bland didn't have a fuel tank, so she rigged up an empty whiskey bottle instead, feeding the carburettor through one of her hated aunt's tin ear trumpets, held by the gardener's boy. They pushed Mayfly out into the rain and started her up, which woke up sleeping neighbours for hundreds of yards in all directions. It ran well, till the gardener's lad let

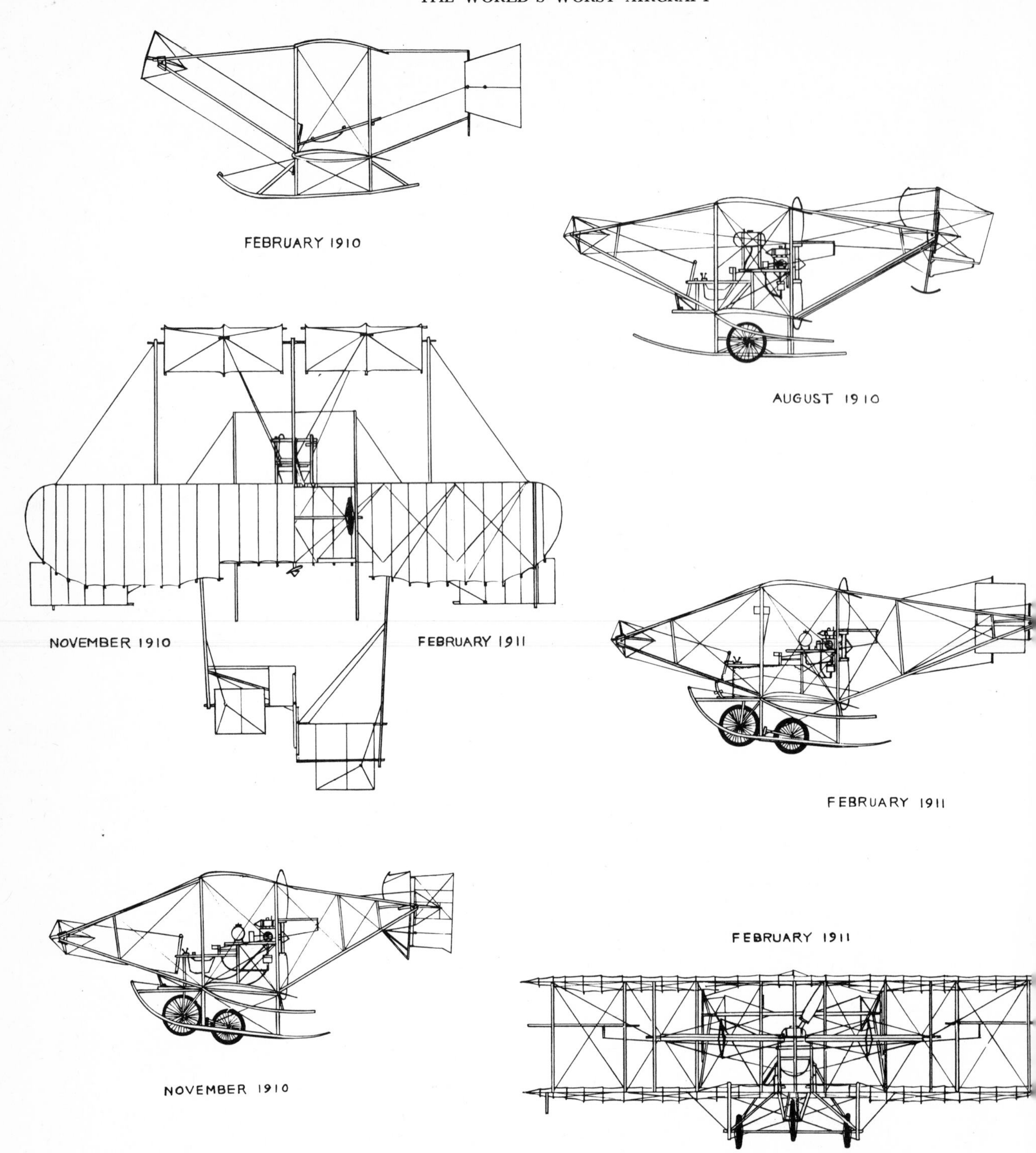

15. Mayfly went through many changes from its genesis as a tethered kite to final success as a powered aeroplane.

his attention wander, and allowed the rest of the fuel to pour away all over the wing.

Later the fuel tank arrived and Miss Bland could conduct more serious tests with it. Her technique for starting was to get the gardener's boy to stand between the tail booms and swing the propeller till one cylinder fired; then wait patiently till it picked up running on the other three as well. 'It was,' she wrote, 'not a good engine, a beast to start, and it got too hot . . . as the engine is English, its sense of humour is not developed sufficiently.'

It certainly wasn't a smooth engine; the vibration it generated was enough to set the nuts dancing on its four mounting bolts, and to shake loose a couple of bracing wires which fell back into the propeller and shattered it again. Nor did the neat steamed curve in the handsome sugar pine ribs endure, and new ribs had to be cut from solid spruce with the curve already in them. Many other changes were also deemed necessary before a flight under power could be attempted: stronger wheel hubs for one thing, as Miss Bland disdained to copy the 'castors on springs' she'd noted on the English aeroplanes at Blackpool, and the only give in Mayfly's suspension came from the flexibility in the tyres.

Her previous testing ground—the side of a hill—wasn't ample enough for powered flight. Happily the local lord, with some prompting, stepped forward and offered her the use of his 800-acre deer park: few trees, but a terror of a bull, which, thought Miss Bland, might serve to terrify Mayfly into the air should all else fail.

Then the weather (it was August, noted for its terrible weather, and traditionally the month for holidays) became very bad. It was not until the end of the month that there was a calm day. Miss Bland, clad in mechanic's overalls, and one of those wide Edwardian hats with a veil which tied under her chin, was intent upon the manipulation of her

16. Miss Bland checks the throttle of her 20 hp Avro engine, "not a good engine, but an English engine with no sense of humour". 17. *Right*, the quarter-scale model Mayfly in kite form in 1911.

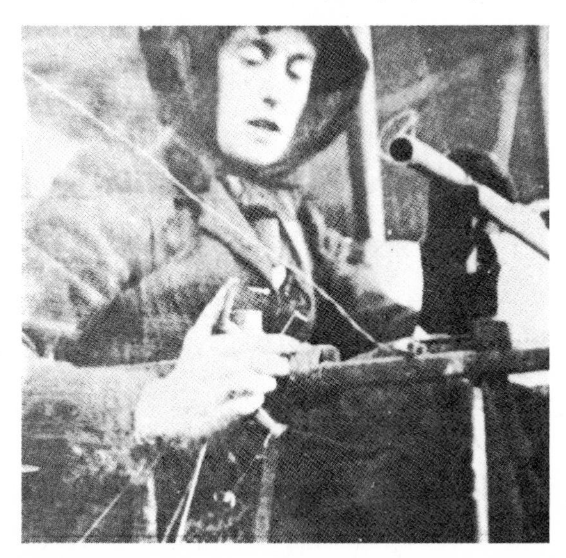

engine and flying controls, when to her utter astonishment she noticed she was 'several feet up in the air!'. She cut the motor and settled back to earth. She ran back to look in the wet grass; no doubt about it, there was a length of quite a few yards where no tracks showed. 'I have flown!' she exulted.

She flew again a few days later, with Mayfly pitching and rolling like a small boat in choppy seas; but then the original Wright Flyer had oscillated too, so she was in good company. She flew regularly up until Christmas. Things broke and things snapped and things cracked, and Mayfly suffered a good deal of modification and change. It also lived tethered out in the open: hence this fine description of it in one reference work: 'No great effort was expended to rig it square or true, and it sagged and bulged in all directions . . . it was underpowered, while at the same time a bigger engine would have shaken it to pieces.' But by the standards of her day, Miss Bland was now an expert, 'able', in the words of another biographer, 'to discourse clearly and adroitly in print on virtually any aspect of aerodynamics'.

She continued flying into frosty February with her sagging biplane, and even planned a Mayfly Mk. II, with longer wings with squared-off tips. She placed an advertisement in *Flight*, The World's First Aeronautical Weekly:

IRISH BIPLANES IMPROVED 'MAY-FLY' TYPE
Standard or Racing
FROM £250 WITHOUT ENGINE
WIRE WHEELS, CONTROL LEVERS (Farman action),
made for Wires or Control Rods,
STRONG & LIGHT STEEL TUBING
ALL AEROPLANE ACCESSORIES, &c.
GLIDERS, full controls, etc., from £80.
As a Glider this Biplane has accomplished glides of over 90 yards, very stable in gusty winds, with the engine it can rise in 30 feet IN A DEAD CALM.
Full particulars on application.
L. E. BLAND, Carnmoney, BELFAST.

But she also believed in hedging her bets, for in the same issue of *Flight* ran this ad: 'AIR-COOLED ENGINE, 20 BHP, complete, propeller, tanks: £80, or nearest offer, Particulars, L. Bland, Carnmoney, Belfast.'

You see, Miss Bland had by now spent some £200 on Mayfly, and frightened the life out of her father, who was offering to buy her a motorcar if only she'd give up aviation. South to Dublin she went, in a train, to pick up her Model T Ford, and halfway home she took over from the company driver for her first and only driving lesson. Her poor father! No sooner was she home than she was taking out a sales sub-agency for Ford motors.

She must have given all her relatives plenty to gossip about. One of them was her cousin Charles Loftus Bland, who'd been in the army till invalided home, when he'd

18. Lilian Bland supposedly in full and glorious flight, one frosty, foggy morning in 1911.

resigned his commission and sailed for Vancouver to work as a lumberjack. Women with 'spirit' were more highly admired in Canada than in Edwardian Britain, and it wasn't too long before Charles proposed. Now any lady will allow that a *proposal* is far more exciting than *aviation* or even a *motorcar*. In a trice the announcement was in *The Times* and the aeroplane had been donated to the Dublin Flying Club for use as a glider.

All Canadians were then popularly supposed to live in log cabins in the forest; and that is exactly what Charles Bland did, out in British Columbia. Arriving there, Lilian Bland set to, manfully, getting a farm going. Her fine husband, unfortunately, hurt his back early on and she had to shoulder his responsibilities too, fixing the motor boat and the power saws and milking machines and driving the tractor. A daughter was born to them, but was killed in a tragic accident when only seventeen.

By 1935 Lilian Bland's back had been hurt too, and she returned to live in England, where the labours expected of ladies were gentler. In 1955 she retired to Cornwall, and spent her time gardening, painting, and gambling a little. She remained indomitably witty and energetic until her death in 1971 aged ninety-two. She was the creator and pilot of Ireland's first powered aeroplane, of which, I am sad to tell you, nothing remains. It has vanished—unless you believe one historian who claims, 'The Mayfly's Avro engine is believed to be the one now in the possession of the Science Museum in London.' A different reference work firmly states, 'The Science Museum engine differs in several respects from Lilian Bland's engine, the fate of which has still to come to light.' Well, it was only an *English* engine, with no sense of humour.

19. Igor Sikorsky's 1914 bomber the Ilya Mourometz had a walkway along its fuselage with ropes to hold on to.

20. The German Staaken R.XIVa: 1,300 hp from five engines but only 80 mph maximum speed.

4

Forssman's Folly

Great fleets of giant bombers raining death from the skies: a curiously *period* image, now, harking back to between-the-wars. The sort of thing old H. G. Wells and kindred soothsayers delighted to curdle our marrow with. *German* bombers, of course; no Anglo-Saxon would stoop to such infamy as wiping out whole cities from above. Yet when giant fleets—one or two thousand aircraft or more—*were* first got together in about 1944, it was the British and the Americans doing it to the Germans. Bombing is one of those things that is no good by halves: modest bombing generates more outrage than surrender, it simply annoys the citizens, and stiffens their determination. No, you must bomb a city to rubble or not at all, for delicacy reaps no rewards.

I suppose the Luftwaffe's raid on Guernica in the Spanish Civil War was the first thoroughly *effective* aerial bombardment. Something about big bombers—perhaps their marvellous lack of subtlety—appealed strongly to the Germans, and they were in the big bomber business as early as 1914.

But they didn't pioneer the multi-engined bomber; *that* had been done by Igor Sikorsky, the Russian. He'd been trying to make helicopters, reaching the conclusion around 1910 that he was forty years ahead of his time. In 1912 he began the world's first four-engined plane, Bolshoi, the big one, or Le Grand in the French that it was smart to speak around St. Petersburg in those days. It was a kind of flying greenhouse, an aerial yacht with four 100 hp engines (flight trials showed they were only just enough), and the wonderful novelty of dual controls. It did set a world record; almost two hours aloft with eight on board, reaching nearly 3,000 feet in altitude. It was amazingly under-powered for its size; its maximum speed was a bare 55 mph, which can't have been much above stalling. The Le Grand's fate was perhaps the oddest of any aeroplane's. One day, while it was parked out on the airfield, the engine of a Voisin biplane which was flying overhead tore loose and smashed through it like a bomb.

Back to the drawing board went Sikorsky, to produce the Ilya Mourometz, bigger still, and only 21 inches shorter in span than the Flying Fortress of World War II. This design had a walkway with a rope handrail down the top of the fuselage to the tail, and there survives a photo of it coming in to land with two Ivans standing on it, coat-tails flapping in the winter chill, while the pilot is using a ridiculous amount of down-elevator to balance his way-too-far-aft centre of gravity.

By 1917, some seventy-five of these bombers were in Russian Imperial Service. They could carry three tons of load, but made small impact on the course of history, being chronically short of engine spares since the Russians didn't make their own aero-engines but begged them from their allies.

These bombers made hundreds of very slow raids on East Prussia and German Lithuania; only one was shot down by a German scout, though a couple of others crashed on their own.

The wily Huns had been following Sikorsky's work with avid interest. Their High Command was bent on aerial bombing with airships, terror weapons under whose bulbous shadows all Europe would cringe. Many German engineers, however, including the airship's inventor (the Graf von Zeppelin), thought *aeroplane* bombers would be more effective. Zeppelin got together with Bosch, the electrical firm, to form the Staaken company, whose giant bombers were the most successful. Staaken bombers had their engines out on the wings (with one in the nose) *à la* Sikorsky, with the propellers bolted directly to the end of the crankshafts. Many of the other designers preferred to keep their engines inside the fuselage (where the flight mechanic could keep a close eye on them), driving propellers on outriggers through long drive-shafts and gear boxes, which in power trains were always heavy and unreliable. Wily old Count Zeppelin's bombers were best.

Staaken aircraft raided England a dozen times, along with smaller Gotha bombers. Here is part of one aircraft commander's account of such a mission:*

'. . . we head off along the pin-marked line on our maps. Inside the fuselage the pale glow of dimmed lights outlines the chart table, the wireless equipment and the instrument panel . . . Before long we spot the signal cannon at Ostende, which fires star shells into the night to assist us on our way. The night is dark . . . under us is a back abyss, no waves are seen, no lights of surface vessels flicker as we head for the Thames Estuary at Margate. On our right, in the distant north, is our only light, the weak pulsating glow of the aurora borealis. Ahead of us is a black nothingness—are we on the correct course?

'Now thin but continually flickering cloud shreds streak past. We climb over the cloud cover, through which holes now and then appear, but beneath nothing is sighted, although we must by now be over England. Suddenly, directly ahead, the searchlights illuminate the sky in their hunt for us, their bright beams making glowing circles in the thin overcast, but they do not spot us. Because all surface lights are blacked out it appears as if we are soaring over a dead land. But the enemy has heard us, and so we are free to request wireless bearings . . . in a few minutes we receive a message from Belgium giving our position: we are south-east of London.

* *The German Giants* by G. W. Haddow and Peter M. Grosz, published by Putnam.

'Can we recognize the docks through the low overcast? Directly ahead, the landing lights of an English airfield flare up as the enemy prepares to intercept us. The machine gunners arm their guns and fire at the searchlights below. Oberleutnant Kamps releases four bombs, and the detonations are clearly seen—this is in retaliation for attacks on *our* aerodromes. All at once through a hole in the cloud the grey band of the Thames appears. Not far ahead we can see a portion of the balloon barrage which surrounds London . . .

[Kamps drops the rest of their bombs, and they turn for home.] 'The banks of the Thames are dotted with anti-aircraft batteries that soon have us under fire. As we approach the coast the undercast becomes thinner and thinner; before long the searchlights catch us and the bursts of anti-aircraft move dangerously close. A shell splinter tears through our upper wing without causing any damage. The flaming shells come so close we can almost touch them. Beneath us we spot the exhaust flames of a pursuing night-fighter, but it does not threaten us. We reach the open sea and steer for Ostende, where well-known signals will guide us home.

'As we come in sight of the coast the steady rhythm of the engines begins to falter, until suddenly all four propellers stop! Some split-second thinking: the fault can only be in the fuel system. The last two fuel tanks have just been selected—the fuel lines must have frozen due to water-contaminated gasoline. To thaw them out is impossible: will we reach the coast, or are we to sink in the sea? Life jackets are strapped on. Fortunately the great gliding qualities of our plane enable us, in spite of stopped engines, to reach the coast behind our front line.

'By means of flares we search the darkened landscape on which we must land, but only trenches and hollows are discernible . . . by pulling sharply at the controls, I stall the aircraft, letting it fall almost vertically against the ground. With a mighty impact it hits a ditch; one landing gear collapses and the wing shatters but no crew member is injured.'

There, in that one account, is shown the tactical uselessness of the German giant bombers of World War I. The heavy but feeble engines of the day meant you could carry only a small bomb-load (only about 8% of your total weight) through the fierce fighter defences of the daytime. Forced to fly by night, you had but the vaguest idea of where you were and what you were bombing. The unreliability of your power-plants meant you might make it home, or you might not. And the lack of weather reporting or forecasting meant that you might find your home airfield completely fogged-in if you *did* get home—and you had no form of instrument approach, but could only descend into the fog as slowly as you could, to a certain crash. (One bombing squadron lost sixty-one aircraft—twenty-four shot down and thirty-seven in crashes and fires—and nearly a hundred men.)

The German giant bombers made a dozen raids on England, dropping some 50 tons of bombs. They flattened the Odhams printing shop that turned out Horatio Bottomley's ultra-patriotic *John Bull*; they knocked a corner off Chelsea's Royal Hospital; they

21. This German Army VGO II bombed the Russians in 1916. It is seen here after an argument with a ditch.

flattened twenty-three houses in Maida Vale with one 1,000 lb-bomb. Matched against the cost and time and effort it took to build and operate the bombers, it can hardly have been worth it. Bombers can easily get so expensive that the damage they manage isn't worth it—they'd have helped the war effort more by staying home. (The Americans found this out later in Vietnam, trying to 'snuff gooks' as they would say, with eight-jet strategic bombers and losing fifteen at $40 million each.)

And if Zeppelin's well-designed, well-engineered Staakens were a doubtful asset, what of the *un*successful designs? You could get money out of the German exchequer for practically anything that might conceivably fly, whilst their bomber programme attracted some very mad scientists. My favourite is Villehad Forssman, a Swedish mad-scientist-of-fortune, who was a builder of airships in Russia in 1910, before moving to Germany in 1914. He was, says *The German Giants*, 'a Jules Verne type, a man with a vivid imagination who invented among other things a one-man submarine, and a shell-proof tank.'

Early in 1914 Forssman had built a monoplane named The Bulldog for Prince Friedrich Sigismund. This, it seems, was enough to establish him as an aeroplane designer, for shortly after the shot that echoed around the world and started lights going out all over Europe, he was hired as a designer by the electrical manufacturing combine Siemens-Schuckert, who'd been manufacturing airships since 1907 as a sideline.

Siemens had also tried winged aeroplanes in 1909, only to abandon the work as unprofitable after a year or two. But war changes everything, and in 1914 the aeroplane department was gleefully re-established. It is very nearly impossible to lose money making aeroplanes in wartime. But Siemens did, at least at first; for their designer Villehad Forssman persuaded them to build versions of his Bulldog monoplane, which flew too badly for even the German military to buy.

In October 1914 Forssman switched his thinking to giant aeroplanes, and designed a, well, frankly it was a *copy* of Igor Sikorsky's famous four-engined design. It had four uncowled Mercedes engines of 110 hp each mounted on struts above the bottom wing, driving tractor propellers; a fair enough arrangement, except that the thing was badly underpowered. The stressing of the structure was terrible; parts of it were *too* strong (and therefore too heavy) while other parts were too flimsy—notably the bracing between the biplane wings, where six extra struts had to be inserted later. But the worst fault was that it was so tail-heavy as to be uncontrollable—little short hops just above the grass were enough to reveal that. So Forssman added a gunner's turret, stuck on to the nose like a preacher's pulpit, to try to balance things. It wasn't enough: Forssman's giant still wasn't fit to fly. They re-rigged the wings to incorporate some dihedral; they added another rudder; they cowled the engines.

Then Siemens let Forssman go; and another engineer, Harold Wolff, was called in. He moved the outboard engines up to mid-gap position, and added spinners to all the propellers to fair them into the cowls. He completely restyled the nose, bringing it to a point like the prow of a yacht, with portholes along the sides and a blister canopy for the pilot. They got another test pilot, who made a few ground runs, hops, skips and jumps, and quit while he was still *ahead*, or at any rate *alive*. They hired a famous pre-war pilot, Lt Walter Höhndorf, holder of the *Pour-le-Merite*—the famous 'Blue Max'. It was September 1915 when he took the controls, a whole year after work had started on Forssman's folly. It was September 1915 when Höhndorf lost control during a tentative hop, and the aeroplane went over on its nose.

But Siemens had spent a year and a good deal of deutschmarks on Forssman's giant bomber, and earned not a pfennig with it, for the German military didn't pay for giant bombers until they had flown, and shown they could carry an operational load up to an operational altitude. Höhndorf's wreck had been less than total, and Siemens had not

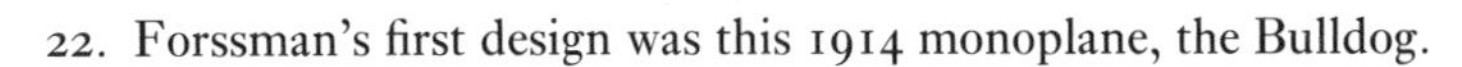
22. Forssman's first design was this 1914 monoplane, the Bulldog.

23. The four-engined bomber that Forssman designed for Siemens.

yet abandoned hope of some financial return from the machine. Their technical director approached another pilot, Bruno Steffen: ten per cent of the military's payment if he would take the acceptance flight. A deal was done with the military who, in return for a price reduction, agreed to accept more modest performance figures: 2,000 metres of altitude in thirty minutes, carrying a useful load of 1,000 kilograms and fuel for four hours.

Bruno Steffen studied the monster closely, and decided (he must have been a brave man) that he'd accept the challenge. He made some changes while the plane was being rebuilt, the principal one being to link the throttles so all could be moved together. His brother Franz Steffen, also an engineer, studied the machine and its drawings closely, and despite real structural weakness in the fuselage behind the wings, decided brother Bruno had a fair chance. No one else did; Bruno's friends and associates did their utmost to dissuade him. He made a short flight, and announced the big flight for the morning. Control in pitch, he said, wasn't too bad; the ailerons were pretty uselessly heavy, but he planned to throttle the outer engines for lateral control.

Came the morn, and all was ready. Steffen planned to carry five passengers as part of his 1,000 kg load; would anyone like to go with him? *They would not*. Someone from the German Air Service acceptance commission party, perhaps? *Nein*. He went alone.

Loaded, the plane had become monstrously heavy—so heavy he had to fly with the control wheel pushed almost fully forwards, even while climbing. Then a powerful up-draught threw the plane into a bank. Bruno Steffen found that with the control column so far forward he just hadn't the strength to turn the wheel to level the wings! He had to release his forward pressure (at which the machine tried to stand on its tail), wind the aileron wheel to its stops, heave forwards again, then when the wings had levelled, reverse the procedure, hoping all the while the wretched thing didn't stall, for with that much of an aft-centre-of-gravity condition it would surely spin if it *did* stall. Steffen

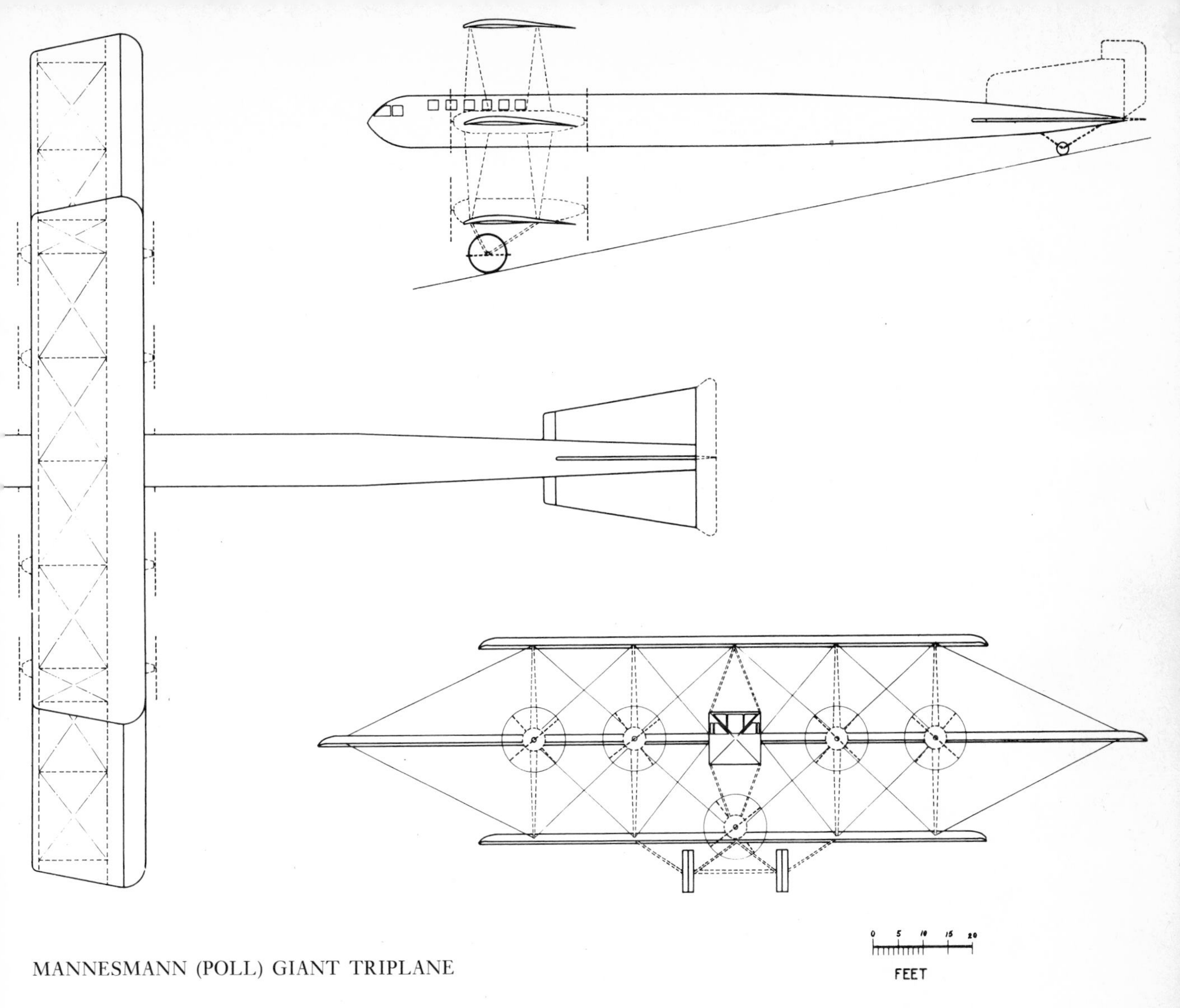

MANNESMANN (POLL) GIANT TRIPLANE

held his breath, and continued upwards. He made 2,000 metres with just two minutes to spare; then he climbed another 100 metres just to be sure. On the way back down one of the engines stopped, through lack of fuel pressure. Steffen wobbled away furiously on the hand-pump; a *second* motor quit, then the *third*, then the *fourth*. It became very quiet in the giant aeroplane. Steffen had to push forward still harder, reaching till he was half out of his seat, to maintain an even glide. He glided down in slow circles, and made a perfect dead-stick landing on the airfield. Fuel and ballast and barometer were checked by the military committee, and the aircraft formally accepted for 'training purposes'.

They rebalanced the machine and flew it again, but it was still impossible. Then one day quite soon after Bruno Steffen's grand test flight, they were making engine runs with the aircraft's wheels chocked to keep it from moving when there came a rending noise and the fuselage slowly broke clean in two aft of the wings—just where Bruno's

25. One giant wheel of the Poll triplane survives, in the Imperial War Museum in London.

brother Franz had predicted it was weakest! Bruno Steffen bravely announced his relief that the thing was finally finished, and would now never kill anybody, but he must have blenched to his bones at the thought of having climbed to 6,000 feet and come back down again in a plane that wasn't strong enough even for engine runs while stationary!

And now, if you have found this story hard to swallow so far, and perhaps think I have made it up, read no further, for it gets *worse*.

After the Armistice, an Allied Control Commission team, poking through hangars in Germany, stumbled quite by chance on the remains of a partly-built triplane of *fantastic* size: 150 feet long and 165 feet in span, with ten engines! The designer's name, they learned, was 'Forstman'. Can this be our old friend from Siemens, with his name mispelled? There are other clues that make this likely, and the colossal triplane *did* bear the stamp of his work. It was intended to carry fuel for eighty hours, which is rather more than *three days*, during which it was to carry leaflets across the Atlantic and sprinkle them on New York. The structure was very heavy yet ridicuously weak: there wasn't any cable bracing inside the fuselage to hold it together. Instead, it was covered with two layers of three-ply, making it as heavy as a boat but still far too weak. The ailerons were far too small; the centre of gravity way aft; and the elevators ineffectual.

Was this colossal mechanical albatross Villehad Forssman's final folly? It seems likely. A little of it has even survived: a section of the fuselage and one gigantic, 8-foot diameter landing wheel are in storage at London's Imperial War Museum, dusty, forgotten monuments to a man who believed in thinking big.

5

The Christmas Bullet

Aviation, as you might expect, attracts more than its fair share of con-men, dreamers, wild nuts whose ability to differentiate between their own crazy dreams and actual reality is profoundly poor. In the design field you can usually spot them thus: all other aircraft designers, they claim, are fools, blind fools incapable of noticing that all they have to do to double the range and triple the speed of an aeroplane, while at the same time making it so easy to handle a child of ten could fly it, is to incorporate this wheeze or that dodge, the patents of which are often held by guess who?

These eccentrics are also notable in that while they may have briefly attended an engineering school, they seldom graduate; that while they never seem to have much trouble in attracting financial backing, it is always from people with no previous aviation experience, but rather from rich lawyers, newspaper owners and the like, men who themselves deal in wild ideas rather than stern reality; and that whenever arrangements are made for their new wonderplane to be tested or examined by knowledgeable authorities, the said wonderplane is always somewhere else, or not quite ready, or in the secret shop for modifications that will make it still more wonderful.

One such glorious eccentric was William Christmas, a doctor of medicine from Warrenton, North Carolina, who also 'found time to dabble in aeronautics'. The answer, he decided, was simple: an aeroplane's wings should be flexible, like a bird's, so that they could flex under load in flight. Their flexibility should also allow the airfoil to change slightly in flight; and the wings must be cantilever, unbraced, just as a bird's wings are. All this at a time (the early years of this century) when orthodox designers were doing all they could to make wings rigid enough to stay on the aeroplane. Only Dr Christmas, it seems, had the genius to perceive that rigid wings were hopelessly inefficient, and he, of course, knew more about the subject than any other pioneer.

Dr Christmas's thinking was just the sort of simplistic tosh that appeals to amateur geniuses. A part of his fantasy was that he had been an early pioneer of flight, making flights in 1907 or 1908 from a farm in Virginia. He used to say that he'd made a number of flights, eventually colliding with a tree, and then burning the wreck 'to prevent others from discovering his secrets'. His second machine was built in Maryland in 1911; and his third in 1912 by the 'Christmas Aeroplane Company' of Washington DC, which was displayed at an aeronautical show in New York City that year. 'Plans were made for a non-stop flight to Washington' (about 200 miles) 'with a packet of mail, but the trip was cancelled.' *Some* of this could be true; so far as I know no evidence survives.

Dr Christmas seems to have gone back to his original calling, for a few years. But there was war in Europe; by 1918 the United States had been dragged into the battle, and was spending millions of dollars on armaments, including building-up a huge air corps. American newspapers gave the whole thing their usual super-colossal jingoistic treatment, and were full of news of fantastic military aircraft being developed and built in vast numbers to show the Kaiser a thing or two, teach him a lesson he wouldn't forget, and no doubt make a few fortunes for American aviation geniuses along the way. All this publicity finally reached Dr Christmas, and he began to believe that his finest hour as an aeronautical authority had come.

First, he needed money. In a trice he had hoodwinked Henry and Alfred McCorey, two brothers, supposedly hard-headed brokers from New York, into backing him. And one day in early 1918 the three of them turned up at the offices of the Continental Aircraft Company at Amityvile, out on Long Island, asking if Continental Aircraft could build a prototype of their wonderplane, the Christmas Scout.

Now as any con-man can tell you, the more fantastic a story you tell, the more likely you are to be believed. Swearing all present to total secrecy, Dr Christmas then explained the true and grand purpose of his revolutionary design: it was part of a plot to kidnap the Kaiser! 'He spoke authoritatively,' says one historian, 'and seems to have enraptured the men with him, as they listened in amazement.' The Continental Aircraft Company had only ever built one aeroplane, an antiquated pusher biplane that attracted no customers. The warplane boom had quite passed them by, and I suspect that Dr Christmas's fantasy was the very salvation and dream of fame and fortune that they had almost given up hoping for.

Next, Dr Christmas needed an aero engine. But all these were in the hands of the military, it being wartime, and were in exceeding short supply at that. But if there's one thing the United States Army has learned to be afraid of, it's politicians, so Dr Christmas got a friend to write to James W. Wadsworth, Senator for New York, seeking help. This friend of the doctor's did a fine job, describing Christmas fulsomely as 'an experienced aero engineer of the old school who was associated with Professor Langley' (which in view of that academic's history of ludicrous failure in aviation should have been enough to damn him for a start, even had it been true) who had 'successfully built and flown a number of these types of machines previous to the year 1913'. The McCoreys were backing the project, the Senator was told, and several thousand dollars had already been spent developing two designs—a single-place fighting scout and a 'high speed three-place fighting machine'. All the Senator had to do was help them obtain a Hall-Scott 5A and a Liberty 12-cylinder engine for the project.

26. Dr Christmas, flanked by his backers the McCorey Brothers, and the Christmas Bullet.

The Senator, thus primed, wrote to the commanding officer at the US Army's McCook Field, Lieutenant Colonel Jesse G. Vincent. Now Vincent was being pestered by dozens of mad inventors seeking engines and, furthermore, he had himself seen the one useless aircraft the Continental Aircraft Company had built. But all he wanted was a quiet life, so he replied asking for detailed specifications of Dr Christmas's two wonderplanes. Dr Christmas at once identified the problem, for he never again made mention of the Continental Aircraft Company in any correspondence with the army, but instead formed his own company, the Cantilever Aero Co, and wrote on their notepaper from then on.

If Vincent wanted a quiet life, he didn't get it. First he got a letter from Dr Christmas saying that work was far advanced; and then two weeks later another letter saying work couldn't start until they got a priority order from the government for materials. Vincent relented enough to write to Dr Christmas saying he could have the loan of a 6-cylinder Liberty engine so long as he promised not to fly the aircraft, but to ship it to the Army for testing, along with a second engineless airframe for static strength testing. Dr Christmas cabled back: 'Conditions satisfactory, please rush motor', and it duly arrived. It was in fact the prototype 6-cylinder Liberty—the first one built!

Unable to believe their luck, the men of the Continental Aircraft factory were ready to start work. Please, they said to the doctor, could they have the drawings of the wonder-plane? But there weren't any—the thing existed only in Dr Christmas's mind! But his money, or rather that of his backers, seemed good, so they started work on building an aircraft pretty much of their own design along the lines of what the doctor seemed, so far as they could tell, to have in mind. They had to use hickory wood and 'saw-mill' steel, for even the doctor's incredible charm and persuasiveness had failed to obtain any proper aircraft materials.

27. Three views of the first Bullet. Note the over-large ailerons, tiny rudder, and no elevator.

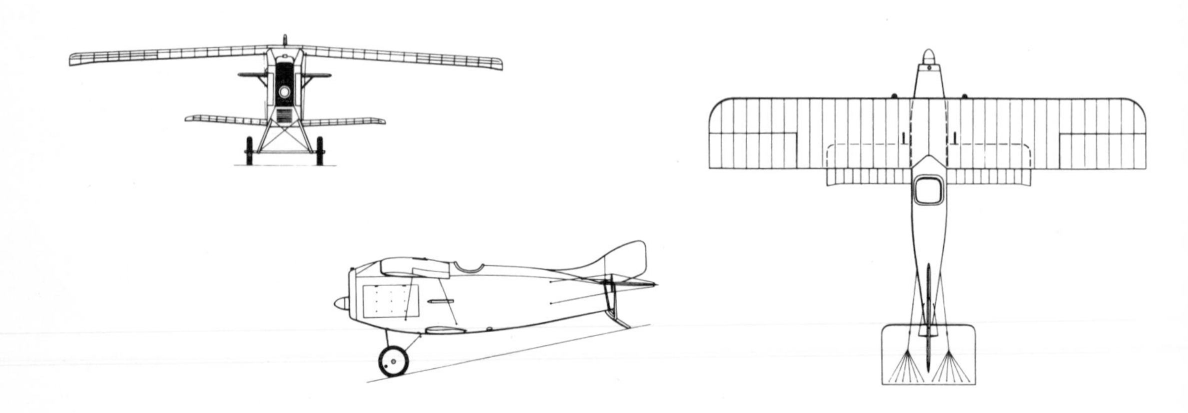

28. The second Bullet was similar to the first, even retaining the warping tailplane.

Chief, or more probably, *only* engineer at the Continental Aircraft Company was a twenty-two-year-old kid named Vincent J. Burnelli, who later achieved fame, if very little fortune, with a mad idea of his own—that of building an aircraft with a wing so fat you wouldn't need a fuselage, but which could accommodate everything, engines, fuel, passengers, inside its huge chord. Burnelli did his best to water down the doctor's worst and craziest eccentricities; he discovered that Dr Christmas had the men fabricating a set of wings that were indeed thoroughly flexible, and he surreptitiously designed and began building a sensibly rigid set of his own. But then one day Al McCorey turned up at the plant determined to take some photographs showing where his money was going. Burnelli's proper wings weren't finished, but Dr Christmas's flexible ones were, though they didn't even fit the attachment mountings on the fuselage. These were crudely modified, the flexible wings bolted on, and the aircraft rolled out of the shop for photographing, with Burnelli trotting alongside protesting for all he was worth. His protests took on an even more horrified tone when he learned that this cobbled-up monstrosity was to be flown!

The Bullet, though seemingly well-built, even if not of aircraft-strength materials, had several nonsenses in its design. At the tips of its flexible wings were inset ailerons, which could have done little more than twist the wing under air loads. A flexible wing might have worked had it been combined with a warp control system. This the doctor had kept for the tailplane, which he'd had built in one piece with wires attached to bend it up or down for control in pitch—but the tailplane was built so stiffly it would hardly bend at all, and there seems to have been no provision for trimming the loads of power and airspeed changes, either. There was a hinged rudder, which, when combined with the very narrow-track landing gear, was far too small to have kept the thing straight on the rollout after landing. What they had done was to paint the thing up in Army cockades and stripes, to give it the semblance of being a real military project.

Dr Christmas seems to have completely forgotten his promise to the Army not to fly his beast before they had a chance to strength-test it, for he wrote to them wildly threatening to fly three Scouts extensively in order to demonstrate 'their advantages over every other machine of the same type'. The Army wrote back firmly reminding him of the conditions under which they'd agreed to loan him the engine. The Army advised its own pilots that none of them should fly the aeroplane until it had been sandbag-tested, but beyond that there wasn't much else they could do; the Christmas Bullet was a civilian project.

Then came the Armistice, which you might have thought would have provided a neat chance for Dr Christmas to abandon his project (without losing face), since there was now no chance of the military buying it—or anybody else. But no; he kept on, and even redoubled the pace.

First, he needed a pilot, for even *his* megalomania stopped short of believing he knew how to fly. He hired a company pilot, an Englishman, who inspected the Bullet, and said, 'You're not getting me up in that,' and then quit, or was fired. Another pilot came and sat in the cockpit and tried the controls, and saw how hopelessly stiff the warping tailplane was, and said, 'No thanks'. Other pilots came by, and all thought unemployment looked better than being Dr Christmas's test pilot, until one Cuthbert Mills, an American returning from France, agreed to take the job. One of the Continental Aircraft employees took him to one side and said 'Look fella, this guy's nuts, don't chance your life', but he didn't listen, and even invited his mother out to the flying field to watch the first hop. The Bullet got airborne, climbed a little, began to turn, shed its wings and dove vertically into the ground, killing Mills instantly. It wasn't only his mother who wept.

The Army were furious; they'd lost their prototype engine, for one thing. They could not believe the doctor's effrontery when he wrote to them in February 1919 asking for propeller drawings, and revealing that he was building a second Bullet, having obtained a new engine from somewhere else. This new aircraft was put on display in the New York Aero Show the next month with this bold label: 'CHRISTMAS BULLET—safest, easiest controlled plane in the world. Speed 200 mph—6-cylinder Hall-Scott 200 hp motor. Cantilever Aero Company, 1265 Broadway, New York City.' Can you believe that?

Once again the Army wrote to Dr Christmas protesting, and informing him that in no way could he test his aircraft at any of their flying fields. Dr Christmas, with his usual ability to ignore what he did not want to know, replied to the general: 'This company will, within a very short time, take advantage of your invitation to bring the Christmas Bullet to Washington. The machine will be flown from New York to Washington and left there long enough to give you and your advisors sufficient time to thoroughly inspect and appreciate all the good qualities of the Bullet. Our factory is situated not very far from Lufbery Field and the writer is asking you to give permission for the Bullet to be groomed up on this field before the trip is made . . .' No, said the Army, no and no and no again.

What happened next is uncertain, but it seems the doctor managed to obtain the use of a farmer's field somewhere on Long Island, and to hire a Captain Allington Jolly, late of the RAF, to fly the Bullet. It seems he got airborne, but found the elevator control was inadequate to make the aeroplane climb, flew straight into the farmer's barn, and died . . .

Dr Christmas was next heard of testifying before a House of Representatives investigating committee; his Bullet, he told them, was the most efficient aircraft ever built, capable of flying 60 mph faster than any other plane in the world. (He didn't tell them both had crashed.) Before the United States had entered the European war, he went on, Germany had offered him one million dollars in gold, payable in advance, 'to go over there and take over her air service development'. And by now, of course, his company was so swamped with orders from Europe and elsewhere that there was no chance of his fulfilling any US order 'for at least a year, even with a large labour force'. Fantasy, all of it.

Equally fantastic was that the US government did, in 1923, actually *pay* Doctor Christmas $100,000 for an aileron patent he had filed, without attempting any litigation to determine if it was valid!

Thus pensioned, Dr Christmas lived to the fine age of ninety-four, dying in 1960.

6

The Tarrant Tabor

Mr W. G. Tarrant came from Byfleet in Surrey. No doubt as a boy he played on the Common and was sometimes late home for tea. Did he make model aeroplanes, and perhaps boast to his friends that one day he would make the largest plane in the world? Maybe, for the seeds of our grown-up dreams are firmly sown in boyhood. And make just about the biggest plane in the world was quite definitely what W. G. Tarrant tried to do.

Tarrant developed a firm of building contractors, noted for the production of wooden buildings. He got some lucrative contracts for aircraft component manufacture—as did just about every woodworking shop in the land, in those desperate days of the First World War.

Then came the official call for a 'bloody paralyser', a machine big enough to carry the fuel (and maybe even a bomb as well) to get to Berlin. *Bomb Berlin!* It was the idea that appealed to Tarrant, rather than the anticipation of causing any meaningful damage. The Germans had succeeded in bombing London, with tiny, lost forces of Gotha bombers and Zeppelin airships. They hadn't done any real damage, nor taken but a handful of lives, but the sheer dastardliness of the evil Hun in thus taking war so far behind the lines, and terrifying the tweenies and costers and civil servants, filled the British with blind rage and the lust for revenge. Regardless of the cost, Berlin must be bombed in turn.

So the call went out for giant bombers, and it was answered by Fred Handley-Page, and Mr Tarrant the building contractor. Handley-Page had designed and built thousands of warplanes, including whole squadrons of bombers, while Mr Tarrant hadn't; but he wasn't daunted and he assembled a staff of engineers to work with him. Furthermore, he somehow succeeded in getting the government's own aircraft factory, the Royal Aircraft Establishment at Farnborough, firmly on his side.

In the end, the war was over before Handley-Page's giant bombers were ready for action, and before Tarrant's own design was anywhere near completed. But by now Tarrant had got the civil servants thoroughly involved; the RAE regarded the Tarrant

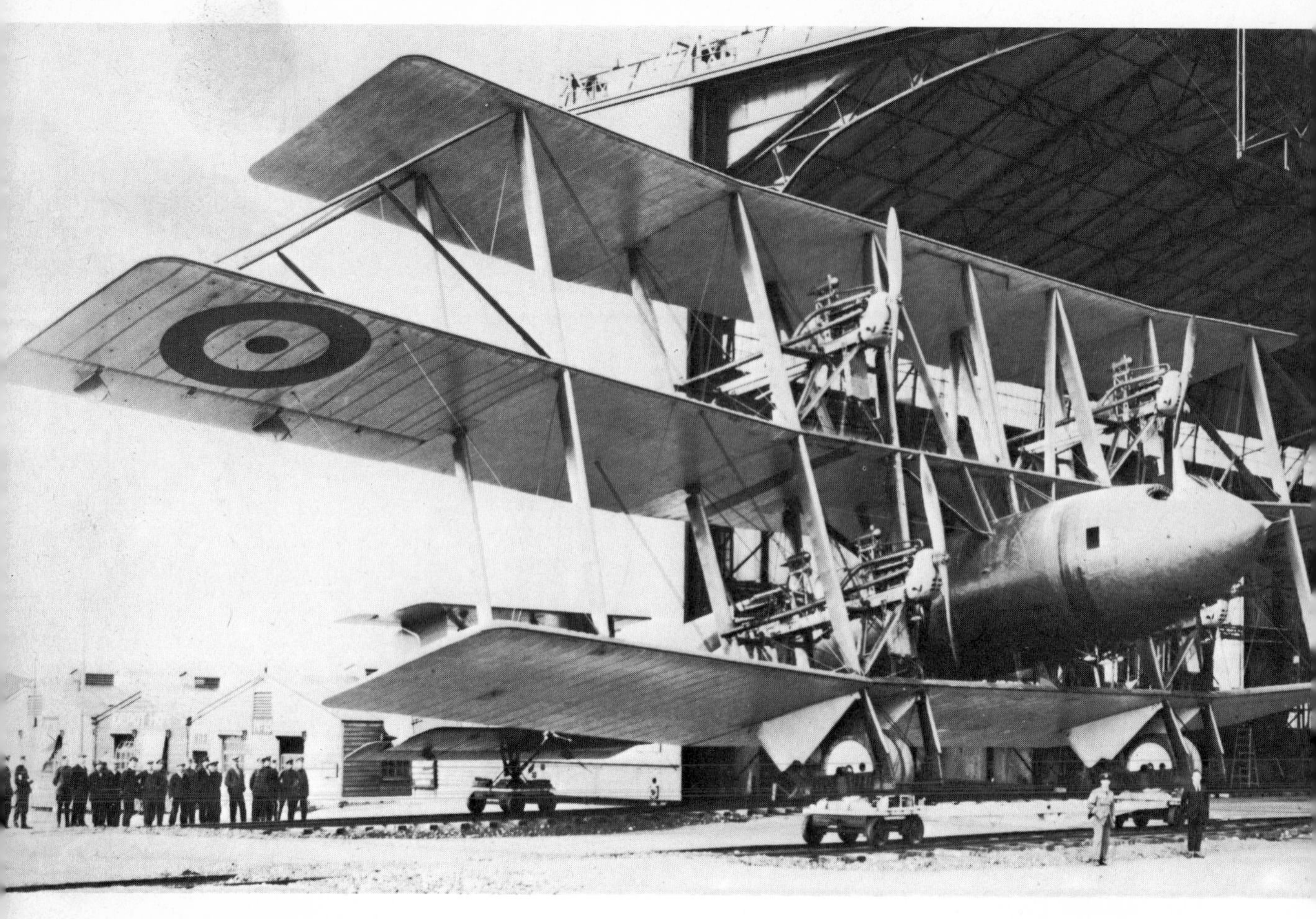

29. The Tabor was a colossal machine, 30 feet larger in span than a Lancaster, and 37 feet high.

Tabor almost as their own, and the RAE's superintendent placed every facility at Tarrant's disposal. War or peace, Tarrant's Tabor was going to be completed. In truth, the authorities had a swords-to-ploughshares dream that big bombers like this one would easily convert to passenger planes, and might soon be coursing through the skies from one European capital to the next, as 80 mph aerial liners.

The Tabor was a colossal machine. Its span of 131 feet was 30 feet larger than that of the Lancaster or Flying Fortress of World War Two; furthermore, the Tabor was a triplane, so that its total wing area of five thousand square feet really put it in the jumbo class. Its weight, empty, was more than twelve tons, and it stood, parked, more than 37 feet high. It was completed in the spring of 1919, in a growing crescendo of press publicity, and finally the world's press were formally invited down to Farnborough to inspect this flying skyscraper. The man from *Flight* magazine thought that Mr Tarrant 'was to be congratulated upon his courage in tackling such a costly experiment in the interests of the development of the large commercial aeroplane of the future . . . He has associated with him a number of specialists . . .' *Flight* forebore to suggest that Mr Tarrant might have preferred to walk before trying to run—the gigantic Tabor was his first aeroplane. Tarrant grew expansive before the assembled journalists, and suggested his Tabor might easily find it possible to fly from London to Bombay with but a single stop; and he allowed that he had a new fuselage on the stocks that would accommodate as many as a hundred passengers.

The man from *Flight* gave the prototype Tabor a most thorough inspection, and his experienced old eyes were, frankly, impressed. Tarrant, his report seemed to imply, might be new to aviation, but he was a demon woodworker. The fuselage was a hollow monocoque, built up of neat circular formers through which the longerons were easily threaded. The skin was formed of strips of wood wound on in two directions to form a stressed ply. (A modern airliner fuselage is built up in much the same way, though using metal instead of wood.) The wings were also all wood, and made extensive use of the bridge-builder's classic Warren girder construction, and Tarrant had evolved (and patented) a particularly neat way of locking the cross-braces to the flanges of the beams. 'The first really practical way of doing this,' was *Flight*'s opinion.

Tarrant's Tabor might indeed have adapted well to passenger carrying, for unlike most bombers of its day, its fuselage was entirely hollow, and quite empty of internal cross-bracing wires and struts to trip over.

'It would appear, therefore,' opined the man from *Flight*, 'that Mr Tarrant has discovered a method of construction which has very much to recommend it; at any rate, for the very large aeroplanes of the future, assuming that wood will remain the material employed . . . for some years to come.' But he added, 'That metal will ultimately supplant it is not unlikely,' which was itself an astonishingly prescient comment for 1919, for it took nearly twenty years for this to happen.

Yet there were aspects of the Tabor's structure that struck *Flight*'s engineer as puzzling, not to say foolish. The ailerons were mounted only on the extra-long centre wing, whose tips were braced only by very long struts that clearly were expected to carry loads in compression as well as tension. But it was the disposition of the engines that bothered him most. There were four between the lower wings, two pulling, two pushing—all well and good. But there were also two more between the *top* wings, quite 27 feet above the ground. What sort of moment, *Flight* wondered, would these top engines exert about the aeroplane's centre of pressure, not to mention its wheels? He even asked Tarrant's engineers pointed questions about this worry; yes, they allowed, he had a point, but they'd done their sums, and found that any tendency those top engines might have to bring the tail up would be counterbalanced by the downdraught from the top wing on to the tailplane. That this might work in flight, but not at low speeds on the take-off run, seems to have occurred to nobody.

This vertical stacking-up of the Tabor's engines was the one real eccentricity of its design. Aircraft engineers like to concentrate the thrust of a plane's engines as centrally as possible; and the Tabor's begetters had originally planned things this way, with four Siddeley Tigers of around 600 hp each clustered neatly between the Tabor's lower wings. But the Tiger, in the words of one historian, 'fell short of expectations' (what engine in those times didn't?), and the Tabor ended up with six Napier Lions, and the two extra engines had to be put somewhere. Up on top.

On May 26th, 1919, the Tabor was ready. One Captain F. G. Dunn, AFC, was the first pilot; he'd been one of the better-known pilots at Hendon in the pre-war days, and had a little time on Handley-Page's giant bomber, the V/1500. Second dicky was one Captain P. T. Rawlings, DSC, an engineer who had flown bombers too, and who was manager of Tarrant's Aeroplane Department. Captain Wilson was technical observer and flight engineer; and three RAE foremen bamboozled their way into being allowed to go along for the ride.

Some last-minute calculations showed that the Tabor might be tail-heavy, so they loaded half a ton of lead shot into the nose for balance. They dragged her sideways out of Farnborough's balloon hangar on her special dollies, and dragged up the special forty-foot high gantry needed to start the engines—all six of which had to be hand-swung, a sweaty routine of shouting and heaving that could take up to an hour, for all six.

Dunn then taxied the giant triplane to and fro about the aerodrome, trying the controls and making turns; then he turned her ponderously into wind to try 'a straight'. He opened up the lower engines, and got the tail up; then he seemed to open up the top engines as well. Abruptly the Tabor nosed over; the nose of the beautiful monocoque fuselage struck the ground and began splintering and crumbling, gouging a deepening furrow through the turf. Further up came the tail, further down went the nose, by now quite disintegrated. The front propellers now began chewing the earth; the A-frame that carried the undercarriage loads up to the engines and wings also dug in, and the Tabor went over on its back in a gigantic rending crash. It came to rest just past the vertical, with the tail sticking in the air like the back end of an impossibly gigantic bomb. One on-looker stayed to call an ambulance, while the rest ran, gasping, towards the wreck. Tenderly they dragged out the three captains, dying of their injuries; the three RAE foremen seemingly escaped harm.

There was an inquest, and they dragged poor Mr Tarrant along to appear. He told the coroner of a sad little quarrel there'd been between his engineers and the RAE over the Tabor's balance, fore and aft. Tarrant had wanted an independent check run by the National Physical Laboratory, but had been convinced by the RAE that his, Tarrant's, engineers were wrong to worry. But worry he did, and so added that half-ton of lead to the nose at the last minute. But it was the sudden thrust from those top engines that surely caused the disaster.

The Tabor was Mr Tarrant's first and last aeroplane.

7

Multiplanes

Nowadays a biplane is something quaint, an obvious antique, a plane you can tell is *old* in one glance: four wings. But in the early days there were more biplanes than monoplanes, and biplanes tended to be more successful. The reasons were structural rather than aerodynamic; with struts and wires you could cross-brace a biplane structure till it was strong, and wouldn't flex. Early monoplane wings tended to flap a bit, sometimes right off the aeroplane, because designers hadn't yet worked out how to make a thin wing rigid. Biplanes, in fact, are still being manufactured in the '70s; Curtis Pitts builds his 'Pitts Special' aerobatic biplanes in Southern Florida (they won the World Aerobatic Contest for the Americans in 1972); and the Russians still build their An-2 utility biplane.

Triplanes, however, are long gone. But they had their day. The English pioneer A. V. Roe began with triplanes, out on the Lea Marshes in Essex in Edwardian days.

'Our general procedure was to make an early start with our experiments. We used to be up at four a.m. when we gathered at our shed under the railway arches. We had boarded up the ends of two of them, but it was hardly an ideal workshop, for there were no windows, and it was necessary to take down the shutters if we wanted light. The arch brick roof invariably leaked as they usually do, the floor was muddy and occasionally we were flooded out. However we had a coke fire to cheer us up, and toast bread, boil water, etc.' [*Hardly the sort of conditions under which they developed Concorde!*] 'The machine would be wheeled out amid occasional excited expressions, sometimes jeers, and sometimes rude remarks from lookers-on.' [*Just like Concorde!*] '"What time are you going up, guv'nor?" was a common remark. We then endeavoured to start the engine, a task which usually took at least a quarter of an hour. When it was started and warmed, I would give the signal "Let's go" and the machine then tore over the ground, followed by my helpers carrying tools, pieces of timber and other necessary appliances to cope with repairs after the almost inevitable crash.'

Then there was the Molesworth triplane of 1911, its wings stacked close as plates on a tray, and *Britannia* in that beautiful shadowed lettering you see on old railway locomotives, all along its fuselage. It wouldn't leave the ground. Nor did the Russian Prince Sergei

30. The famous Fokker triplane climbed like the devil and was as agile as a monkey. Light on the controls and unstable in flight, it would do amazing flat turns without banking.

31. The Red Baron, von Richthofen (on the left in the photo below) flew an all-red triplane, and was eventually shot down in it.

de Bolotoff's huge triplane, unless you count the occasion when a gust of wind overturned it. I could go on for ever.

Two triplane scouts were extremely successful in the First World War: our Sopwith and their Fokker Dr.1. They weren't too fast, due to interference drag as the air flowed between the three sets of planes, but they climbed like the devil, and were highly manoeuvrable and light in pitch—due to the very narrow-chord wing giving only a small centre-of-pressure travel as the angle of attack changed. You didn't have to pull hard to turn. Sopwith's test pilot Harry Hawker looped the prototype triplane three minutes after take-off on its first flight. Oliver Stewart wrote of the aerobatic prowess of the Sopwith triplane: 'Although it did not appear to do the manoeuvres with the suddenness of the biplanes, it did them with infinite grace. The triplane spun rather slowly, and its flick roll was also rather slow compared with other machines of the time; but what it lacked in quickness it made up with the smoothness and grace of its manoeuvres . . . Irreverent pilots said it looked, when doing aerobatics, like an intoxicated flight of stairs.'

Anthony Fokker's famous triplane was not only light in pitch but unstable in yaw as well, due to its short fuselage with no fin, and only a small rudder. Verner Voss battled alone with seven Se-5s for long minutes, shooting holes in all of them with his Fokker. 'His machine was exceptionally manoeuvrable and he appeared able to take flying liberties with impunity . . . I put my nose down to give him a burst, perhaps too soon; to my amazement he kicked on full rudder without bank, pulled his nose up slightly, gave me a burst while he was skidding sideways, and then kicked on opposite rudder before the results of this amazing stunt appeared to have any effect on the manoeuvrability of his machine.' They finally got Voss, but another of the Se-5 pilots remembered: 'As long as I live I shall never forget my admiration of that German pilot, who, single-handed, fought seven of us for ten minutes and also put some bullets through all of our machines. His flying was wonderful, his courage magnificent . . .'

And the bloody Red Baron himself, von Richthofen, was flying a Fokker triplane when he too was shot down. His squadron had re-equipped with faster biplanes, but he had kept on his triplane, for its lightness and manoeuvrability.

Almost every aeroplane designer of the First World War tried a triplane; most quickly abandoned the layout. The only successful triplanes were those with 'forward stagger'—with the top wing a mite ahead of the centre wing and the bottom one a mite back—which gave something approaching stability. The Russians built a triplane with so much forward stagger that the wings were effectively in line astern; there's a picture of it flying, but it might be faked. A Nieuport with the top wing well back was noted as 'extraordinarily unstable'.

The Belgian ace Willy Coppens has described the typical fate of one of these wildly experimental types: 'The three mainplanes, supported by one strut only on each side, could be pivoted on their axis in order to vary the incidence. I can now see the weakness of this form of construction.' One of the pioneers of Belgian aviation, Jules Vedrines, was hired to do the test flying, and made some carefully tentative hops. One day when

32. This Nieuport triplane had the top wing set well back, and was quite extraordinarily unstable.

Vedrines was away, 'the designer of the machine and the madmen who were financing the enterprise' persuaded a different pilot to have a go. 'He took off boldly, and started climbing steadily, but when he tried to flatten out to fly level, the machine started "bucketing" like a wagtail. Thereafter things happened quickly. Unable to hold the machine in, and seeking safety in speed (instead of by reducing power) he dived straight into the ground at something approaching 150 mph. From a distance we saw a column of dust rise from the spot, and heard the dread sound of wood breaking into a thousand fragments—a sound that sends cold shivers down the spine . . . And then that awful deadly silence.'

The triplane layout appealed to early bomber designers; if you have engines of poor power-to-weight ratio, as they did, about the only way you can give an aeroplane the capacity to carry any sort of bomb load is to give it a huge wing area, while at the same time keeping the structure light. So the triplane was an obvious solution. Certainly it was to the Italian Count Gianni Caproni di Taliedo, whose huge designs flew so slowly they practically went backwards in anything above a strong breeze: no overwhelming disadvantage, since their effect on the poor Austro-Hungarian soldiers in the trenches was principally psychological. But even in 1916 a maximum speed of 78 mph was really too slow.

And if three wings, why not four? Why not indeed, thought 'tall, slick, monocled, iron-jawed' Noel Pemberton-Billing, a wealthy Englishman who was afraid neither of being thought eccentric or of throwing his money around. He had learned to fly in

33. The Italian Caproni Ca 42 was very slow, and difficult to fly, and vulnerable despite an arsenal of defensive weapons.

twenty-four hours for a bet of £500 with Fred Handley-Page, a notable skinflint who was obliged to pay up when Billing did it, gaining his Royal Aero Club certificate within the time. Billing was an ardent mariner who'd made his wealth by yacht brokerage and quiet gun-running, so it was to build seaplanes that he'd originally started his aircraft company on the shore of Southampton Water. For it he chose the telegraphic address 'Supermarine', and that later became the name of the business too, and you are right, this was the same business which produced the Schneider Trophy winners and the Spitfire.

Pemberton-Billing's great quadruplane was no boat but a landplane, conceived as the answer to German Zeppelin raids. There'd been twenty such on England in 1915, and while the damage done by their bombs and the numbers of British civilians hurt were tiny by World War II standards, this was the first time since 1066 that any damned foreigners had inflicted any damage at all on the British mainland, and the public outcry was fantastic. Billing had always nursed a strange hatred of Zeppelins.

In 1914 he had joined the Royal Naval Volunteer Reserve and organised the first real bombing raid—an attack by four Avro Tabloids on the Zeppelin hangars by Lake Constance, which had succeeded in blowing up one airship in its shed. But Billing was far from being an organisation man, and 'his tempestuous temperament had resulted in officially-sponsored retirement from the RNAS'. In January 1916 he was back running his aeroplane works—and standing for parliament for Mile End in East London, where he must have been thought an unusual toff indeed. He did his best to cash in on the anti-

34. Pemberton-Billing's Nighthawk, designed as a Zeppelin-terrifier, had posts for three gunners, one with a $1\frac{1}{2}$-pounder; it also carried an aerial searchlight with its own generator.

Zeppelin feeling: 'In parliament I shall be able to enforce such vigorous air policy that German aircraft will be attacked wherever they are built or harboured', he promised. 'They will be fought in the air before they reach our shores, and the sky over London will be so well guarded that if any escape they will never dare return . . . The British airship which flew over London a few days ago would not be much good against a Zeppelin; but we have a machine—it flew for the first time this morning—which carries an armament before which a Zeppelin would turn back and never come here again.'

What was this wonder? None other than the Supermarine P.B. 9: four sets of wings, two pusher engines, two pilots in separate cockpits just in case any lucky Zeppelin gunner might manage to wing one of them, and a streamlined nacelle just under the topmost wing where sat the demon gunner. It flew just seven weeks after its construction had begun, and crashed just a few days after that. But the Admiralty were interested enough to give Pemberton-Billing an official contract for a four-winged Zeppelin-straffer.

So Billing turned out a second quadruplane, similar to the P.B. 9, but with tractor engines and a redesigned top turret. There was only one pilot, who sat inside the fuselage just behind the wing, from whence he can hardly have seen anything at all—particularly when trying to land—and posts for three gunners. One, up top and facing back, had a Lewis gun on a Scarff ring mount, just in case any dastardly Hun dared be so bold as to attack this attacker; another could pop his head out of a hole in the forward fuselage and operate another ring-mounted Lewis. But the real bite belonged to the forward upper turret gun, a $1\frac{1}{2}$-pounder Davis gun on a traverse mounting, which should knock any Zeppelin out of the sky. To assist in aiming at night there was a searchlight on gimbals in the aircraft's nose, driven by its own 5 hp motor attached to an electric generator. So that if nothing else this Supermarine Nighthawk (they called it that) embodied the world's first auxiliary power unit and the world's first aerial searchlight. It also carried a ton of fuel which was supposed to give it an endurance of eighteen hours, which I doubt, but there was a sleeping berth provided for the gunner or gunners just in case. The point of the quadruplane layout was to enable the Nighthawk to loiter, flying very slowly, throttled well back, and its speed range was from 75 mph down to as low as 35 mph on its two Anzani 100 hp radial engines.

The Nighthawk was not proceeded with, perhaps because it was just too slow and top-heavy, nor did Mile End elect Pemberton-Billing, despite his having paid Horatio Bottomley, the con-man and publisher of *John Bull*, to give him support. Mr Billing was too modest, wrote Bottomley: he was the true inventor and builder of this wondrous machine, and the day he was elected to Parliament he would fly over Mile End in it and drop his thanks from the skies to the voters. Perhaps Billing was too good for the Mile End; at any rate East Herts duly elected him in a by-election two months later.

Three wings, four wings, why stop there? Count Caproni didn't, with his Ca 60. Nine wings it had, attached to a kind of gigantic houseboat of a hull, and the whole thing was the size of a block of flats, and, says one Italian historian, 'would not have looked

35. Count Caproni's most ambitious freak was this Ca 90, a kind of flying houseboat with eight engines and nine wings, and about the size of a block of flats. It was wrecked on its first flight.

out of place sailing up the English Channel with the Spanish Armada in 1588'.

It had eight 400 hp American Liberty engines, four at the front pulling, and four at the back pushing. The centre two were mounted in the same nacelle and connected to the same propeller, while the nacelles for the outer pair ran back the full length of the structure, through the centre wings to join up with the outer nacelles at the rear. The idea of this was to help brace the unwieldy triplane wings, and to provide a walk-way for mechanics to rush about in servicing the engines in flight—which if you know much about Liberty engines, makes some sense. The poor mechanics could either crawl down the inside of the nacelles, or dance around on top of them.

The Ca 60 was launched on Lake Maggiore in January 1921, and they invited the American ambassador, since it had American engines. They began trials in the spring: the very first hop was enough to reveal that the monster was viciously unstable, which is about what you would expect it to be, with all those wings and no tail surfaces. The test pilot was a Signor Semprini; a photo of him survives, and a most worried looking young man he was, too. However, they seem to have over-ruled his nervous doubts about the Capronissimo, for they loaded ballast equivalent to sixty passengers aboard (nothing really, since the Ca 60 was supposed to be able to carry 100) and told him to take her away. Who says Italians are not super brave? Semprini gunned his 3,200 hp, and took her up to sixty feet—which is as high as she got; the Ca 60 put her nose firmly down and headed for the deep. Semprini did his best, but the ballast shifted, the centre wings snapped loose, and in she went. There survives a photograph of the wreck, still half afloat, with a cluster of boats around her, and one of the boatmen is *laughing*. There was something to be pleased about: Semprini, despite the fact that his pilot's cabin was right at the front of the machine, and therefore hit the water first, managed to escape the wreck unhurt.

They did plan to rebuild the Ca 60 and try again, but a mysterious fire destroyed it before they could begin. I doubt that anyone, except possibly Count Caproni himself, was too sad.

But nine wings was by no means any kind of record. What was? Probably one of the venetian-blind efforts of Horatio Phillips, a 'clever but somewhat dogmatic' Victorian engineer who had patented a marine hydrofoil with multiple vanes, and had then gone on to an aerial version of the same. (But air and water do not behave similarly: air is compressible, while water, as you will know if you have ever belly-flopped into a swimming pool, hardly is. Multiple vanes lift well in water, poorly if at all in air.) Horatio Phillips built four helicopters and five or six aircraft and spent £4,000, all his own, before he gave up. He should have done better than he did, for he was a pioneer aerodynamicist who as early as 1884 had taken out a patent for 'wings with slightly thickened leading edge, so curved on the top surface that a vacuum is produced', which is certainly thinking along the right lines.

He was perhaps as sensitive to ridicule as A. V. Roe *wasn't*, for he kept on the move, testing his weird aircraft variously in such romantic locations as Battersea Park; at

36. Horatio Phillips' 1904 multiplane had twenty vanes hand-carved of yellow pine, and a water-cooled engine that Phillips made himself. Tests proved the craft impossible to control, but he went on to make others with 50 and 110 slats.

Norwood; by the Crystal Palace; near Streatham and at Mitcham. Phillips's 1904 multiplane had a framework of twenty vanes all hand-carved out of yellow pine, plus a 4-cylinder water-cooled engine of 22 hp that he had made himself; the man was a fine engineer. The craft 'lacked longitudinal stability and control, and underwent a number of design changes'. In 1907 he finished another, with fifty slats in each of four frames. This monstrosity is supposed to have made one hop with over 500 feet passed while airborne, which would make it the first powered aircraft to fly in Britain.

'Evidence exists', boldly states one reference book, 'of another Phillips man-carrying multiplane.' With a single venetian-blind wing but containing 110 slats or winglets. Twenty, fifty, 110: one wonders by what scientific process he chose the number of slats to make? It must, I am sure, be one of Phillips's multiplanes in that old clip of film they trot out on television occasionally, wherein this mad contraption runs like a headless chicken towards the camera and then stops, sags, rolls over and folds up in a dead tangle of wreckage. There's also a shot of a helicopter that bounds up and down on its wheels like an energetic puppy till bits fly off and it too topples over, flaps feebly and disintegrates. Could this be one of Phillips's machines, too?

Even more preposterous was a 1918 affair (and they should have known better by 1918) named the John Multiplane, started with wartime funds by the American military, and assembled for test at Langley Field in Virginia in 1919. It had seven wings assembled in no particular obvious order, but all at sixes and (literally) sevens with each other, some up, some down, some forwards, some back. More than sixty struts, every one beautifully polished, were used in that birdcage of wings, and more wire than in a dozen Bechstein grands. It was, said one wit, 'the first split level airplane'. From surviving photographs I would say it stood fully 20 feet high, and was probably 40 feet long and 60 in span. To power this monster: one pathetic little Liberty engine in the nose! Of course it never flew above a few feet, which is a mercy, for the craft's tailplane looks far too small to have been capable of controlling it in flight. Herbert F. John, may your name live for ever, even though your multiplane didn't.

37. The 1919 John multiplane, built with US military funds, had seven wings in a cluster, and more than sixty polished struts. Unbelievably, it did get airborne.

8

Gee Bees

Nowadays, if you want to be in the aeroplane designing business, you must go to school for about a hundred years first. Finally you graduate, festooned in degrees, and go to work in a fluorescent-lit drawing office, a beehive somewhere in southern California, in the smog. That's where you spend half your life; the other half you're out of work.

It wasn't always so. Once a little native wit and ingenuity was enough. Take the five Granville Brothers—farm boys from Madison, New Hampshire, and I don't think more than about one of them got much beyond the third grade. The eldest was the wildest, the born organiser in the family. His name was Zantford Granville, a very New England-Puritan name, but everyone called him 'Granny'.

Granny was one of those kids who is always inventing. He hooked up a little gas engine to the water-well windlass; he fixed the barnyard gate so it could be raised in winter, above the snow level; he built an adding machine; and a wooden bicycle, to save walking. All these, note, were labour-saving devices—but if Granny was physically lazy, his wits were alive enough.

Granny was fascinated by flying, but terrified, *petrified* of heights. 'Climbing to the top of our barn,' remembered brother Tom in an interview with Bill Sweet for the Experimental Aircraft Association's *Sport Aviation* magazine, 'just scared the life from him and he was numb with fear for several days.' But one day Granny screwed up his courage and went for a flip in an old Curtiss, and found, as have many other surprised kids, that a fear of heights often doesn't translate into a fear of flying.

Around 1922, Granny was running a garage in Arlington, Massachusetts. By 1925, he was working for the Boston Airport Corporation, and brother Tom was minding the garage. Granny promptly got into an argument with his boss, which is an employee's privilege, and promptly got fired, which is the boss's. Granny went back and hung around the garage, 'driving me nuts with his restlessness', remembers Tom.

If no one wants to hire you, what do you do but go into business for yourself? So Granny pulled out his severance pay and put it down on an old car. He put a truck body on the frame, and equipped it with a work bench, tools, welding gear, dope and fabric,

38. Granny Granville and the barrel-shaped Gee Bee racer. Farm boys with only a grade school education, the Granvilles' design was briefly the fastest plane in the world. Every one built crashed.

nails and lengths of sitka spruce, and it became Granny's mobile aeroplane-fixing service—you call, we come; you bend 'em, we mend 'em. He succeeded, too, and soon added a roof rack for wing panels and a tow-bar for fuselages, so he could tow any damaged planes home for repairs.

And if fixing planes for a living does one thing for you, it is to convince you how *bad* most of them were even before they needed fixing. And most planes in the 1920s weren't bad, they were rotten. So before long, Granny began to have ideas about designing and building his own aeroplane. His four brothers all loved the sound of that, and soon it became a spare-time, weekends-and-evenings project for the five of them. Six, really, for they took on a friend who had just enough cash for a used 60 hp motor.

The Gee Bee ('G.B.'—Granville Brothers) Model One was a perfectly ordinary biplane. Well, no, it wasn't quite. It had flaps on all four wings, for one thing. The tail-wheel swivelled through 360 degrees but had a flat spot on the cam to keep it straight on the rollout. It had a hanging control stick to give more leg room, a landing gear with universal joints that would swing away in a dud landing without taking out the bottom longeron with it, a quick-disconnect on each control stick so if your pupil got panicky and froze, you could cut him out of the loop. So the first Gee Bee was bursting with bright ideas, even if it was fairly conventional in layout.

You know how for the first flight of a new design it is usual to wait for perfect weather, dead calm and unlimited visibility? Granny's impatience so got the better of him he ended up first-flying the first Gee Bee in the middle of the night, in a thunderstorm. He simply couldn't wait; no chute, either—couldn't wait for that to arrive. Granny later allowed that part of his reason for the midnight flip was he didn't want anyone laughing at him if things went wrong. But they didn't, and the Granville Brothers were now in the aeroplane-building business.

First, they needed premises, for they couldn't get any kind of lease at Boston. This was the heyday of May 1929, and the nearby city of Springfield welcomed them with open arms, financing them, and giving them an old dance pavilion for a factory. Eight more of these Model A biplanes were quickly turned out before the Wall Street crash arrived, to teach the Granville Brothers the lesson that when things are bad on Wall Street, the first thing people stop buying is private planes.

But they soldiered on as best they could. They had by now hired a real engineer, Bob Hall, who helped them design a really modern plane, a little low-wing monoplane. Figuring that publicity might help them sell a few of these Sportsters even in those hard times, they put a Cirrus engine in the plane and entered it in the 1930 All-American Flying Derby, a gigantic 5,541-mile sort-of-race and reliability trial organised by the manufacturers of the Cirrus engine as a promotion piece for planes powered by their product.

The first Gee Bee Sportster was flown in the Air Derby by one Lowell Bayles, a local barn-stormer. Bayles didn't win, but he did come in second at 116.40 mph; not bad for 110 horsepower.

They stretched the Model X single-seater Sportster into the two-seat Model Y Senior Sportster, but they still weren't making money. In those times, who was? It was in the early summer of 1931 that Granny had the idea that was to bring fame, fortune, tragedy, horror and downfall to Granville Brothers Aircraft. About the only loose cash still lying around in aviation, he reckoned, was the prize money being offered at the National Air Races. They'd build a racer and win some of it. They began in mid-July, and Hall went out and pounded Springfield's pavements looking for backers for the racer. It flew in late August—a flying pickle-barrel of an aeroplane, painted a waspish yellow and black, and powered by a racing Wasp borrowed from Pratt & Whitney and souped up to 535 hp. Lowell Bayles, who'd flown the Sportster in the Aerial Derby, had put $500 of his own cash into this new Model Z racer, so they let him fly it. He won the Goodyear at 206.001 mph; the Thompson at 236.239; and the Shell Speed Dash at 267.342—the highest speed of the whole meeting. The designer Bob Hall won a mixed free-for-all race in the new racer, and other races flying one of the Model Y Senior Sportsters.

It was an incredible performance. These five farm boys, with grade school education, had produced about the fastest plane in the world, a bare two and a half years after setting up their business. The plane had been built in six weeks and had flown for the very first time just one week before the air races began! If only they had left it at that! But no: with the fastest plane in the world, they wanted the world airspeed record too. They prized out of Pratt & Whitney an even bigger Wasp—a 1,340-cubic-inch, 750 hp monster—stuck it in the Model Z, and took off for Detroit to do their record runs.

The record attempt went badly. They had to do four runs on a single flight, and

39. Lowell Bayles won three major races in this Gee Bee in 1931, then was killed attempting a world record.

40. In cutaway, (*below*) Gee Bee Number 11 took the record in 1932 and won the Thompson Trophy, flown by Jimmy Doolittle.

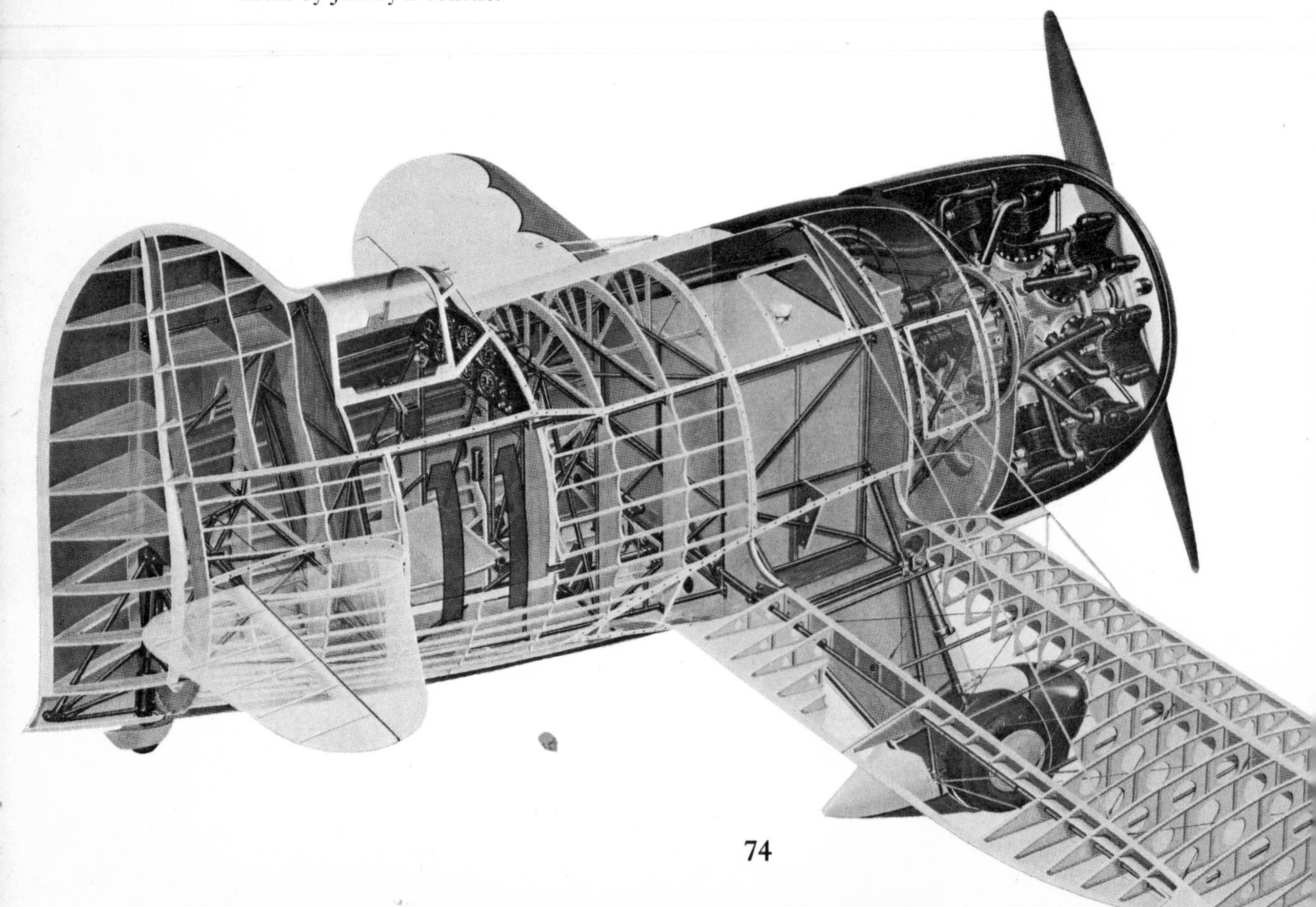

nothing ever went quite right, with even the timing apparatus quitting on one attempt. They did hit 314 mph on one run. Then, on December 5, during one last go, a fuel cap came loose and smashed into the windshield, clouting Bayles in the eye. Dizzily he started to pull up, but the Model Z pitched up on him. One wing folded back, and the Gee Bee snapped and snapped and snapped, rolling over and over till it hit the ground, disintegrated and burned. They found Lowell Bayles's body 50 feet from the wreckage; and all America mourned, for in those distant days, air racing was the very frontier of science and excitement.

They were to go on mourning. More of these Super Sportsters, the true racing-barrel Gee Bees, were built, and crashed, and rebuilt, and crashed again. The Springfield Air Racing Association had shown a profit of better than 100 percent on their original 1931 programme, so for 1932 they built two more racers, the R-1 and R-2, of still more exaggerated barrel form. A man named Russell Boardman had become the major stockholder in the SARA, so they let him make the first flight in the R-1, on August 13th, 1932. The R-1 had absolutely no vertical stabilizer at all—simply a rudder tacked onto the end of that cavernous fuselage, but one hop in that configuration was enough for Boardman; so horrendous was the lack of lateral stability he made them add a small fin before he'd fly it again. A month later Boardman, testing one of the regular Sportster models, spun in, putting himself in the hospital over race week. Who was to race the new plane?

This question resolved itself neatly when the great Jimmy Doolittle had to make a wheels-up in his Laird Super Solution during a test flight; Doolittle would fly the Gee Bee. In September, he set a new world landplane speed record of 296.287 mph in the R-1 over a 3-km straight course; and two days later he won the Thompson at 252.686. Doolittle's handling of the monster has been described as 'gentle but firm'. With 800 hp and one of the new controllable pitch propellers it 'fairly leapt off the ground to take the lead almost immediately'. The plane had 'plenty of brute power but less maneuverability' than the slower contestants.

Soon after, Doolittle announced his retirement from air racing to devote all his time and energies to the affairs of Shell. About the business of air racing, he later wrote, 'I have yet to hear of the first case of anyone engaged in this work dying of old age.' Had the R-1's handling persuaded him there was no future in it? Maybe. Forward visibility for take-off and landing was clearly nil. Elevator and rudder blanketing at high angles of attack must have been desperate; they were, after all, trying to fight the torque of 800 hp with a fuselage less than 18 feet long to the back of the rudder!

Why were the Gee Bee racers such a grotesque shape? There are fashions in aerodynamics as in most kinds of art and science, and the fashion in the early '30s was the 'perfect streamline form', a bulbous teardrop shape, rounded at the front, reaching maximum thickness at maybe a third of its length, and tapering from there to a pointed rear. The word was, this form was the thing for minimum drag. But this shape clashed with the latest fashion in engines, the new radial air-cooled powerplants, which put the maximum *necessary* cross-sectional area right at the front of the beast. So to approximate

41. Russell Boardman, the Granville Brothers' backer, was killed in Number 11 at Indianapolis.

the supposed perfect streamline form, the fuselage had to get still fatter aft of the engine, till it could begin tapering to the tail. (Most of a racing Gee Bee's fuselage was simply empty space. The rudder was a foot thick at the hinge line.)

And to cut down on wetted area, they made the fuselage as short as they dared—the R-1's fuselage was actually shorter than that of the lower-powered Y Sportster model. And racing pilots in those days were supermen; racing planes weren't supposed to be easy to fly. Because of the weight of the engine they put the pilot away aft for balance, right where he couldn't see anything. And they put the wheels way forward, too, so their huge 'perfect streamline form' fairings gave them still more side area up front, just where they didn't need it.

In 1933, things really began to go cruelly sour for the Gee Bees. The National Air Races that year were in Los Angeles, so the transcontinental race ran from east to west. Coming in to refuel at Indianapolis, boy racer Russell Thaw in the R-2 lost it on touch-down, hit a wing tip and ground-looped. They dragged the aeroplane into a hangar and patched up the crumpled wing. Next in was Boardman in the R-1, by now powered by a colossal 900-hp Hornet.

Boardman found Thaw thoroughly upset by his near-crash, nervously pacing up and down in front of the hangars while time went by, and by. Boardman gassed up and took off. A wind change caught him as he broke ground; he stalled, rolled and slid 200 yards upside down. They dragged him out and off to the hospital, with a broken skull; they couldn't operate because of the injuries he'd sustained in the crash a year earlier. Thaw, sensibly enough would go no further. Boardman died without regaining consciousness.

Two Gee Bee pilots were now dead. There was to be a third before the year was out: a twenty-six-year-old girl named Florence Klingensmith, flying a 450 hp Whirlwind-powered Model Y Senior Sportster in the Chicago races, had the fabric open up on one wing. She flew a mile away from the course, struggling to regain control, but eventually jumped, too low for her chute to save her. They found her in a nursery garden, surrounded by flowers.

The Granvilles patched up their remaining racer, Thaw's R-2, and later in the year, one Jimmy Haizlip did some test flying in it. On one landing, he touched down a mite crooked, and the R-2 dropped a wing, snap-rolled, dug in a wing tip and went cartwheeling, over and over down the field. Virtually nothing was left of the plane except the cockpit area, from which they pulled Haizlip, cut about and rather bruised. 'The blamed thing,' he is supposed to have explained, 'kept trying to bite itself in the tail.'

Effectively, 1933 finished Granville Brothers Aircraft. They'd wrecked both their special racers. They'd won less than $2,000 in prize money that year, and they'd lost their wealthiest backer, Russell Boardman. In February 1934, they lost Granny himself; he spun in trying to deliver a Warner-powered Sportster in bad weather to one of the very rare customers for Gee Bee aeroplanes. But the company kept on; they'd carted home the wrecks of the R-1 and R-2 and combined the best bits of both in a new racer. They called the new plane *Intestinal Fortitude*, which was doubtless what its building had taken. They shelved their ambitious plans for four-, six-, and even eight-seat Sportster models.

They started building a new and bigger racer, which they named the *Q.E.D.* (it's a Latin tag much used by mathematicians in algebraic problems, short for *quod erat demonstrandum*, 'which has already been proved'.) Then they went broke.

Granville Brothers Aircraft was sold up soon after Granny's death. But somehow money was found to finish the *Q.E.D.*, for coming up was the world's greatest long-distance air race, the $50,000 MacRobertson race from London to Sydney. Built for Jacqueline Cochran, the *Q.E.D.* was a stretched Gee Bee—a long-range racer whose fuselage was extended to carry 400 gallons, enough for a 2,400-mile range. For the big race, she took along Wesley Smith as co-pilot. For all its lengthened fuselage and more sensible dimensions, it was still a Gee Bee.

There was something funny about the airflow over the double-hinged flaps that caused the plane to quit flying just as they were beginning to think about rounding out for landing. It would fall the last 30 or 40 feet with a tremendous crash. It did so when they arrived at Mildenhall outside London for the start of the race. 'Don't think too much about it,' Wesley Smith told the English reporters. 'It always lands that way.' It landed that way in Bucharest in Rumania, even though they couldn't get the flaps down, and they were out of the race with damaged elevators. Smith stayed on in Bucharest, and even set up a local speed record with a Rumanian prince named Cantacuzene for co-pilot.

Meanwhile, back home, the R-1/2 hybrid had been taxied into a ditch—perhaps the kindest thing that could have happened to it. For 1935 it was once more rebuilt and christened *Spirit of Right* by its pilot Cecil Allen, whose backers, of all people, were a religious magazine. But even the power of prayer wasn't enough to save Allen: taking off in a fog for the start of the 1935 Bendix, he lost it, and fell into a potato field.

The *Q.E.D.* soldiered on for four more years. It was finally bought by an ace Mexican flyer named Francisco Sarabia, who on May 24th, 1939, set a speed record by flying nonstop from Mexico City to New York in 10 hours 47 minutes. Taking off from Bolling Field in Washington, D.C., on his homeward journey, a rag casually left inside the cowling was sucked into the carburettor. The *Conquistador del Cielo*, for that was how Sarabia had renamed her, stalled, fell into the Potomac, and Sarabia was drowned.

So ends the prodigiously tragic history of the Gee Bees. At least, I hope it does, for the *Conquistador del Cielo* still exists; it is on public display at the Mexican Air Force base at Santa Lucia. I don't know what sort of state the ship is in. Bad, I hope, lest anyone should ever be tempted to try to rebuild her and fly her once more. Enough is enough.

The Gee Bee is amongst the finest, best engineered planes ever made.

42. This rebuilt hybrid of the two racing Gee Bees was bought by Mexican ace Francisco Sarabia. He drowned in her after a take-off accident.

This plane was made after the Gee Bee Co went into liquidation and is not a hybrid of any previous machines.

9

The Barling Bomber

If at first you don't succeed . . . why then, *give up*, of course, and try your hand at something different. However: some people are dumb and courageous enough to try, try and try again—among them Walter H. Barling, who had designed the Tarrant Tabor, so vividly described in chapter six. He went off to America, still dreaming of giant triplane bombers, where he met General Billy Mitchell, who had risen to fame as the commander of the American air services at the Front in France in 1918. Mitchell was a complex, explosive character. The official history of the USAF calls him 'the outstanding American air combat commander of the war', but allows that he was as well as 'colourful and dashing' also 'determined to cut red tape and get things done no matter how'. Other historians go further, saying he 'also possessed some less endearing traits—a touch of arrogance, a streak of flamboyance, and tendency to exaggeration and verbal intemperance'. Said the US Navy Admiral Richard E. Byrd of him: 'I believe he was sincere, but his sincerity was the ruthless pertinacity of a zealot . . .'

In 1919 America's front line of defence against the envy of less wealthy lands was her battleships. 'The supposed invulnerability of a battleship was echoed in its alternate title of "dreadnought"', notes C. R. Roseberry in his history *The Challenging Skies.* 'To suggest that one of these vessels might be sunk by bombs from above was rank heresy.' Thus rank heresy was exactly what Billy Mitchell began to propound. You can imagine what the admirals felt about *him.* But to the Englishman Walter Barling, he must have seemed heaven-sent. In no time at all Mitchell had obtained for Barling a $375,000 US Army contract to build, yes, you've guessed it, the world's biggest aircraft, a triplane bomber. This nonsense was so huge that it had to be built in sections. It stood 37 feet high and weighed 21 tons, just standing there empty. It bore a more than casual resemblance to Barling's earlier design, the Tarrant Tabor; but this time there were no overbalancing engines on the top wing, and there was an extra set of wheels under the nose to stop the thing nosing over. But it was a monstrous machine, looking 'more likely to antagonise the air than to pass through it' in the words of one who saw it.

The Barling Bomber's first flight was on August 22nd, 1923. Unlike the Tabor it *did* actually fly, but as to performance, the thing could hardly get out of its own way. It wouldn't even do 100 mph, or fly the 400 miles from the Army Air Corps' Dayton headquarters to Washington. Bombed up, the Barling Bomber had a range of under 200 miles. Too much drag: interference drag between all those struts and wires and wings and things, and not enough power, even for six Liberty engines. The Barling Bomber flew around, very slowly, for several years, often being on display at air shows, and even setting up eight world records. The proposed second aircraft was never built and the first one was scrapped in 1928.

General Billy Mitchell went on to prove that you could indeed sink battleships with bombs from aircraft—and was court-martialled for 'conduct to the prejudice of good order and military discipline'. The prosecutor at the trial had a field day, describing Mitchell as 'the charlatan and demagogue type' and 'a good flier, a fair rider, a good shot, flamboyant, self-advertising, widely imaginative, destructive, never constructive except in wild, non-feasible schemes, and never overly careful as to the ethics of his methods'. And the Barling Bomber was surely the wildest, least feasible of his schemes.

43. The 1923 Barling Bomber was the world's biggest, but so slow it could hardly get out of its own way.

10

The R101 Airship

Friedrichshafen in March, still under the icy pall of a particularly bitter northern European winter: the invited guests for Dr Eckener's airship cruise aboard the *Graf Zeppelin* are well wrapped and furred. They need to be, for the airship is unheated. But by next morning they are sailing up the sunny Mediterranean, warm as summer, from Marseille past the French Navy dozing at Toulon; past St Tropez, then a simple fishing village unknown to any outsiders except a few lotus-eating painters; on up the Riviera, low and slow, time for all aboard to soak up the sights of Cannes, and Nice, and Monte Carlo sheltering at the base of its mile-high mountain. The guests, who include the minister of this and the president of that, are just enthralled.

'It was as if we were softly gliding through an infinity of surrounding misty blue. Air and sea merged imperceptibly into each other. We flew on, as if set free from hard, rough material things, in a world of fragrance and soft light. As in a dream, the passengers sat at prettily decorated coffee-tables and, in a mood of wordless ecstasy, enjoyed good Friedrichshafen pastry together with the fabulous panorama of the sea. Yes, an airship voyage is wonderful!'—the words are those of Captain Eckener himself.

From San Remo he heads the airship south, out to sea. It's only seventy sea miles to Corsica; thence to Ostia and inland to Rome, where they circle, again slowly, and send Mussolini a telegram. Southwards to Naples 'where the city itself, Vesuvius, Capri, Sorrento and Amalfi competed for the prize of beauty'. Darkness falls as they reach the Straits of Messina, and soon they sit down to dinner. 'We had turtle soup, ham with asparagus, roast beef with vegetables and salad, celery with Roquefort cheese, and an excellent nut cake from Friedrichshafen.' Together with a fine hock and Mosel wine in abundance.

By breakfast time they are over the coast of Crete. A straight flight throughout that day south-eastwards to Haifa in what is then called Palestine, where they cruise above Jerusalem, getting a god's-eye view of those earthbound holy places. That evening Captain Eckener takes them (in bright moonlight) out over the Dead Sea, which is well below sea level, and he takes the *Graf Zeppelin* down, down till it is flying a thousand feet below sea level!

44. The *Graf Zeppelin* made some fantastic voyages, including one around the world.

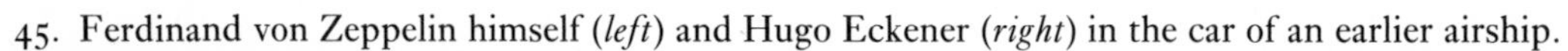

45. Ferdinand von Zeppelin himself (*left*) and Hugo Eckener (*right*) in the car of an earlier airship.

'The barely risen moon shone still with little power, so that the great lake lay reflected in semi-darkness, as mysterious as the nether world. We slowly sank down, carefully feeling our way lower and lower, until we hovered a few hundred feet over the surface of the water. We looked up to the heights towering around us as if from a cellar.'

The measly British ran Egypt too, in those days, and they refused Eckener permission to head for Cairo: they don't want the wily Hun impressing the *fellaheen* with their technological prowess. So Eckener steams up the coast just out beyond the three-mile limit, and wryly sends King Fuad a wireless cable regretting that 'contrary winds prevent us from flying over the land of the wonders of a thousand years'. What a diplomat! There'll be questions in the British House of Commons about that, you mark my words! Then northwards, sailing over those dreamy Homeric islands of the Aegean to Athens, where they drone twice round the Acropolis in one morning. Then homewards over the Austrian Alps, where it's winter again, and snowflakes twirl past the cabins and plaster wetly against the forward windows. The President of the Reichstag, who is perhaps *the* guest of honour, is brought to the wireless microphone to broadcast midnight greetings to the gay midnight waltzers of Vienna. Back to Friedrischshafen early that morning, in perfect comfort and safety (except for the northern chill) from an Odyssey that lasted a glorious three days and four nights.

This fantastic journey took place in 1929. And if you consider just how little advanced aeroplanes were in 1929—small, rattly, unreliable, uncomfortable, short of range and ability to navigate—you can see at once why the airship then seemed invincible for all long-range flight. Nothing to match it. No winged aircraft had that sort of range for another twenty years; or that endurance to this day. Also, airships could cope safely with bad weather such as fog or low cloud; whereas aeroplanes could barely stay upright in the clouds let alone find their way safely down out of them. It is avionics such as the 'instrument landing system' that make airliners safe today: in 1929 there was nothing much but the old turn-and-slip instrument. But piloting an airship, you could slow down, hover, back up, creep up slowly in any sort of visibility. You had the time even to take radio cross-bearings and work out your position, even though you couldn't see the ground.

Hadn't the airship already proved itself as a passenger vehicle? The old DELAG company had carried 10,000 passengers in admirable safety over its route network between principal German cities during the years 1910–14. True, the Zeppelin's history during World War I had been little but tragedy and death; but what branch of any service on either side hadn't?

The airship was always very much a German art form. Ferdinand von Zeppelin, called the 'Crazy Count' because of his reckless bravery, had been a Junker, as German as they come. He was in his sixties, rich and retired from the Prussian Army, when he began his airship experiments—no 'too old at forty' for him. In his soldiering days he'd even been to America to see and fight in the Civil War—things being rather quiet, battle-wise, in Europe, at that time—and had been introduced to President Lincoln, who didn't impress him one bit. 'A tall, gaunt figure with a large head and long, unkempt hair and beard' was how he described Lincoln. Why, anyone in the Prussian Army knew you had to have short hair to be efficient. No doubt the Count appeared very much the heavy Hun to the President. 'We Zeppelins have been counts for centuries,' he told him, pompously. 'That will not be in your way,' replied Lincoln gravely, 'if you behave yourself as a soldier.' The Count was baffled. 'What in the world did he mean by so strange a remark?' he later asked.

By 1929 the old Count was dead, and Dr Hugo Eckener was chairman of the Zeppelin company. Eckener had got into the airship business by a roundabout way; a philosopher and amateur yachtsman, he'd also been a correspondent of a German newspaper who had scoffed (in print) at the Count's earliest experiments. Then he changed his mind about the airship's possibilities, and sold his services to Count von Zeppelin as a kind of public relations man; he stayed to become the greatest, most skilled airship captain of all time, with an utterly uncanny 'feel' for weather, as well as chairman of the Zeppelin company's board. He'd got the 1929 ship, the *Graf Zeppelin* built largely by public subscription—which is really successful PR!

Later that same year, 1929, Eckener took the *Graf Zeppelin* on the ultimate journey—around the world. It was the first time this was done by any airship, and only the second by any kind of flying machine. It was a curious journey, sponsored by the American newspaper owner William Randolph Hearst and innumerable postage stamp collectors as well as German newspapers. At Los Angeles, Eckener had a chance to display his skill and, frankly, *daring* as an airship commander after he'd had trouble getting the ship down through the 10 degree temperature inversion that holds the famous smog down. He had to valve great amounts of hydrogen to make the ship heavy enough. Then, for take-off that night, the ship was too heavy, with little replacement hydrogen available. Eckener off-loaded ballast and as many crew members as he dared (to join him by rail on the East Coast) and made a running take-off, seeking extra dynamic lift. With the elevators full up, the bottom fin was ploughing a groove in the dirt. Just off the airfield was a high tension line, picked out by red marker lights. Eckener waited till his control car had cleared the wires, then ordered full *down* elevator, and was just able to hoick the stern over the wires, and begin to climb. But it was a very close thing.

Hugo Eckener understood better than anyone the nearly mystical, magical appeal of airships to the public. He called it 'Zeppelin frenzy'. An airship, he wrote, 'was not, as generally described, a "silver bird soaring in majestic flight", but rather a fabulous silvery fish, floating quietly in the ocean of air and captivating the eye just like a fantastic, exotic fish seen in an aquarium. And this fairy-like apparition, which seemed to melt into the silvery-blue background of sky, when it appeared far away, lighted by the sun, seemed to be coming from another world and to be returning there like a dream—an emissary from the "Islands of the Blest" in which so many humans still believe in the inmost recesses of their souls.' Those airships were huge, as big as the ocean liners of their day, too; and their sound in flight was an unearthly fantastic droning noise, from

46. 'Walking' an airship from its hangar was a tricky operation requiring many hands.

the exhaust impinging on pusher propellers and reverberating off the overhanging envelope much as light reflects off a mirror.

Yet the dangers and difficulties of airship operations were every bit as great as the magic. Hydrogen is explosive in mixtures with air of anywhere from 2% to 80%, and therefore a desperately dangerous fluid to handle and contain. There was also helium, lighter than air too, and non-inflammable; but on earth it only occurred in certain natural gas flows in Texas, and the US government had totally banned its export, classifying it as 'war material'. Which it was: how else could you have bombed New York in the thirties but from an airship? 'Your Hitler,' that old curmudgeon Harold Ickes, US Secretary of the Interior later told Eckener, 'is going to make war.' No helium. In any case, helium's lifting power wasn't as good as that of hydrogen.

An even greater menace to airship safety, perhaps greater than anyone at the time knew, was the violence of vertical air currents in thunderstorms and line squalls. We know now that these can often reach 100 mph or more vertical speed; and up and down draughts of this force can exist in close proximity. If the bow of an airship ran into a powerful updraught while the tail was being thrust violently down, the forces could be strong enough to rend the ship into pieces. (It had to be lightly built in any case, to take full advantage of the inherently-limited lifting power of its gas.) You tried wherever possible to avoid squalls and thunder cells, but there were times (in an age before weather radar) when there was nothing for it but to batten everything down and plunge in. Eckener did just that while flying the *Graf Zeppelin* east of Cape Hatteras one day. He met 'the wickedest squall line I have ever experienced, and I don't believe there could be a worse one'.

'What happened next stands out clearly in my memory in every detail. The airship was suddenly thrust upwards so violently that we felt as if we were being forced to our knees. Immediately the bow plunged downward so fast that it felt as if the gondola floor was being jerked out from under our feet. At the same time the ship trembled in every part, and we wondered if the framework could stand the enormous stress.' It could.

He had a worse moment still inside a 'small' thunderstorm in the Rhône valley: 'A terribly dangerous situation, which I look back on with horror even after many years, and which came within a hair's breadth of being fatal for the ship and for all on board her.' Here's how it was described in Douglas Robinson's book *Giants in the Sky*:

'Flying blind in cloud, the *Graf* began to pitch and bump, while lightning flashed close aboard. Suddenly an unprecedented cloud-burst, far more intense than those of the tropics, poured down on the ship. Next, the large raindrops changed to hailstones the size of walnuts, and these, beating on the taut cover, began slowly but inexorably to force the airship to the ground although she was developing maximum dynamic lift with an up-angle of 12 degrees. Feeling that a crash was inevitable, Flemming wanted to stop the engines. "No!" cried Eckener. "We need them more now than ever! Set them on flank speed!" and just then the ship, though she was ten tons heavy, began to climb slowly . . .'

In all, 173 rigid airships were built, 152 of these by the Germans. I think they were always marginal vehicles from any safety point of view, whether they used hydrogen or helium, even in German hands, despite their unique know-how, world-wide airship operating experience, and engineering and structural design skills. But when the inherent risks were compounded with inexperience, politics, and ruthless ambition, and the ship was built by an inefficient civil service, then the venture came close to being madness. Such was the case of the British R101.

The British had built a handful of airships in the Great War, generally copying the structures of wrecked German ships, the sophistications of which they hardly understood. One such, the R38, was completed after the Armistice, to the order of the United States Navy, who so far had no airships of their own. On a test flight, with a mixed British and American crew, full rudder was recklessly applied while at full speed, and the R38 broke in two and blew up. Only one American aboard survived; the other sixteen were given an impressive funeral service in Westminster Abbey. The R38 had been built (by the Air Ministry) along the lines of the war-time German 'height climber' Zeppelins, which were very lightly built; the R38's designer had only calculated static loads, hoping that a static load factor of 4 might cover dynamic loads; and he was ignorant of the high bending moments existing in a turn.

Most of the other British war-time rigids had been built by Vickers; and Vickers in 1923 proposed to the British Government that airships might be ideal for passenger services to distant parts of the Empire; that six airships might do; and that naturally Vickers should build and operate them. Before the matter was decided, the Conservative Government of the day was defeated and the first-ever socialist Labour Government under Ramsay MacDonald came in. Nationalisation and state ownership was an essential tenet of the socialist dogma, and while the idea of airships appealed to them, they were reluctant to let profoundly capitalistic Vickers have it all their own way. Furthermore, there were still officials at the Air Ministry who, despite the tragic end of their own R38, still thought they alone knew how to build airships.

So MacDonald's government made the curious decision to commission *two* ships to the same specification, one each from Vickers and the Air Ministry, to see which might be the better. There was no doubt in the government's mind that the socialist ship had to be the best; but at least making a contest of it would prove this to the whole world. 'The controversy of capitalism versus State enterprise,' wrote the capitalist team's chief calculator, Nevil Shute Norway,* 'has been argued, tested, and fought out in many ways in many countries, but surely the airship venture in England stands as the most curious determination of the matter.'

As work proceeded each team's feelings about their rivals became more bitter. In Norway's words, 'The Air Ministry staff at Cardington considered that they were engaged upon a great experiment of national importance, too great to be entrusted to commercial interests . . . it was impossible to suppose that any private company could compete with Cardington . . .' while the Vickers team, under the leadership of Barnes Wallis, 'the greatest engineer in England at that time and for twenty years afterwards', felt 'the bitter experience was not yet at an end. These were the people, these very same men all but one who had killed himself in R38, who were to be entrusted with the construction of another airship when by rights they ought to be in gaol for manslaughter. In the five years that were to elapse before either airship flew, neither designer visited the other's works, nor did they meet or correspond upon the common problems that each had to solve.'

Norway had been horrified by the disclosures in the report on the R38 disaster: 'I sat stunned, unable to believe the words I was reading . . . It was inexpressibly shocking to me to find that before building the vast and costly structure of the R38, the civil servants concerned had made no attempt to calculate the aerodynamic forces acting on the ship, and I remember going to one of my chiefs with the report in my hand to ask him if this could possibly be true. Not only did he confirm it but he pointed out that no one had been sacked over it . . . indeed, [it was] the same team of men [that] had been entrusted with the construction of the R101 . . .'

Over the long five years both ships grew slowly. The 'capitalist ship' was built at Howden in Yorkshire, in an old wartime airship shed: 'A more unsuitable locality for airship manufacture would be difficult to find. Very frequently the shed was filled with a wet

*Better known under his first two names as a superb novelist.

The R101—the 'socialist ship'—anchored to the mast at Cardington.

mist so that every girder became coated with water; mould attacked the fabrics in the store, and the corrosion of duralumin became a serious matter. We became experts in corrosion.' There were problems with the locally-recruited female labour. 'The lads were what one would expect, straight from the plough, but the girls were an eye-opener. They were brutish and uncouth, filthy in appearance and habits . . . the lowest types . . . incredibly foul-mouthed . . . promiscuous intercourse was going on merrily in every dark corner . . . problems we had not contemplated when we started to build an airship.'

The Air Ministry team's problems were rather more of their own making. They spent two years testing hull and fin shapes in a wind tunnel and eventually chose a hull form of nearly perfect streamline shape—and real beauty of line. The rakish swept fins were handsome, too, but the designers failed to notice that this shape of fin stalled at small angles, becoming ineffective. (The Zeppelin company could have told them this.) They chose stainless steel instead of duralumin for the main girders: stainless steel is difficult to work. They designed an unusual form of gas valve, mounted on the sides of the gas cells and hard to get at. The valves were so sensitive that they opened automatically if tilted more than three degrees; and the R101 later proved to roll more than this often in flight, and in consequence lost gas steadily, becoming chronically heavy throughout flight when she should have become lighter (through burning fuel).

For some strange reason approaching superstition they decided that petrol engines were 'unsafe' in high temperatures in the tropics, and elected to employ diesel engines. They chose a Beardmore 8-cylinder in-line engine, originally developed for railway locomotives and in consequence needlessly heavy: each engine weighed nearly 2½ tons, and the airship's entire power installation totalled 17 tons as against the R100's 9 tons. The engines were unreliable, and came nowhere near producing their design power, which was 700 bhp at 1,000 rpm. At 900 rpm severe torsional vibration sprang up in the long crankshafts; the maximum usable power was under 600 hp even after stiffening the cranks (and further increasing the weight!). The head of the design team, Lt Col Richmond, tried to switch to lighter petrol engines, but could not get permission to do so from the Air Ministry, and fell to moaning that 'it was as absurd to blame the R101 for her heavy engines as it would be to blame a man for wearing heavy boots if he were not allowed to change them.'

Nor was that the sum of power troubles. An airship, like any ship, is sometimes required to go astern; it was first planned that this would be taken care of in the R101 by variable-pitch propellers. The propellers kept breaking on the test bed; and in the end they had to carry a fifth engine with a reverse pitch prop; with its power car three tons of dead weight that was shut down at all times except when approaching or leaving the mooring mast—a minute or two at the beginning and end of a flight! The Vickers team, when they learned this, 'were left staring at each other, speechless . . . In spite of their past record, it was incredible to us that our competitors should perpetrate such childish follies.'

At the Air Ministry establishment at Cardington an entire section of the ship was built for experimental purposes and then scrapped, at a cost of £40,000.

Early in their work the capitalist team had discovered 'a curious aerodynamic feature in the stability of these huge ships; not only could they both easily be steered by hand without the assistance of a servo motor, but no balance was required upon the rudders although they were over a thousand square feet in area. At a comparatively late stage in the design we learned on sure authority that R101 not only had balanced rudders but had servo motors fitted at great weight and cost to assist the helmsman in the steering of the ship. Out flared the inferiority complex; we suspended work on the rudders and spent three days in checking through our calculations to find our mistake. At the end of that time we knew that our figures were correct, and we were left dumbly staring at each other.'

The engineering glories manifesting daily at Cardington were at all times trumpeted to the waiting world by a zealous Air Ministry press department. 'There is no denying,' wrote Norway, 'that the incessant publicity of the competing staff had its effect upon our spirits . . . Our puny efforts at a counterblast could not compete . . . moreover we had little energy to waste on matters of that sort.' But it meant that the Air Ministry team could hardly ever change their minds on anything without therein branding themselves as fools. They spent money like a drunken sailor, on research, 'innumerable experiments on such accessories as gas valves, servo motors, steam heating of the passenger quarters, evaporative cooling of the engines, etc. All these researches were admirable in themselves, but unnecessary . . . It was difficult for them to change their minds; if public money had been spent upon an article for the ship, into the ship it had to go.' For the capitalist team it was very different: 'We changed our engine policy three times during the construction of the ship . . . we bought our gas valves for R100 from the Zeppelin company . . .'

And there seems—incredibly—to have been neither control nor running tally kept of the weights of everything going into the R101! It was not until the ship was complete and inflated and undergoing lift and trim tests that they discovered the useful lift, planned to be 60 tons, was more like 35. This meant that she did not have intercontinental range. The capitalist ship, too, was heavier than hoped, but not by much; she still had 51 tons useful lift, and at 81 mph she was more than ten mph faster than her contract called for.

Both ships had trouble with their fabric envelopes, and the gas cells. The R100 had a fabric sealing strip on her rudder which became unglued during her first speed test; and while at full speed near Montreal on a transatlantic proving flight she ran into rough air and shed fabric from her fin coverings, 'a hole large enough to drive a bus through'. But she was repaired and safely flown home.

During flight testing of the R100 she was based at Cardington—the only place in England with an airship mooring mast—and it was here that the capitalist team got their first good look at the rival ship. 'We found her an amazing piece of work,' wrote Norway. 'The finish and the workmanship struck us as extraordinarily good, far better than that of our own ship. The design seemed to us almost unbelievably complicated; she seemed to be a ship in which imagination had run riot regardless of the virtue of simplicity and utterly regardless of expense. The servo motors were there, large as life and every bit as heavy . . . The feature of the design that perturbed me most of all was the method of taking the thrust of the engines in the power cars to the hull. The engine in each car drove a pusher propeller. A large thrust bearing was mounted in the boss of this propeller, from which a heavy steel cable ran straight aft to a point on the hull fifty feet back . . . it seemed most dangerous and quite unnecessary. A competent engineer should be able to do better than that.'

Soon the R101 was back in her shed. Everything that might be superfluous (such as those servo motors) was removed to lighten her; and the wiring cradles that contained her gas bags were let out to increase their volume. This had a disastrous effect on her

48. Barnes Wallis's R100—the 'capitalist ship'—after her return from Canada.

longitudinal stability, which had hitherto been good, for the loosened gas bags could now surge forwards and back by as much as fourteen feet, with the centre of lift moving with them. The R101 became statically unstable, divergent in pitch; if she began to go nose-up she would immediately try to pitch *more strongly* nose-up, and vice versa. For the rest of her short life she followed an undulating flight path, up and down, with the sweating elevator helmsman forever rolling his wheel hard forwards or hard back as he tried to fight the instability.

When they next walked her out of her gigantic shed, the airship's outer cover immediately split, in a tear 140 feet long. It, and others similar, were patched up.

They took her to the big RAF air show at Hendon—after all, publicity really mattered to them—where she nearly got out of control, suddenly going into a dive that was only stopped when she was down to 500 feet (no more than half her own length) above the ground.

She continued to make sudden dives all the way back to Cardington. On board as a guest was the first officer of the competing R100, and he later admitted it was 'the first time I've ever had the wind up in an airship.' He said to the height coxswain, 'The ship seems to be heavy?' Sweat poured down the latter's face. 'It's as much as I can do to hold her up,' he said.

Back at Cardington they discovered a new problem: more than sixty small holes in the loosened gas bags where they had chafed and worn on the structure and on each other.

There was some official concern about these gas leaks; a brave Air Ministry inspector even minuted: 'Until this matter is seriously taken in hand and remedied I cannot recommended to you the extension of the present "Permit to Fly"'[test flying certificate] 'or the issue of any further permit or certificate.'

But within the Ministry itself no one knew much about airships, so they passed the buck, and sent the inspector's report back to Cardington; thus in effect the ship's builders were asked to decide themselves if their own ship was safe or not! Of course they whitewashed over the inspector's doubts: gas bags in airships always chafed, they claimed, and a little padding would doubtless take care of it.

And they rolled the R101 back into her hangar again, this time to cut her in two and insert a new bay with extra gas bags, to increase her lift; to change two of her engines for new ones with reversing gears; and to renew much of her outer cover.

From that time on, says Norway, 'the atmosphere at Cardington became very bad . . . There was an atmosphere of cynical disillusionment in the place, very depressing.' One day, two of his colleagues had something to show him: 'They shut the door, looked out of the window to see that no one was about, and pulled out from under the desk a couple of square yards of outer cover fabric . . . It was ordinary outer cover, linen fabric, silver doped on a red oxide base. On the inner surface two-inch tapes had been stuck on with some adhesive, evidently for strengthening. I . . . turned it about in my hands, and suddenly my hand went through it. In parts it was friable, like scorched brown paper, so that if you crumpled it in your hand it broke up into flakes. I stared at it in horror . . .

'They told me that [it was] the new outer cover of the R101, [and] had been doped in place upon the ship. When it was finished, it was considered that it ought to be strengthened in certain places by a system of tapes stuck on the inside, and for adhesive they had used rubber solution. The rubber solution had reacted chemically with the dope, and had produced this terrible effect.

'I said, "I hope they've got all this stuff off the ship."

'He smiled cynically. "They *say* they have."'

This was a bare three weeks before the final disaster, and, says Norway, there was undoubtedly someone, may be at Farnborough or in the company manufacturing the dope, who could have told them that dope and rubber solution did not agree. 'I think that they were floundering, making hurried and incompetent technical decisions, excluding people from their conferences who could have helped them.'

Now they were under extra pressure, from above. Christopher Thomson, the Secretary of State for Air, was determined to fly to India in the R101, and then to be back in London in time for the opening of the Imperial Conference, of which the date was firmly set. 'I must insist on the programme for the Indian flight being adhered to,' he minuted downwards through the Air Ministry, 'as I have made my plans accordingly.' But experimental work, said Norway, 'is not susceptible to such pressures; if a gas bag chafes and leaks or an outer cover splits, no vapourings of a Secretary of State will put it right. To rectify such troubles a designer must be given time to think and to experiment; it does not help for an impatient politician to bedevil the designer by pointing out that the delay is inconveniencing the politician, the great man himself.'

Who was this 'great man'? An army general, a man otherwise 'gracious and cultured', from military families on both his parents' sides, who had, against all odds, grown sympathetic to socialism, resigned from the army, twice stood unsuccessfully for Parliament as a labour candidate. Ramsay MacDonald, the first Labour prime minister, must have been short of men with administrative talent, for he resolved to make General Thomson his air minister (though he had no experience of aviation); and since the general could not persuade the electors to elect him, MacDonald made him a baron, and he chose the title Lord Thomson of Cardington, as if to show more clearly which airship he favoured. Indeed, it was largely he who had scotched the original plan to have Vickers build six ships, and had substituted the civil service-versus-capitalism plan instead. But there were suggestions that perhaps he had ambitions to be the next Viceroy of India, and wished to make a stir in his new empire by arriving there in his own airship. Did he never have a moment's doubt about the R101's safety, or detect even a glimmering of that dreadful 'atmosphere' at Cardington that so bothered Norway? Perhaps, towards the end he did, for during a final conference at the Air Ministry, he said: 'You must not allow my natural impatience or anxiety to start to influence you in any way. You must use your considered judgment.' But it was far too late in the day for his harassed and exhausted airship men to suddenly develop 'considered judgment', and no one chose to say anything in reply.

Test flying was far from complete when the time came for the India flight; indeed, the R101 had never flown at full power! Nor did she have an airworthiness certificate; her simple 'Permit to Fly' was only valid for test flying within the United Kingdom. 'But,' wrote Norway, 'when every safety precaution, including the 48-hour flight trial with its six engines at full power in bumpy weather had been abandoned, a scrap of paper could not be allowed to hold up the Indian flight.' The Air Ministry officials wrote out their own Certificate of Airworthiness on their own aircraft: the R101 had never been subjected to any independent engineering check or scrutiny of any kind!

The officials, including Lord Thomson and his valet, went aboard on a miserable evening, with a falling barometer. The leaking airship was already heavy, and had to drop four tons of water ballast to get away; she was climbed to 1,500 feet, although her pressure height (at which gas began to valve out automatically due to expansion) was only 1,000 feet, so that even before being on her way she had lost nearly half her ballast and excess lift—her ability to manoeuvre in altitude.

Over London she received a revised weather forecast for the first part of her journey: the wind would freshen from 20 to 30 mph to 40 to 50 mph, almost on the nose, reducing her groundspeed (even at maximum cruise, a speed she had never been flown at before) to maybe 20 mph. Here was a nearly perfect excuse to turn back to Cardington, to abandon the insane journey. With blind optimism, the R101's captain elected to continue.

By two o'clock in the morning, more than seven hours from take-off, the R101, flying dangerously low, had gone only just over 200 miles, to Beauvais in northern France. In low cloud, driving rain and rough air it seems the forward part of the ship's envelope split again, and a gas bag deflated; she dived steeply, was levelled off, then dived again, quite gently, into a wood. Perhaps it was a spark from a broken electrical circuit which ignited the leaking hydrogen; there was a flash that lit the whole area like daybreak, and then a rumble like an earthquake, as five million cubic feet of hydrogen exploded. The R101 the world's biggest airship, the half-million pounds she had cost, and forty-eight of the fifty-four men in her, were gone.

The British airship programme was over, too: though the capitalist ship, the R100, had met her contract specifications and seemed safe enough, she never flew again and was soon dismantled. In Britain at least, 'Zeppelin fever' was cured.

To Nevil Shute Norway, now out of a job (like all the Vickers team, but not of course the civil servants), there was at least a powerful moral to be drawn from the dreadful history of the R101. 'The one thing that has been proved abundantly in aviation is that government officials are totally ineffective in engineering development . . . The disaster was the product of the system, rather than of the men themselves. The worst that can be said of them is that they were not very good engineers. They suffered, too, from having no contract to fulfil. No financial incentive to meet the performance specifications. No penalties if they were not met. No independent check or inspection of their work. And all the time, 'looming over them like Destiny' was Lord Thomson of Cardington, 'who had taken his title from his confidence in them, who had made them and had power to unmake them. It was impossible for them to admit mistakes without incurring discredit far exceeding their deserts, for everybody makes mistakes from time to time. Surely no engineers were ever placed in so unhappy a position.'

Free industry, on the other hand, 'is ruled by Boards of Directors whose function is to prevent the engineers that they employ from taking on work that is beyond their powers . . . they do this by virtue of their own long industrial experience, which enables them to assess the difficulties of the job and to engage staff suitable to do it. The men at Cardington had no comparable restraint . . . the civil servants and the politicians above them . . . were quite unfit to exercise that type of control.

'I am very willing to recognise the good in many men of these two classes, but a politician or a civil servant is still to me an arrogant fool till he is proved otherwise.'

The R101 had been Britain's first awful experience of socialist 'nationalisation'.

11

The Maxim Gorky

'In Ryazan, in the year 1731, in the presence of military governor, sub-deacon Kryakutnoi, from the town of Nerekhta, inflated a hide into a great ball and filled it with smoke . . . he slung a loop from it and seated himself in it; the powers of darkness lifted him up higher than the birch trees . . .' So to the old church in Mother Russia, aviation (or at least, hot air ballooning) was the obvious work of the devil. I've seen a fine engraving of old Kryakutnoi and his balloon, rising up to the level of the onion domes of his handsome church.

Every Russian schoolboy knows that a Russian was first to build a successful powered manned aircraft, two decades before the Wright Brothers. This is not totally impossible; the Wrights used to say that the trick of powered flight had been, in theory, perfectly possible for fifty years before *they* first brought it off. The Russian Wright was one Alexander Fyodorovitch Mozhaiski, a naval officer who is described in Nowarra and Duval's *Russian Civil and Military Aircraft 1884–1969* as having 'an income quite adequate for his needs'. You needed this to be a pioneer aviator; one British experimenter in Edwardian times estimated his repair bills at £1,500 a *month*—and £1,500 then was real money.

Mozhaiski's flyer was a monoplane—big, with a span of forty feet—and powered by two lightweight steam engines, one 10 hp, one 20 hp. The first drove a tractor airscrew mounted conventionally in the nose; the second, through chains, two propellers mounted in slots cut into the wings. Mozhaiski, like any true aristocrat, did not deign to take the controls himself, but deputed a man named Golubev to do this. Tests were made after a take-off run down an inclined ramp, and it is reported that the machine did leave the ground for a few feet. But though it had twice the power of the later first Wright Flyer, it was far too heavy—almost a ton—to be able to *sustain* flight. But it was a valiant effort: even if its two steamers *were* British-made, which they were.

Thereafter, Russian aviation languished sadly behind the West. The one Russian aircraft designer of real talent to have flourished during the First World War, Igor Sikorsky, later fled the revolution to America: Sikorsky is famous for having developed

49. This machine was reputed to have been airborne two decades before the Wright Brothers' aircraft.

50. Alexander Mozhaiski—the Russian who built it.

the first truly practical helicopter in World War II; but he had started experimenting with rotary wings as early as 1909 in St Petersburg. Here his dreams inspired a colleague, O. K. Antonov, who also built a helicopter. But it didn't fly, and Antonov, 'suffering from the stresses of overwork during the project, became distraught and destroyed the machine'. One can just imagine the poor fellow, his usual Russian manic-depression heightened by despair and no doubt a little vodka, falling upon his idiot helicopter that refused to fly, with an axe or a hammer.

By 1930 Russian aviation had settled down to be composed mostly of big bombers. At one point in the 1930s the peace-loving peoples of the Soviet Union had the largest bomber fleet in the world—over 1,000 aircraft. The favourite design was Tupolev's big four-engined monoplane, the ANT-6, known to the Russian military as the TB-3 or -5, or the G-2 in a troop-carrying rôle. They were perhaps the world's last big bombers still to be flown from an open cockpit. There was also an Arctic version with, mercifully, the cabin glazed over and heating installed. There was also a version equipped to be a mother-ship to no less than five little fighters, which could be released in flight and even hook back on! An ANT-6 did once take off with four fighters attached, then while airborne join up with a fifth and make several circuits of the airfield, with all nine engines turning. Then all five fighters were released at one moment. (The thing about events like that is, you always wonder how they entered the flight in their log books afterwards. I mean,

51. A TB-3 bomber with three biplane fighters mounted on top of it.

52. A TB-3 in the act of catching a fighter in flight.

if you were the pilot of one of the fighters, you could hardly log the take-off because you hadn't made it, except as a passenger. But how can you log a landing with no prior take-off?)

In 1933 there appeared a new Tupelov giant, the six-engined, 175-foot span ANT-16. It was a six-engined flop, with no performance, and they scrapped it. Furthermore, the Soviet Government made it clear that it was not inclined to pay for any more giant aircraft. But Tupelov had got the giant aircraft bug, badly. He wanted to build something even more giant than the ANT-16, *the biggest aeroplane in the world.*

Help came from what must have been, even in Soviet Russia, an unlikely source: the Union of Soviet Writers and Editors decided to celebrate the fortieth anniversary of the commencement of the literary career of the author Maxim Gorky by launching a public subscription for the construction of a giant aircraft to carry his name, and for the creation of a 'Maxim Gorky Propaganda Squadron' to immortalise his name and works. You may think this the silliest reason for building an aeroplane ever; and I would not disagree. But where there's a Soviet will there's a way, and in no time they had collected six million roubles, in small donations from workers all over Russia, and were showering them upon Tupelov and his workforce, a modest crew of some 800 lads.

The ANT-20, when it was built, wasn't huge, it was *VAST*. Its span was 260 feet, which is a full 65 feet bigger than a Boeing 747! It had eight huge 900 hp engines, six arrayed along the leading-edge of the wings and the other two mounted as a tractor-and-pusher pair in a pod above the fuselage. The wheel pants alone stood about twice the height of an average crew member. It required a crew of twenty for normal operation; and had variable seating for up to eighty passengers—a lot in 1933, when the DC-2 managed only a dozen. There was a cinema in the Maxim Gorky's rear fuselage into which the populace were invited to watch propaganda movies during ground stops. There was a newspaper office complete with rotary printing press in the left wing; and a photographic dark-room in the right. The aircraft also contained a café, its own internal telephone exchange, and sleeping quarters and toilets. Four auxiliary engines were required to generate the power to run the huge loudspeakers that broadcast the Soviet message down upon the astonished peasants over which the aircraft flew, and at night to power a system of lights along the underside flashing slogans.

The Maxim Gorky first flew on May 19th, 1934. About a year later the employees of the Central Aerodynamic Institute in Moscow, where it was designed, were delighted to be invited to come down to the airport with their families for joy-rides in the giant machine. Thirty-six passengers were to be taken at a time. The first group went aboard, while the others lined up in a long Soviet queue to wait their turn.

This mission was to be as much for propaganda as anything else, and therefore a small fighter was deputed to fly alongside the Maxim Gorky to show just how big it was, while a photographer in another plane recorded the event. The fighter pilot decided to liven up the proceedings with a few manoeuvres. He tried a barrel roll, got disorientated upside down, and came crashing down on top of the Gorky's wing, becoming lodged between two of its engines. To the absolute horror of all those friends and relations waiting their turn on the ground, the Maxim Gorky came apart in the air, spewing out bodies and

53. The Maxim Gorky had a span bigger than a 747, eight engines, and needed a crew of twenty.

equipment from a height of several thousand feet. All passengers dead; the pilot of the little fighter plane, dead; three people on the ground, dead, struck by falling wreckage.

The *New York Times* was moved to write a leader on the wisdom of building ever bigger aircraft. 'How far is it desirable, and how far is it possible, for this process to go? Clearly it has definite limits. National pride, and the human desire to own or construct the "largest airplane in the world", just because it could be called that, have probably had a great deal to do with the matter.'

The Soviet authorities seized upon Comrade Blagin, the dead pilot of the little fighter, as a suitable villain, and heaped all kinds of abuse on his memory. The new Russian word 'blaginism' was coined to denote selfish exhibitionism and the lack of proper socialist disciplinism, and for all I know may still be in the Russian dictionary.

The Russians, however, didn't seem to be readers of the *New York Times*, for they immediately began a new public subscription campaign to build three *more* ANT-20s. Eventually they built sixteen of them; slightly different to the original Maxim Gorky in that more powerful engines had come along, of which six would suffice, so that there was no need for the two-in-pod on top of the fuselage. They served as pure transports, crew of eight and sixty-four passengers, and some at least continued to fly right throughout the Great Patriotic War, 1941–5.

Nearly forty years after the disaster to the Maxim Gorky, another giant aircraft with Tupelov's name on it exploded in mid-air with the whole world watching—the Tu-144 supersonic airliner that crashed at the Paris Air Show in 1973. My photograph of its spectacular end ran on the front page of just about every newspaper on earth: I seem to have been the only still photographer at the show to realise the Tu-144 was doomed, in time to focus on it. I wish I hadn't; the image of that huge white bat, intended as proof that the Soviets had at last caught up with the hated West in matters of aeronautical design, so cruelly and publicly disproving that proud dream, will live in my mind's eye for ever. Yet the Tu-144 may still go on, like the ANT-20, to become a serviceable transport. Let us hope so.

12

Dornier's Giant Flying Boats

An aircraft salesman once invited me out to New York's La Guardia airport for a flight in a Skyservant, a modern Dornier light twin. 'Delighted,' I said, and then added, thoughtlessly, 'I've never flown any Dornier. Been bombed by them, though.' This, I think, the American salesman thought in poor taste; at least I never did get to fly the Skyservant. And although it's for the wretched WW 2 bombers that we British tend to remember Dornier, it was as a flying boat designer that he made his name.

Claude Dornier joined the Zeppelin airship works in 1910 when a young man of twenty-six, after several years with various steel construction firms. Old man Zeppelin rather believed in metal for building aircraft himself, and after young Dornier had done spells on stress calculation, propeller design, metal-clad airships, and had designed an airship hangar that could be rotated so that you could always walk the airship out into wind, the old man set him to work on building all-metal seaplanes. Here he would have been working at the newest frontiers of technology. For one thing, there wasn't much available then in the way of light alloy. In Haddow and Grosz's *The German Giants* a Dornier engineer is quoted thus: '"Dural" was a brand-new material in 1914, available only for experimental use. It had many drawbacks. For instance, it was not produced in consistent quality; more often than not a rolled "Dural" sheet would exfoliate like the leaves of a book. Impurity inclusions caused frequent imbrittlement cracking, and after brief periods of storage, the "Dural" sheet had the unpleasant tendency to disintegrate in spots to a white powder.'

Wisely, Dornier decided to use familiar steels for the highly stressed parts of his first boat, and the new 'Dural' only where stresses were low. Mostly he used strips of steel alloy drawn or rolled into profiles such as Us and Vs and built up with rivets to form cross-braced structures like those used in bridge, or crane booms—or Zeppelin skeletons. As you might expect of an engineer so burning with youthful ambition, his first seaplane, all-metal of course, was no modest little venture, but simply, The Biggest Aeroplane in the World. One hundred and forty-two feet in span, and a biplane with three pusher engines and no less than 33 struts at crazy angles to hold the top wing to the bottom one.

54. The Rs.I; because of the lack of a 'step' in the hull it wouldn't leave the water. 55. Eventually it was driven on to the rocks in a wind-storm and destroyed.

Now water exerts a suction on boat and seaplane hulls, and to break loose from it your hull must have a break or 'step' sharply cut into it, to let air in to break the suction. Young Dornier didn't know this. Bad luck, really, because in other respects this first of his big boats wasn't a bad design—a good deal neater than those that followed. But leave the water it wouldn't. The Zeppelin factory where it was built was at Seemos on Lake Constance (on the borders between Switzerland and Germany), and they taxied the great thing up and down the lake so long, and so often, that the local inhabitants developed their own little doggerel about it. Freely translated, it ran:

'Das ist der flying boat from Seemoos.
From zer lake it can't come loose . . .'

Then one day a Föhn wind sprang up, and the big boat jammed on its slipway in the gusts. So they towed it out into the lake and tied it to a buoy, all engines running, hoping they could keep it headed into wind and so ride it out. In the early morning the mooring let go and the flying boat was driven on to the rocks, to be thus shipwrecked without having ever flown.

'Spurred on,' it says in *The German Giants*, 'by the sudden loss of the Rs. I, Dornier and his staff worked vigorously to complete their second flying-boat, the Rs. II.' This device looked even less like an aeroplane than Rs. I; it was really a motor-boat hull with a great plank of a wing held aloft by a cat's cradle of struts, and a structure, not unlike a trellis up which roses grow, extending back to hold the tailplane. The engines were three 240 hp Maybach Zeppelin engines buried inside the boat hull and driving outrigger propellers through shafts and chains and things, and what transmission problems they had. But it flew.

'With precise motion,' claimed test pilot Schröter, 'I gently pulled the wheel towards

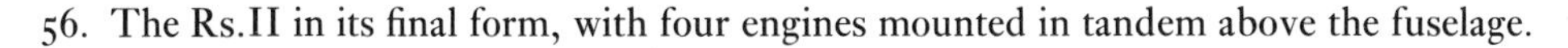

56. The Rs.II in its final form, with four engines mounted in tandem above the fuselage.

my chest. Now a springy jump from wave to wave. The jolts ceased; we were in the air. How easy it all was, almost as if I had a fully-proven aircraft in my hands!

'Carefully I prepared to land. With throttled engines, the Rs. II willingly lowered its nose and glided to a landing. A sudden splash, a lurch forward and we came to a halt.' The entire tail assembly whipped about, for it wasn't nearly rigid enough.

They rebuilt the tail boom and bought a fourth engine, took the other three out of the hull and mounted them all halfway up the superstructure, in pairs—two pulling, two pushing. By now the Rs. II embodied three features that were to typify Dornier's subsequent seaplane designs: this paired-engine arrangement, one pulling, one pushing; very broad, low-aspect-ratio, plank-like wings; and the use of 'sponsons'—stub wings projecting from the side of the hull, to give stability on the water, obviating the need for wing-tip auxiliary floats.

It was by now August 1917, and the German Navy wanted delivery of the Rs. II, and they wanted it at Nordeney in the North Sea, a very long way from Lake Constance. In September Dornier and his men held a practice flight over the waters of the lake to see if she would stay aloft long enough to make it up the Rhine to the North Sea. She wouldn't; an engine backfired and its propeller disintegrated in a hail of flying splinters. The Rs. II descended in a nervous glide back down to the water. Shortly after this she was scrapped.

Dornier hardly cared, for he was well along with Rs. III. (The 'Rs.' by the way, is simply an abbreviation for the German word for 'giant aeroplane'.) Taking no chances, Dornier cut no less than *three* steps into the boat hull of this one. The aircraft was on three levels: above the boat hull, mounted on the usual jungle of struts, were the same two pairs of Maybach engines; then more struts went up to the huge wing, this time with a proper fuselage running back to the tail. The fuselage, as well as a pilot's position also contained a soundproof cabin for a radio operator and a little nest for a machine gunner. (There was also a gunner's station in the bow of the boat hull.) A light ladder ran up the centre of the craft so that the crew could clamber about. This Rs. III was a monstrous device: 75 feet long and 121 feet in span, it weighed nearly nine tons empty and twelve loaded. Despite having almost 1,000 hp, it was paralysingly slow, with a maximum of just over 80 mph.

The Rs. III actually made it to Nordeney, where it passed Navy tests and was released for front line service—just a fortnight before the Armistice. It did serve afterwards: as late as January 1920 it was still listed on a roster of aircraft used for spotting mines in the North Sea and the Baltic. The Rs. III was finally destroyed by the Allies at the end of July, 1921, at which time the German government rather hopelessly valued it at exactly one million marks.

There was also an Rs. IV, similar to the III, which was not completed till after the war was over. We on the Allied side should be grateful to Herr Dornier, for all the money, men and materials that went into his useless flying boats might otherwise have gone into deadly Fokkers.

57. The Rs.III on the slipway turntable. It was on three levels, with a ladder joining them.

At the war's end Dornier had also been working on a more sensible project: a twin-engined metal flying boat of reasonable size, named the Gs. I. It first flew in 1919, and was promising enough for the Allies to take notice of it; they ordered it to be sunk, and banned further work on a nine-seat Gs. II development of it. So all was placid on the waters of Lake Constance once more.

But a couple of years later, in 1922, a new aircraft company, the Societa di Construzioni Meccaniche Aeronautiche SA, was setting up in Pisa. The company was building a twin-engined flying boat named the Whale, which had a broad plank-like wing, sponsons projecting from the sides of its hull, and carried its two engines in a pair, one pulling one pushing. It's not difficult to guess that it was Claude Dornier, getting round the Allied ban on aircraft manufacture in Germany by doing it in Italy. The Whale was, at last, an outstanding success for Dornier. More than 150 of them were built in Italy, some by Piaggio, who are the same people who in more recent times built the Vespa motor-scooter. In the end, fully 300 Whales were built, some in Spain, some in Holland, three in Japan, and many by Dornier himself at Friedrichshafen back in Germany, when the Germans felt strong enough to defy the terms of the Versailles Treaty. Dornier Whales served with many airlines, more navies, some air forces; one almost reached the North Pole. Another, flown by Franco's brother, made a spectacular crossing of the south Atlantic to Buenos Aires. Dornier went on to a four-engined Super Whale, which was equally successful.

But Claude Dornier could not rest content to be building simply *successful* seaplanes; his old dream of the world's *biggest*, hugest seaplane still obsessed him. So he began on his most magnificent folly of all: the Do-X. The 'X', it is said, stood for 'unknown quantity'.

Dornier didn't rush into this project as he had his First World War giants. He made much of only employing 'technically proven' ideas in the machine. He built a full-size wooden mock-up of it in a hangar, to make sure everything would fit—common practice now, but revolutionary then. He built a rig on which to test the engine installations, in the familiar push-pull pairs. He ran static tests to see if the main spar was strong enough.

The Do-X was incomparably the biggest aeroplane in the world. It weighed 33 tons empty, 61 loaded. It spanned 157 feet. The duraluminium hull had three decks, and when you boarded you first passed along a corridor lined with doors that opened into little sleeping cabins. You then entered a luxurious lounge full of deep carpets and fine furnishings, with a gramophone you could play if the other passengers didn't mind. There was also a 'recreation room', a bathroom, a smoking room, a kitchen, and a little dining room. The Do-X was powered by twelve air-cooled radial engines together putting out a magnificent 6,000 hp. They were mounted in six paired nacelles on the usual Dornier thicket of struts, high above the wing, and all linked by a kind of auxiliary stub wing.

The Do-X first flew in the summer of 1929. It was intended to carry about seventy-two passengers in normal service. But one day that autumn, a day cold enough for the engines to be giving of their best, it got aloft from Lake Constance with a jumbo load of ten crew and 150 invited passengers—plus nine determined stowaways! This was really one in the eye for the Graf Zeppelin airship, which was also based on the lake's shore: *she* could only carry seventy passengers. And what next, of course, but a flight across the Atlantic to America?

First, there were a few little problems to be resolved. The Do-X was desperately short of puff: loaded up, it couldn't climb any higher than 1,400 feet. And although the front six engines worked fine, the rear six, operating in their turbulent wake, overheated all the time, showing dangerous oil temperatures and terrifying cylinder-head temperatures. They were Jupiter air-cooled radials, British designed but built under licence by Siemens in Germany. Dornier decided he must have more power, and it had better be water-cooled power at that, so he pulled out the Jupiters and installed twelve American Curtiss Conquerors instead—100 or more horsepower each, but a good bit heavier due to the plumbing for the water cooling. At the same time he did away with the stub wing that joined the engine nacelles: it had interfered with the lift generated by the main wing.

They set off from Lake Constance in November 1930, with a crew of nineteen (I wonder what they all *did*?) under the stern command of Captain Friedrich Christiansen, and carrying a magnificent load of mail. They stopped at Amsterdam, and Calshot on Southampton Water, and everybody came and ooed and aahed. Then they flew into fog and had to taxi ignominiously into Bordeaux harbour. At Lisbon a fuel tank in the wing caught fire, but they put it out, and settled down to an idle month while it was repaired. They tried to take off from Las Palmas in the Canaries in a high sea, and battered the hull so badly that repairs this time took *three* months.

In truth, what the Do-X gained on the swings of more power from its new engines, it mostly lost on the roundabouts of their extra weight. The ceiling was still under 2,000 feet, and the cruise was under 120 mph. Even to achieve this she burned some 400 gallons an hour, which is 0.295 mpg.

It was 1,400 miles from the Cape Verde Islands to South America, and to do this, they had to leave behind half the crew and everything else expendable, even down to surplus clothing. Even so, for the first part of the flight the Do-X could not climb out of 'ground effect'—when air is cushioned between the wings and the waves—and flew along just 20 feet above the sea! But she made it to Brazil.

By now the Do-X was really in the headlines, and an order came from Germany that she was to linger awhile impressing one and all and giving joy-rides up and down the coast of South America. Captain Christiansen didn't approve of this, and didn't keep his disapproval to himself, and in no time he was on his way back to the Fatherland on a boat. His co-pilot Captain Fritz Hammer became the new captain. They went as far as Rio, before turning northwards and following the Pan Am flying boat route up through the West Indies to Miami. The Do-X arrived in New York harbour on August 27th, 1931, to a ticker-tape welcome, in which everybody tried to forget that the journey had taken ten months, 12,000 miles at an average speed of 1.6 mph. Jimmy Walker was the mayor of Fun City in those days, and he pinned fun medals on all the Do-X's crew.

The Do-X went into dry dock in Queens for 'overhaul'; the truth was, Dorniers were hoping to sell her. *No* such luck.

So on May 19th, 1932, they towed her out into Manhasset Bay for the start of her long, long take-off run. She went via Newfoundland and the Azores. Coming into Horta she got very short of fuel and they put her down and taxied her the last six miles. Back in

58. The twelve-engined Do-X was in 1929 the biggest aeroplane in the world.

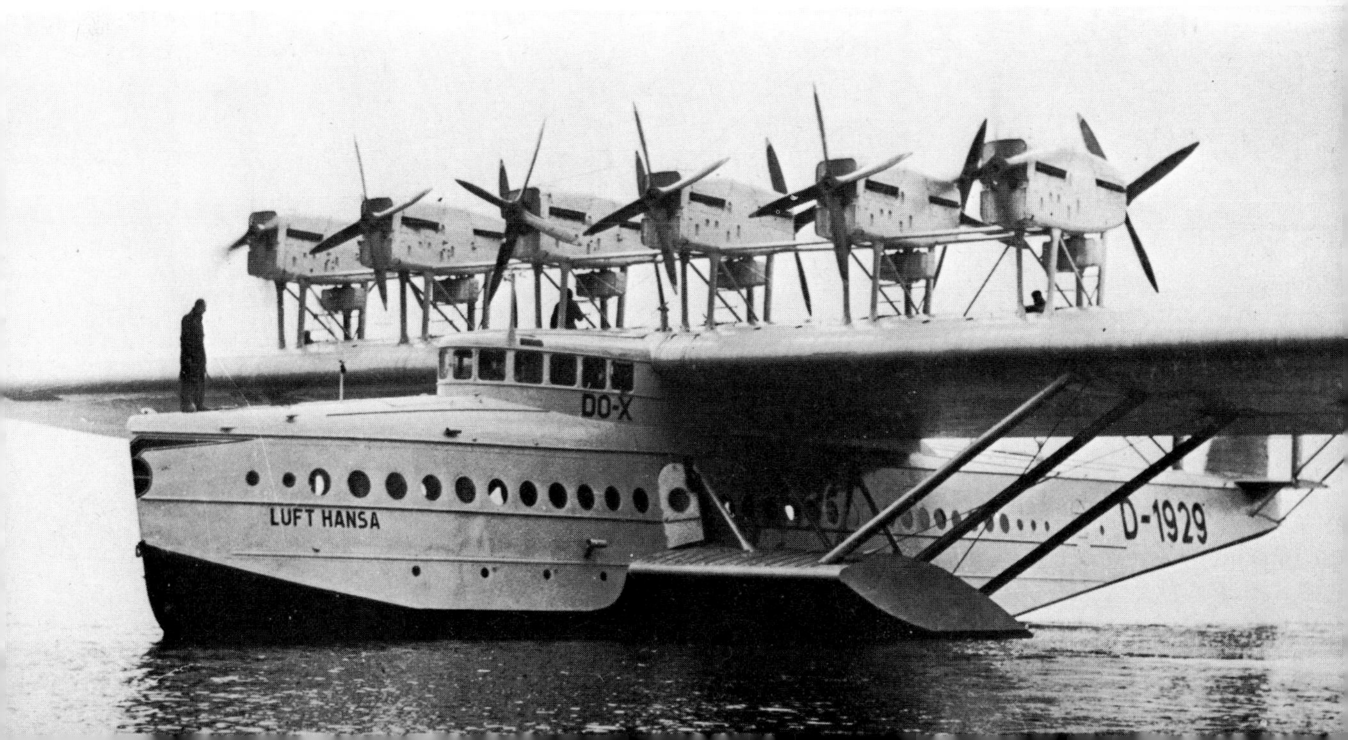

Germany they gave her a grand welcome, and then set about forgetting about her. Actually two other Do-Xs were built with Fiat engines and sold to the Italians, who planned to use them as airliners, till they found out how thirsty they were. The Italian air force used them for 'experimental flying' for a while; then Mussolini finally admitted to himself that he'd been sold two pups, and they were broken up. As for the first Do-X, she went into the Berlin air museum, where an Allied Bomber raid got her in the Second World War.

Says C. R. Roseberry of the Do-X in his *The Challenging Skies*. 'The best that could be said of her was that she was a fairly creditable freak. Her appetite for fuel was much too gluttonous to permit of a payload except on short hauls.' And 'elephantiasis of the airways' is what he calls it.

Her problems were the old ones of weight and drag. That broad wing that Dornier liked so much couldn't have been very efficient; broad chord wings never are. The fuselage wasn't the most streamlined structure you ever saw. There would have been massive interference drag between the wing and the sponsons and the struts and wires that cross-braced them. But far the worst drag-generator must have been the row of engines running across the top of the wing. Just where you wanted smooth undisturbed airflow to generate lift there were pylons and struts and wires and ladders and radiators. And even though the nacelles were set so close together that the propellers overlapped, they still took up fully half the span. That's half the span developing hardly any lift at all! The push-pull nacelle mounted over the fuselage worked very well on the Whale, where there was only *one* such nacelle, over the fuselage where the wing wasn't developing much lift anyway. Mind you, it's hard to see where else Dornier *could* have put his engines. Later big flying boats had them buried in the wings—perfect—but aero engines weren't very powerful in 1929, and Dornier found that even twelve engines weren't enough to give the power his huge boat needed. He certainly couldn't have buried twelve engines inside his wing—it wasn't long enough. I suppose he should have waited till you *could* get 6,000 hp from four or maybe six engines. But 'waiting till' is never an aircraft designer's strong point.

Old Claude Dornier died in 1969, but the company continues, run by his son Claudius. It must be one of the oldest aviation enterprises in the world. They now make STOL twin-engined aircraft, still with high-set plank-like wings, still with the engines out on their own in pods. Dorniers still hanker after flying boats: they proposed a three-turbo-prop boat, the Do 24/72, to the Spanish Air Force for air-sea rescue duties. Claudius Dornier still has dreams of building a giant flying boat freighter, a flying container ship with a gross weight of a thousand tons, a length and span of about 100 metres, and a range of over 4,000 miles. The engines would be ten huge turbofans, though later versions, said Dornier, could even be nuclear powered.

13

The Flying Flea

Henri Mignet was a French schoolboy when Wilbur Wright came over and flew at Le Mans; the silhouettes of the birdcage aeroplanes of the day were on all the front pages—and in Mignet's scrapbooks. He would steal away to a photographic darkroom when he should have been in class, and there he built a crystal set. He built a kite and a camera for it to carry, and was able by aerial photograph to utterly astonish his mother as to how many gutters their roof had. In the school holidays he constructed a glider of paper and bamboo braced with household string. He strapped it on, and ran up and down in a field, maybe leaving the ground for a skip and a jump. Then he made a better glider, a biplane, and left his father holding it down one windy day. Father sneaked a moment to roll a cigarette, and the wind took the glider, made it fly half a loop and dropped it neatly on Mignet's little sister, who hopped from the wreck 'like a circus dog jumping through a paper hoop'.

Mignet went to the Bordeaux School of Electricity where he had to work more seriously. Then came the war, and he was drafted into a signals unit. Here the discipline was far from strict, and he was able to slip away to a military aerodrome where, fascinated, he made friends with the mechanics and was allowed to become their helper. If it was so easy to join the mechanics, couldn't he just as easily become a *pilot*? One day a friendly sergeant let him taxi a SPAD scout, and it seems Mignet tried to fly it, ending up with the SPAD on its back in a cornfield. The sergeant clipped his ear and sent him back to the signals unit, disgraced. 'No drums or trumpets for Mignet' that day. Wounded in the war, Mignet spent his convalescence making thermionic valves. Then he went home.

Mignet's father was a wild-life painter and somewhat of a nature mystic, who instilled part of his love of nature into Henri. The two of them would watch the buzzards, and Henri amused himself by counting how many seconds they took to soar through a full circle, and how many minutes since they last flapped their six-foot-span wings. 'For years I tried to combine my notions of mechanics from my schooldays with my observations of the free life of the wild. Birds flew all around me. Occasional aeroplanes and dirigibles from a nearby air base flew over. I *must* possess wings, live in a cockpit, experience again

59. A rare photograph of a Flying Flea actually in flight. But not for long—see page 114.

the atmosphere of that military squadron, but *all in my own way*.' If orthodox aviation had rejected him just because he'd wrecked one miserable SPAD scout, then he'd show them, and would take to the skies all unaided and uninstructed.

The thirty-foot span of his first powered aeroplane almost filled the family paddock. Mignet found a bigger field for it, and began to 'make aviation'. The craft wouldn't fly, but its engine and propeller made plenty of noise and wind, and that for a start was enough for Mignet.

He constructed more aeroplanes, a glider, even a helicopter, all remarkably unsuccessful. At night he'd talk to his friends the radio hams—one as far away as Saigon, halfway round the world. He needed encouraging. 'I knew only too well the sound of breaking wood and the seconds of silence and stillness that followed it. Many times I made my little walk around the latest wreck and pronounced this sincere promise: "This time is positively the last. I'll abandon aviation for ever!"'

He had bought some books on aircraft, but it seemed to Mignet that conventional ideas were all wrong. Why have pivoted ailerons and elevators? Why not simply pivot the whole wing, as birds did? He thought with twisted logic back to his disaster with the SPAD. 'If I hadn't tried to fly, I wouldn't have crashed. And I had the accident not through my fault but because the whole conception of the ordinary aeroplane was wrong.'

With his eighth machine, he began to have a mite of success at last. He would run it endlessly across the meadow, up and down, across and back, while his wife sat in the shade of a tree doing her embroidery. Mignet began to make little hops, at first perhaps being simply thrown up by a bump, then gradually getting the feel of the simple controls until he could skin along in ground effect.

Encouraged, he wrote an article and sent it to an aviation magazine. Its theme: that amateur aviation was possible, that without any experience or engineering skill you could build an aircraft for no more than the cost of a ham radio, and (without any formal flying tuition) run it up and down a meadow till you could pilot it.

The article was a wild success. Mignet's proud claim was exactly what every amateur inventor, every ten-thumbed do-it-yourselfer, every spotty kid who fiddled with motor-bikes, every lazy uneducated dreamer had been waiting for. You must remember that in 1928 aviation was not the everyday thing it is today, but still the stuff of heroism. 1928 was the year of Lindbergh. But real aeroplanes were expensive, and a course of flying lessons was real work as well as being costly. Here was this simple uneducated middle-aged Frenchman saying that you could knock together your own plane, and as to piloting, it wasn't any harder than learning to ride a bike. Hadn't he proved it? The stuff of dreams.

The article, 'Is amateur aviation possible?' generated wild controversy; for every reader in whom it lit a fire of desire there seems to have been a sceptic, a scoffer. So Mignet published another article full of diagrams telling how to build his HM 8 aeroplane. That really got everybody going. The first amateur-built aeroplane based on Mignet's work flew the next spring.

The HM 8 was almost a conventional aeroplane in its layout: at least it had wing-shaped wings and a tail. By the time Mignet was up to his fourteenth design, five years after the HM 8, it had evolved into a horrible-looking tandem wing object with no real tail and a fuselage like a coffin with an outboard motor attached to the front. Proper aerodromes wouldn't let him in sight, so all his flying machines were arranged to fold or dismember so they could be towed behind Mignet's motor-bike to a meadow where he would camp, and camp, through autumn mists and winter frosts till spring came round again, while he 'made aviation'. By dint of sheer persistent fiddling and changing and never giving up, he got the HM 14 to the point where he could actually take off and fly in a circle back to his starting point.

Mignet by now had become an amateur publisher as well; he'd written a book about his adventures 'making aviation' and printed and published it himself. He didn't print nearly enough, and it soon sold out; he had it reprinted, this time by a proper publisher. It was translated into English by the Air League of the British Empire, a curious organisation that still exists today, pontificating to itself and forever telling the authorities how aviation in Britain should be run. Mignet's book was called in French *Le Sport de l'Air*, but in English *The Flying Flea* because Mignet had decided to call his HM 14 aircraft Pou du Ciel (Sky Louse) because, he said, it was 'a small insect which had made people scratch their heads'.

The book, no two editions of which are the same, since Mignet was forever tinkering with it in the same way that he tinkered with his aircraft, is a rambling dreamy philosophical account of his mystical infatuation with the sky. Its dedication runs: 'To all those who dream of having wings . . . To the memory of those who have loved them so greatly.'

Inside he explained: 'I built the Flying Flea because I have a passion for things of the air; because I cannot live far from wings; because I love to fly this little machine which is both docile and full of life, to live the magnificent sport which is Aviation; because I was inescapably drawn by the poetry of large spaces, of the open air, of the clouds, of the light, of colour, in a single word—I am under the spell of the air.' If that didn't get you, elsewhere he spelled out his message in a form you couldn't fail to understand: 'It is not necessary to have any technical knowledge to build an aeroplane . . . If you can nail together a packing case you can construct an aeroplane.'

He explained why conventional aeroplanes were so expensive: 'Designers have adopted bad habits from association with the client "WAR". Since they have turned their attention to the private buyer, they have not changed their ideas.' The problem with piloting,

KEY
1 Scott Flying Squirrel two-stroke, 25 b.h.p. at 3,500 r.p.m.
2 $\frac{3}{4}$ in (20 mm) square spruce frame
3 3 mm birch plywood skin
4 Mild steel tube
5 $\frac{1}{2}$ in (12 mm) rubber bungee cord
6 Spruce spar booms
7 3 mm ply web
8 Laminated ply
9 Rear spar: two laminations $\frac{1}{2}$ in $\times$ $\frac{3}{4}$ in (12 mm $\times$ 20 mm)
10 Spruce laths $\frac{1}{4}$ in $\times$ $\frac{1}{2}$ in (6 mm $\times$ 12 mm)
11 1·5 mm ply rib
12 Spar boom $\frac{5}{8}$ $\times$ $2\frac{1}{2}$ in (15 mm $\times$ 60 mm)
13 1·5 mm ply spar web
14 Wing pivot
15 25 cwt bracing cable
16 Control torque tube
17 15 cwt wing incidence control cable
18 5 cwt rudder control cable
19 Telescopic tube limit stop
20 Wing static-balance bungee
21 'Test-tube' fuel contents gauge
22 0·4 mm (24 swg) brass fuel tank
23 450 $\times$ 100 low pressure tyres
24 Foot-well
25 Baggage compartment
26 Rubber spring instrument mounting

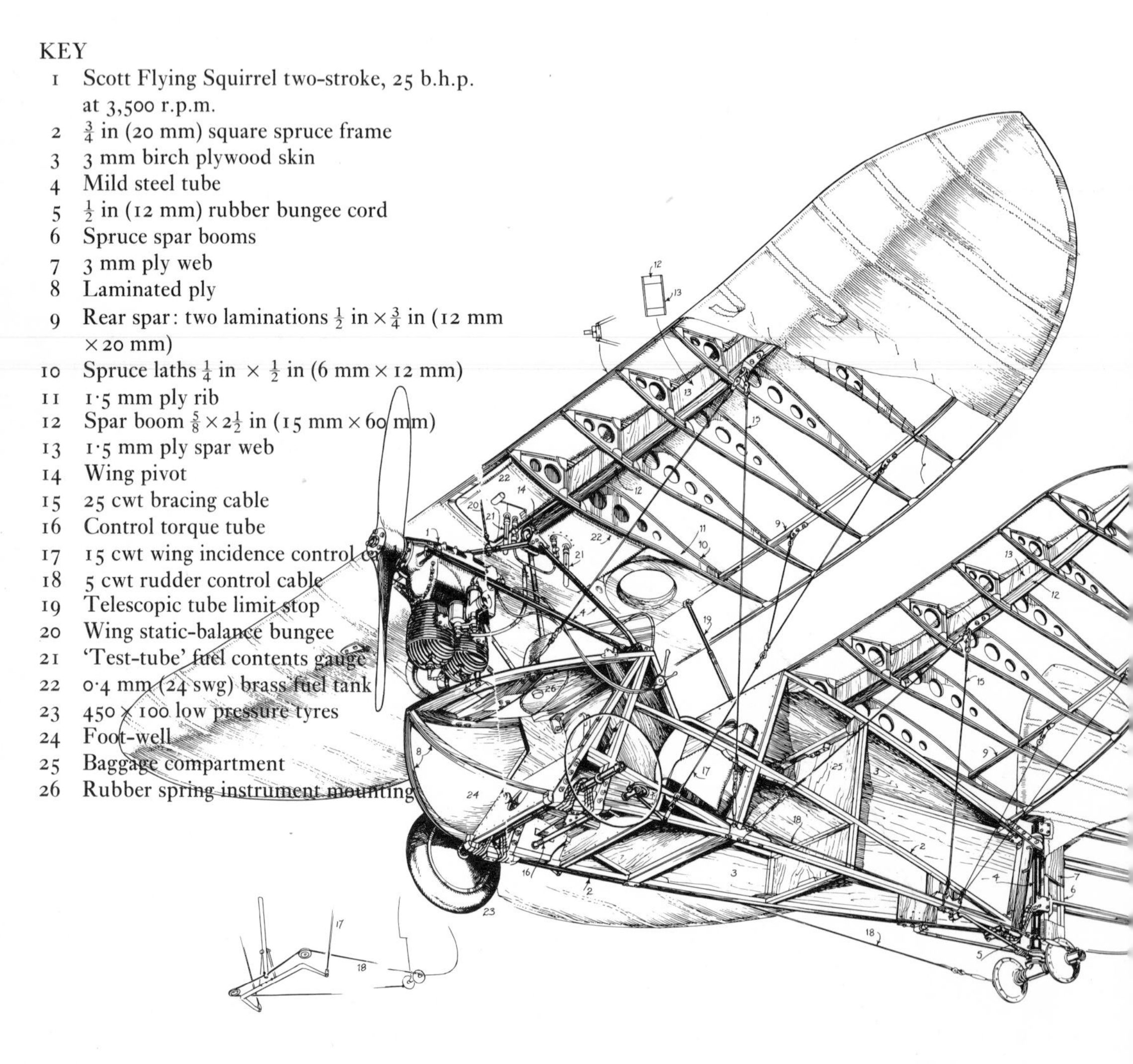

60. The Flea was built of wood with wire bracing. It had no ailerons—or roll control at all.

wrote Mignet, was simply the spin. 'Put a young man, interested in sport, in an aeroplane,' and 'he will not have flown 100 yards before he is in a spin.'

He listed fifteen other factors as to what was wrong with aeroplanes but 'balance' was the biggest. 'Road vehicles, ships, dirigible balloons—things which go on the land, the sea and in the air—are all stable machines . . . and do not possess any apparatus for lateral control . . . Alone among all transport machines the aeroplane has to be supplied with lateral controls. It is only the one which is unstable and dangerous by reason of its design. That strikes one as the aberration of a mad enthusiast.' He should know. Mignet had read somewhere in one of his books on flying that the spin was caused by 'crossing the controls'. The answer, to him, was stunningly simple, almost apocalyptic. 'Do away with one control.' Mignet chose to do without ailerons.

As to construction, 'I refuse to use the ordinary aviation metals such as alloy of aluminium and magnesium. In my opinion these are treacherous metals . . . There are two poisonous things in an ordinary machine, the ailerons and the cowling of the engine. I have cut them both out. No more sheet metal which flies off or rattles! No more cowling. No more of the sight of an overheated engine. And what heavy work is this of hammering and fitting! That's the way to save time! Ailerons and engine cowls represent weeks of labour and are never very successful.' The Flea was to be built of old reliable wood—like packing cases.

Mignet managed without ailerons, without any direct roll control at all, by giving his Flea very short wings with turned-up tips and a powerful rudder. You banked by using the rudder—so powerful was the rudder-induced-roll in the layout. There were no rudder pedals, as on conventional aircraft, but instead, moving the stick to the left and right (which would move the ailerons in an ordinary aircraft) worked Mignet's rudder. Moving the stick fore and aft tilted the whole front wing for control in pitch; the rear wing was fixed. A horrible-looking arrangement to any real aviation engineer, but, claimed Mignet, 'Our little bus is handsome in its ugliness. Its appearance is striking . . . it is indeed a Flying Flea.'

Perhaps the oddest thing about the Flying Flea was that it did fly. *Just*. Its performance was pitiful, and the motion horrible. 'You needed a strong stomach in a Flea', remembered a friend of mine who had flown several. 'They swung from side to side all the time in rough air.' My friend knew Mignet well. 'He was pig-headed. He had the light of madness in his eyes. Very piercing eyes. He wouldn't listen to advice on aviation. His thinking though was ingenious and empirical. His workmanship was appalling.' The most surprising thing was that 'the bloody thing actually flew—almost by a freak'.

Henri Mignet, said my friend (who is now himself a highly respected aeronautical engineer), 'had at best a half-truth. He had a little knowledge, and as the poet said, it became a dangerous thing.'

But the appeal of Mignet's writings was enormous. 'You can't imagine the excitement, it was unbelievable. That yellow book [the English translation] was a best-seller. You just couldn't buy it anywhere.' The Air League's first printing of 6,000 sold out in a

61. Fleas were prone to go over on their noses in mishaps. But the fatal defect was aerodynamic interaction between the tandem wings. 62. The front wing of the Flea on the right has been raised to avoid this.

month. Says Terence Boughton in his book *The Story of the British Light Aeroplane*, 'Throughout the summer of 1935 the craze for the Pou spread all over the British Isles. In sheds and garages, basement, attics and living rooms, amateurs were glueing and nailing their way towards their objective of cheap and simple flying for all.' I've seen it estimated that at one time 600 Fleas were under construction in Britain; that 500 were actually built in France and many in the USA.

There was even a Flea on display in the window of a dainty teashop in Piccadilly. And the *Daily Express* newspaper, ever quick to spot a new band-wagon on which to climb, decided to sponsor the Flea movement and may be do its own circulation a bit of good along the way. When the first British Flea made its maiden flight, on July 25th, 1935, ending up wrecked and on its back in a cabbage patch, the *Express* provided its owner with the cash to rebuild it, and they invited Mignet to visit Britain and show us how.

By August 12th he'd got as far as Calais, his Flea ending up on its nose with a wrecked engine. 'It was' noted one account of the trip, 'with a mixture of disbelief and derision that officials there greeted his pronounced intentions of setting off for England the next day.' But the next afternoon he reappeared with a replacement motorcycle engine, fitted it, made a quick test hop, landed, tied an inflated bicycle inner tube around his waist just in case, and took off into the teeth of a strong head-wind for England. The *Daily Express*'s chartered airliner met him in mid-Channel and escorted him to a more orthodox landing and 'a waiting crowd of not quite Lindberghian proportions' at Lympne. There followed an *Express*-sponsored tour of south-coast resorts, with fully 14,000 people turning out at Shoreham to watch the Flea's antics.

The first truly British Flea meeting was held in April the next year. Most of the Fleas attending were still only partly built; all came by road. Those that were complete and could be started spent the afternoon charging up and down across the grass, Mignet-fashion, in any direction regardless of attempted traffic control or wind direction. There were numerous ground collisions, though no one was hurt. One enterprising operator had a special non-flying short-span Flea there that you could hire for half-a-crown, and the inevitable equally enterprising small boy managed to get this device airborne and firmly lodged forty feet up a tree; it was the best flight of the day.

Very few of the Fleas ever did fly. 'The people who built them were mostly so ignorant.

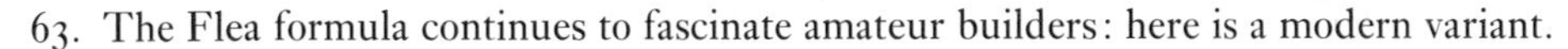

63. The Flea formula continues to fascinate amateur builders: here is a modern variant.

They built them too heavy, through misunderstanding Mignet's French plywood sizings. Or their nominally 30 hp motor-cycle engine was so out of tune it was only producing 10 hp. People copying Mignet made an awful lot of mistakes. They'd get the wings twisted, for instance. They didn't realise when rigging an aircraft like the Flea that one centimetre can make a difference. Or they'd carve their own awful propellers which generated little thrust. Most Fleas would taxi with the tail up and that was about it. Or at best they would finish stuck halfway up some tree.'

Their builders should have been grateful for failure, for the Flying Flea had a dreadful flaw in its behaviour in the air: once in a dive, the stick force reversed and the dive grew even steeper. If you were high enough when this happened (usually you weren't) you ended up on your back, flying upside down, when the Flea became so stable you could not recover! There were eleven fatal accidents like this: four in Britain, one of them killing the Air League's own test pilot. 'In normal flight at positive incidence,' says Boughton, 'the Pou was both stable and controllable, and could be flown satisfactorily for months or years until one day, due to a down-gust or a rapid push on the control column to initiate a dive, the critical incidence was attained. Thereafter no amount of pulling back would produce a recovery, and the little machine would carry its unfortunate pilot into the ever-steepening dive which had so often been reported by eye-witnesses.'

The effect was aggravated by an aerodynamic interference between front and rear wings: put simply, when you tilted the front wing trailing-edge down, you could suddenly increase the airflow over (and hence lift from) the fixed rear wing, producing a nose-down couple that ran away with you. This was the killer defect; there were others of lesser danger, such as the inability to sideslip, which made landing any way but straight into a gentle breeze hazardous. The interference effect between the two wings was eventually discovered by French government wind tunnel tests, and, says Boughton, 'could not have been predicted by any other method.

'The results brought the great Pou fever to an abrupt end in England. British "Permits to Fly" were withdrawn and most of the aircraft built met with an obscure fate, though one or two survive to this day collecting dust as somewhat pathetic curiosities.' Eventually a 'fix' was developed for the problem: you could either articulate the rear wing or fit a trailing-edge moveable flap to it—but by this time the craze to build Fleas had withered. Henri Mignet himself was never seriously hurt in any of his aircraft, and continued experimenting and building new versions of the Flea until his death in 1965.

To the end, though often hungry, sometimes short of cash, even reduced to sleeping under the wing of his Flea in the back of some hangar, he continued to 'love aviation as he loved his children, as he loved his wife, with all his heart'. To this day, versions of his no-aileron, tandem-wing concept continue to be built and flown by French enthusiasts. And the 'home-built aircraft' movement which he inspired continues in every industrialised country, but most notably in the United States, where it is huge. Today, home-built aircraft must be approved by government inspectors, and their pilots must be licensed; amateurism quite as amateurish as that which Henri Mignet fostered is no longer allowed.

14

The Brewster Buffalo

'The Brewster fighter turned out to be a perfect dud' wrote the American fighter pilot 'Pappy' Boyington. Pappy was lucky enough to be flying Curtiss P-40s himself, or he probably would never have survived to write those words.

Pappy Boyington was based for a while at Rangoon, alongside the RAF. 'As we talked and drank' (on his first evening there, in the officer's mess), 'the ceilings and walls around us in this mess bore mute evidence that this was no game. The Nips were playing for keeps. Although this mess had been spared by bombs, it was perforated with machine-gun fire. You even had to watch your elbows upon the bar, or you were apt to pick up splinters.'

Boyington politely enquired how alerts were announced. 'Long before the RAF gets around to announcing the alert, you will see two Brewsters take off in a *westerly* direction regardless of the wind sock. That's the signal,' he was told. 'The Japanese were flying in from the east.' Said Boyington: 'In my heart I couldn't blame the two English pilots of the Brewsters that remained, considering that this aircraft had already proved its inadequacy.'

'A Brewster squadron of my old buddies at Midway had only one survivor out of an entire squadron. And but for the grace of God I could have been in that squadron. This lone survivor was my old friend Slim Erwin. And he said: "The Japs had riddled my Brewster with so many bursts they gave me up for dead, or I'd never have gotten back either."'

The worst carnage was at the very beginning of the Midway Battle (June 4th, 1942) when the US Marine squadron VMF-221 (on its first-ever combat mission) put up twenty-five fighters (nineteen of them Brewsters) against 107 attacking Jap bombers and thirty-six escorting Zero fighters. Thirteen of the nineteen Brewsters were shot down in a battle that lasted less than half an hour; and of the eleven fighters that did get back down in one piece, eight were so shot up they never fought again. Captain Philip R. White was one lucky pilot who did get his crippled Brewster down in one piece. 'It is my belief,' he averred, 'that any commander who orders pilots out for combat in a

64/5. The Buffalo (*above*) and its adversary the Zero (*below*). The Buffalo was a ton heavier, slower, less manoeuvrable, and with lighter armament.

Brewster should consider the pilot as lost before leaving the ground.' In one dreadful blow the island's fighter defences had been wiped out, and even the few survivors were utterly demoralised.

It seems the Americans had made the awful mistake of believing their own PR. It went further than simple fanfares of publicity to the effect that their fighters were the greatest in the world. Pappy Boyington remembered being thus briefed by a recruiter for the American Volunteer Group, before he sailed for the Far East: 'The Japs will be flying antiquated junk over China. Many of your kills will be unarmed transports. I suppose you know that the Japanese are renowned for their inability to fly. And they all wear corrective glasses. Our technical staff determines this from the remains after a shoot-down.'

In September 1941 the American magazine *Aviation* informed its readers that the Japanese had the world's highest accident record and it trained fewer than 1,000 pilots a year; and 'America's aviation experts can say without hesitation that the chief military airplanes of Japan are either outdated already, or are becoming outdated . . .'

The truth was that the Japanese fighter pilots were superbly trained, already experienced, from battles over China and Manchuria, and flying Zeros—marvellously lightly built and manoeuvrable fighters. It was not until they got the Grumman F6F Hellcat late in the war that the Americans had anything to match the Zero. Certainly the Brewster Buffalo couldn't.

Here's how the Zero and the Buffalo compared:

Mitsubishi A6M2 Zero-Sen		*Brewster F2A-3 Buffalo*
5,300 lbs	*Weight, loaded*	*7,160 lbs*
950 hp	*Power*	*1,200 hp*
330 mph	*Maximum speed*	*300 mph*
22 lbs/sq.ft	*Wing loading*	*34 lbs/sq.ft*
1,900 miles	*Range*	*900 miles*
Two 20 mm cannon, and two 7.7 mm machine guns.	*Armament*	*Four 'point five' machine guns (0.5 in, 12.7 mm).*

So the Brewster was a big barge, full of armour plate but with rotten little guns; while the Zero was extremely light, with fantastic range, and two big cannons firing explosive shells. A Zero could out-turn a Brewster without even trying; and if you did try and mix it in a Buffalo it was inclined to snap-roll if you pulled any g. Even that 300 mph maximum speed is suspect; there's one story of Buffalos being sent out to escort some Blenheim bombers; the Blenheims had to throttle back so that the Buffalos could keep up! The power output of the Wright Cyclone engine fell off markedly with altitude; it could take you half an hour simply to reach 21,000 feet!

The Japanese Navy commander, Masatake Okumiya, wrote: 'The unforgivable error of "underestimating the enemy" made by the Americans and the British was perhaps best illustrated in the reliance placed upon the antiquated Brewster F2A Buffalo fighter plane, which American aviation experts boasted was "the most powerful fighter plane in the Orient" and a "fighter plane far superior to anything in the Japanese Air Force". Against the Zero fighters, the Buffalo pilots literally flew suicide missions.'

The Brewster Buffalo had begun happily enough, as the very first monoplane fighter project for the US Navy—its competitor for the production contract was a Grumman biplane. Orthodox Navy thinking in those days was that you probably couldn't operate monoplanes off carriers. In those days, too, one of the final acceptance tests for Navy fighters was the horrible 'terminal velocity dive', where some reckless fool of a test pilot was offered a large bribe to take the prototype aircraft as high as he could, and slowly push over into a vertical, full-power dive. If the wings stayed on through the recovery pull-out, you got the Navy order. If they didn't, you hoped the wreck came down in a cemetery and not through somebody's roof. I'm not saying that the Brewster Buffalo was ever subjected to such a crazy test, but that its excessive weight came from it being built far too strong, as were all its contemporaries.

The Buffalo's tubby shape came, no doubt, from the current aerodynamic fashion of trying to design fuselages that approximated to the 'perfect streamline form'—something akin to a fat raindrop. This required that the maximum cross-sectional area be a third or even half-way back from the nose; and since the nose itself contained a big round engine, the maximum further aft of it was going to be very maximum indeed. The shape of the Zero's fuselage (it also had a round engine) shows what rubbish this theory was; if nothing else, the drag from all that unnecessary wetted area was punitive.

66. The Buffalo prototype on an early test flight. It proved to be 25 mph slower than promised.

The Buffalo's career went badly from the start. It was 25 mph slower than promised. So they put the entire aircraft in a huge wind tunnel, and were only then able to clean it up and get 300 mph. Then the prototype's engine quit during another test, and it was quite badly damaged. The first Navy squadron to get Brewsters took them to sea on the carrier *Saratoga*, only to find that the landing gears kept collapsing with the shock of arrested landings. The Brewster company said it was all the fault of ham-fisted Navy pilots—nothing wrong with their landing gears.

There did seem to be a lot wrong with the Brewster company, though: 'Serious managerial problems, production bottlenecks, and reports of sabotage.' Typical sabotage was to the arrester hook—the swivel fitting within the fuselage (where you could hardly see it) would be found to be drilled with holes to weaken it. I think the US Navy might have given up on the Brewster Buffalo, except that the fighter they really wanted—the Grumman F4F Wildcat—wasn't nearly ready. In the end the Navy did reject the Brewster for carrier flying, and turned all their first batch over to the Finns to fight the Russians with.

In 1939 and 1940 you could sell any kind of fighter to a desperate Europe. The Brewster company got export orders from Belgium, Britain, and Holland. The British, having ordered the thing, then flew it, and concluded that it was quite hopeless for fighting Me-109s in Europe. They tried to fob the planes off on an RAF squadron of volunteer American pilots then being formed, but the Americans made clear their dismay, and their preference for Hurricanes. In the end, the RAF's Buffalos were mostly sent to defend Singapore, Burma and Malaysia, the RAF then sharing the American view that the Jap Air Force wasn't anything much to worry about. The Brewsters were, though: they didn't like the tropical climate: there was valve-gear trouble with the engines; the landing gears would stick down, and the electrical gun-firing mechanisms would rust and corrode. (The Dutch were having similar problems with theirs, across the water in the East Indies—what we now call Indonesia.)

It was a hellish task, trying to defend those far eastern colonies against the Japanese. There was no radar, or any kind of control-and-reporting network which made such a difference in the Battle of Britain. The first warning you got of a raid was when the bombs began crashing around you. You'd run like hell to your Brewster and try and strap in and get it started while you were being bombed and straffed all the while. If you *did* get airborne you were likely to be picked off by Japanese fighters waiting for you. If by some miracle you had time to climb high enough to get anywhere near the Japanese bombers, well, some of them were faster than you were. And if by some further miracle you managed to find one that wasn't, and to get into a position to attack it, you might well find your guns wouldn't fire. (One flight of three Buffalos did intercept some bombers, only to find that only one out of their combined total of twelve guns was working.) The Japanese had an uncanny knack of catching you with a bombing raid when you had just landed, weary and out of fuel, from a desperate battle with an earlier force.

The Brewsters did shoot down a few Japanese aircraft; too precious few. The RAF

67/8. A squadron of Buffalos flown by Australian pilots in Malaya in 1941. Every one of 154 Buffalos there was destroyed inside three months.

(with the Australians and New Zealanders) had begun with 154 Buffalos in Malaya, Singapore and Burma on December 7th, 1941—the day the Japanese declared war. In three months all these (plus some reinforcements) were gone. The Dutch had thirty in the East Indies, and these lasted no longer.

What it was like to fight Zeros in a Buffalo is described in the American aviation historian Martin Caidin's book *Zero*. It is in the words of an Australian pilot, Gregory Board, who described how, before the battle opened, there were '"Intelligence briefings almost daily by the most learned of men, who came in from the other side of the Japanese bamboo curtain, and told us that the best of the Japanese fighters were old fabric-covered biplanes which wouldn't stand a chance against the Buffalos. With this ringing promise of slaughtering the Japanese in the air should they get too big for their britches, we concentrated on flying and learning different methods of drinking gin-and-tonic."'

The reality of fighting the Japanese was chilling. 'The entire squadron was wiped out to a man. Suddenly we realized what we had in the Buffalo—a barrel which the Zero could outfly, outclimb, outgun, outmanoeuvre and outdo in almost anything else that was in the book for a fighting aircraft.'

The end of Board's own Buffalo, as Caidin describes it, was typical.

'A Zero had latched on to his tail, and the world went to pieces under him. The instrument panel erupted in his face. Instinct made him hunch down in his seat and the move saved his life. Japanese bullets crashed off the armour plate and exploding cannon shells tried to drive the plating right through him. Without that armour he would have been killed instantly. He said it was like a bad dream in slow motion, or attending your own funeral. The Zero shot the surface of the Buffalo's wings off until Board could see the naked ribs beneath. He could feel the fighter coming apart under his hands. Frantic, he went wild, trying every trick he knew in the Buffalo to shake his pursuer. "But whoever was in that Zero was good, damned good," Board recalled grimly, "and he had a hell of a better aircraft under his hands. He chopped that Brewster into ribbons . . . I had nothing left but to try and get out by going straight down. I was pulling all the power the aircraft had and I shoved the stick forward and tried to save my life by diving vertically."

'It did not work. The Zero was a nightmare glued to his tail, snapping out short, neat bursts that continued to chop away at the Buffalo. Board felt the heat as the fighter exploded into flames. The fuel tanks belched fire. Ammunition exploded in the wing racks. Acrid fumes filled the cockpit, choking him.

'He had just enough time to plunge into a cloud where he chopped power and pulled up the nose to slow down; he rolled onto his back and released the hatch. Flames thundered into the cockpit and then he was gone, into the blessed relief of cool air. He fell for long seconds, far clear of the battle, before pulling his ripcord to open his parachute.'

So far as I can discover, only one Brewster Buffalo survived the Far Eastern battles, and the fall of Singapore, Malaya, Burma and the Dutch East Indies. It was to be shipped home by the victorious Japanese for testing. One wonders what they thought of it?

And now, the surprise, the twist in the tail of this story. Remember that the Finns had also received Buffalos, to fight the Russians with? The Finns liked their Buffalos very much, and were extremely successful with them! Their Brewsters were an early model, a whole ton lighter than later machines; and they had an improved 'export' version of the Wright Cyclone engine, which in any case would have been less prone to its worst fault—overheating—in Finland's climate. Even so, the Finnish pilots had their moments while getting used to their Brewsters. Here's Eino Luukkanen in his book *Fighter over Finland* describing his section's first landing in a Buffalo.

'Immediately my fighter's wheels touched the sloping runway the aircraft tried to ground-loop. I used each toe brake to keep the Brewster straight, my progress down the runway accompanied by awful screeching noises as the tortured tyres skidded on the hard surface, but finally I managed to bring the aircraft to a standstill. The second and third Brewsters made identical landings to mine, but the fourth got into trouble when the pilot over-corrected in his attempt to keep the aircraft straight on the runway, the starboard wing-tip brushing the ground. Fortunately the damage was slight . . .'

Once the Finns got used to them, their Brewsters 'roamed far and wide over the battle-field, enjoying one of the best kill-to-loss ratios of any fighter.' Perhaps in truth it was because the Finnish fighter pilots were very good, and highly motivated, whereas the Red Air Force wasn't too hot. (The Russians were still flying *biplane* fighters.) Here's Luukkanen describing how he dispatched a dozy Russian biplane pilot to his socialist Valhalla:

'I closed with the Russian until I could make out clearly the individual details of the fighter; the bright red stars on the pale blue-grey under-surface of the wings, the small puffs of black smoke emitted by the exhaust stubs, the bracing wires and even the lines of the wheel-well doors. Ivan was still unaware of my proximity, for he did not deviate a fraction from his course. At fifty yards I opened up, my first burst striking the underside of the engine cowling and then raking along the belly of the fuselage. The Tchaika clawed into a vertical stall and then fell away on one wing, plummeting into a meadow below.'

15

The Fairey Battle

H. A. 'Tony' Taylor in his book *Test Pilot at War* says:

'The Battle was designed to meet conditions of a period earlier than that in which it finally went into brief action. In 1933, when its specification was approved, the Battle had seemed to be a very good aeroplane. Its performance more or less doubled that of the (biplane) Hawker Harts and Hinds which it was to replace. But by the time it was necessary for the Battle to go into action in 1939–40, it was hopelessly outclassed in speed and lacked necessary defensive firepower. A very large number of Battles were built—mostly by Austin Motors under the "shadow factory" scheme.

'Hindsight is all too easy—and mass production of anything is very difficult to stop quickly without serious social and other disturbances—but I wonder now why something could not have been done about it. It should have been practical for someone to have decided on available knowledge during 1939 that the time had come to try to divert this enormous effort to something more useful, and to stop the mass production of aeroplanes which, good though they were when originally developed, had obviously become easy meat for the known fighters. After brief, heroic use as a bomber the Battle, as such, was taken out of service . . .'

The Battle's tragedy, in a word, was its defencelessness. 'The Battle' says John Nesbitt-Dufort,* 'was supposed to be a "fast" day bomber, but I am afraid in view of its very poor power-to-weight ratio this was not the case. A top speed of 241 mph was alleged, but I certainly never succeeded in winding one up to this in level flight.'

The petrol tanks weren't self-sealing, and the entire fuel system was easily breached and ignited by enemy fire. The Battle had little armour plate, and was vulnerable even to light machine gun and rifle fire from the ground on low-level missions. And its defensive armament was pitiful: one fixed .303 Browning in the starboard wing, firing only directly forwards, and a Vickers gun of similar calibre which the gunner in the rear cockpit could

*See bibliography

swing about on a swivelling mount—much as air gunners used to do in the First World War. From anywhere behind-and-below the Battle was defenceless—and behind-and-below is the easiest area from which to attack a bomber!

The prototype Battle first flew in 1936; production models were ordered the same year, and the first went into service with RAF squadrons in 1937. It wasn't disliked at first; it was stable and extremely easy to fly—important then, when new pilots joined operational squadrons with extremely few flying hours to their credit. The Battle was sluggish, a little slow and heavy to respond to the controls, but safe enough and very easy to land. Its one nasty habit is described thus by Nesbitt-Dufort:

'One would be stooging along quite happily with all temps and pressures at normal when there would be a sudden loss of power. As one looked around for a suitable forced landing field the Merlin engine would metaphorically put its hand to its mouth, belch out a cloud of black smoke, utter a loud bang, a deep cough, belch out a cloud of black smoke and then run on again quite sweetly pretending nothing had happened.

'If I was asked to compare its handling characteristics with that of a car, I would say that its rather heavy and woolly feel was very similar to the old Austin 12.'

Ten Battle squadrons were sent to France during the 'phoney war' of 1939–40. They were tried out on reconnaissance work over the Siegfried Line, and a gunner in one even managed to bring down an Me-109. That Battle got home to tell about it; its two companion aircraft didn't. Ten days later the Luftwaffe did even better, shooting down five out of five Battles. Frantic efforts were then made to fix, somehow, a machine gun underneath the Battle, firing back aft, but it seemed it couldn't usefully be done.

The big German assault finally came on May 10th, 1940, and the Battles were sent in to straffe German troops invading Luxembourg. There apparently weren't enough fighters for any to be spared to escort the Battles, so it was decided to send them in low, to bomb from 250 feet using delayed-action fuses in their bombs. It was now that the Battle's extreme vulnerability to ground fire was discovered: out of thirty-two that went out that first day, thirteen were lost, and those that did get back were all damaged. The Battles, in Group Captain Townsend's words, 'with tragic swiftness had proved their reputation as "flying coffins".'

'One Battle pilot, Flying Officer Bill Simpson, approached a German column at tree-top level. The flak ripped a hole in his engine. He staggered on, dropped his bombs, noting despite his own predicament that they "fell on helpless mules as well as men"—and with flames and molten metal streaking past the cockpit he crash-landed a few moments later in the Ardennes. The aircraft immediately exploded and before he could undo his straps, sheets of flame rushed up at him.'

In his own book *One of our Pilots is Safe*, in a passage of which H. E. Bates wrote: 'I have not read the equal in terror and pain', Bill Simpson describes waiting for death by fire in his crashed Battle:

69. The Battle was stable and easy to fly, but almost defenceless against fighter attack.

'Great sheets of searing flames rushed between my legs and up to thirty feet above me. In that first rush of heat my hands were burned and they seized up solid. They were completely useless. I was trapped by my straps and could not move. The awful realisation that I was about to be burned to death took possession of my mind. A tremendous white heat enveloped me. I could feel my flesh burning, but the pain I felt was mostly mental . . . I let my hands drop on to my knees and curled myself up, waiting for the release of death. My whole mind was full of a bloodcurdling scream; but no sound came . . . Behind my head the electric klaxon screamed out its strident note, reminding me to lower my wheels before making a landing.

'As I sat there waiting to die my mind raced back over the years. I saw a kaleidoscope of scattered, ever-changing scenes. Some were happy, some sad—the most vivid moments of my life. Afterwards I was surprised to find that it was really true that on the point of death life is lived in vivid retrospect, the mind grasping for the last time at the memories which had stimulated it in life . . . But I did not die.'

Still burning, Bill Simpson was dragged clear by his observer and gunner (he heard one of them gasp in horror at the sight of him) and rolled in the wet grass while the Battle exploded and burned and exploded again.

'There was a peculiar drawn feeling about my face; the left side of my nose and left eye felt completely distorted—as indeed they were. Ragged clumps of blackened clothing hung on me. The smell of burning was everywhere—above all, the smell of my own burnt flesh—very frightening, this . . .

'What horrified me most of all was the sight of my hands. I stared at them with an unbelieving terror. They were the hands of a ghost, bone white. The skin hung from them like long icicles. The fingers were burned and pointed, like the claws of a great white bird—distorted, pointed at the end like talons, ghastly thin. What would I do now? What use would these paralysed talons be to me for the rest of my life if I *did* live?'

Live he did; Bill Simpson survived to become one of Archibald MacIndoe's 'guinea pigs'—those dreadfully burned airmen who were salvaged by new techniques of plastic surgery—and after the war, to be BEA's first public relations officer.

Next day, May 11th, and only the second day of the big German drive, eight more Battles were dispatched to bomb the invaders; only one came back. By May 12th, two Panzer divisions were pouring across two canal bridges in Belgium (near the Dutch border town of Maastricht) in a vast thrust that looked exactly like what it was—the beginning of the end for the Allies on the continent. If those bridges could be destroyed, might the German drive be halted? They'd been repeatedly bombed at night or by day from altitude, to little effect: could a low-level daytime attack do it? The job was given to 12 Squadron, RAF, known as the 'shiny twelfth' or else the 'dirty dozen', depending on whether they were in favour or not. No bones were made about the raid being anything but a suicide mission; the C in C sent out the order that only volunteers were to be asked for.

'Our squadron has been specially chosen,' the deputy squadron commander told his chaps in their operations hut in the French woods, 'to destroy a particularly vital target. Six crews are to take off immediately to bomb these two bridges—three against each bridge. The Germans have had time to get their flak defences into position—you can expect the most obstinate defence, both from the ground and from fighters. But these bridges must be destroyed at all costs.'

Air Marshal 'Ugly' Barratt, the C in C, had said that only volunteers were to go on the raid. But Squadron Leader Lowe phrased the order rather differently: 'The raid will be carried out on a volunteer basis. Will anyone who *doesn't* wish to go step forward.' But it wouldn't have made any difference how he phrased it: the 12-Squadron crews were all young, still inexperienced of the horrors of a bomber crew's death, and quite recklessly brave.

'There was complete silence, with no movement of any kind. Then a volley of shouted appeals came from all parts of the hut, developing into a hubbub of pleading and cajoling as one by one the crews pressed their individual claims for going on the raid. The most vociferous and insistent claims came from the six stand-by crews. "It's our turn," they objected, "and we're ready to go. There's no need for volunteers."'*

And go they did. Their two flight commanders got in an argument about tactics: 'I'm

*From *Strike Hard, Strike Sure* by Ralph Barker.

going in at low level,' said Don Garland. 'You'll get shot to pieces,' said Norman Thomas. 'I think dive bombing is the answer.' The argument grew heated, till in the end they agreed to differ, each to his own technique. One crew had aircraft trouble, so in the end five set out. None returned. The bridges, though damaged, survived; the German advance continued unchecked. Thomas and his crew were shot down, and captured unhurt; they were taken no less than three times across the very bridge they had come to destroy as the Germans tried to evacuate them to the east, away from the fighting.

Strangely, to this day the Maastricht bridges raid is revered as one of the most glorious moments in the RAF's history, for the other flight commander, Garland, and his observer were both awarded posthumous VCs. But no award went to the third member of the crew, the gunner Reynolds, 'who had as willingly as they accepted the risk of almost certain death. What a gross mockery of their noble deed to discriminate between the sacrifices of these three young heroes. Was it a question of rank, or the scarcity of VCs? Not that either mattered in the world where they had gone—any more than they do in this one, where most saints and heroes go unsung.' So said Group Captain Peter Townsend.

None of these five Battles returned to base, though one crew got back later on foot. Of the original bomber force of 135 aircraft, that evening only seventy-two remained. Two days later the entire remaining force of sixty-three available Battles was despatched; only twenty-eight returned. No higher rate of loss was ever sustained by the RAF. 'Their sacrifice was quite in vain, however . . . two hours later the Germans were off again on their race to the Channel coast.' And the Battle's battle was over.

The few surviving aircraft were withdrawn to England. Mostly they were given to the Poles to fly—the Poles didn't seem to mind how risky anything was, so long as it gave them a chance to attack Germans. But even so, they were only sent out at night, against Hitler's fleet of barges massing in French and Dutch ports to invade Britain. Battles were also used in coastal patrols around Ireland and Iceland—far from the Messerschmitts. Battle production continued unabated till late in the year, over 2,000 being built. Uses were found for them as target tugs, or engine test-beds, or as bombing and gunnery trainers. But the aircraft is remembered principally for the raid on those bridges: 'One of the great tragic operations of war, a gallant but pointless sacrifice which, like the Charge of the Light Brigade, will remain an inspiration to Britain long after many more brilliantly successful operations are forgotten,' said Ralph Barker.

70/1. The Me-323, the powered Gigant, could lift twelve tons, but was very slow and appallingly vulnerable to fighter attack.

16

Floundering Elephants

Operation Sealion, Hitler's bold, crude plan to jump on Britain, was never actually cancelled or abandoned; merely *postponed*. England was put on one side while the Germans dealt with the more pressing problem of Russia. Once a final solution had been worked out in the east, they would turn their attention back to Britain, which would be well-defended—the Germans knew that. What would be needed would be an initial blitzkreig attack made as fierce as possible, with guns, vehicles, even tanks supporting the paratroops. Let us not do things by halves, they decided; let us make *tank-landing gliders*.

So in October 1940 the German Air Ministry sent specifications for such a giant glider to Junkers and Messerschmitt, with requests that design studies and some calculations be worked out, and quickly: the two companies were allowed just fourteen days to do it. One hundred such gliders were to be built by each company, and preparations must start immediately. Then a week later each company got a telegram: 'Production must start immediately! Double the quantity, make 200! Rapid completion of order vital!'

At the Junkers factory at Merseburg, all was panic. For some unfathomable reason their instructions were to build their gliders all of wood, while Junkers were of course the original pioneers of all-metal aircraft structures. They had no wood-working experience at all. No carpenters. No glue. Not even a saw. No timber of any kind in stock, let alone aircraft grade timber, and being wartime, there was not much chance of being able to commandeer enough for 200 gigantic gliders.

The design office and the test department were soon spitting venom at each other when the test people managed to snap a sample wing spar at only half its design load. 'Let's have a look at it,' said the design staff. 'Look at this,' they said to the test people, 'it's got sap rot, and the glueing is defective.' So they made another test spar, and this time it failed at sixty per cent of the design load . . . By this time several of the Junkers Mammoth gliders were partly built. Horrible looking things they were, with no proper noses, but more like huge flying wings, with a minimum rear fuselage stretching back to support the minimum tail surfaces. 'Much too minimum, those tail surfaces,' said General Ernst Udet, on a visit to Merseburg. 'You mark my words: she'll be unstable as an autumn leaf if you ever do get her in the air!' And of course the design office didn't like *that* either.

The glider was designed to land in simple skids, so of course it needed some kind of droppable trolley on which to take off. The Junkers engineers tried different trolleys, one with thirty-two wheels, before discovering that the glider tended to jump off the trolley too soon, and it had to be attached firmly to the glider so it could be dropped from a goodly height. The trolley ended up a complex structure of steel tubes weighing all of eight tons.

Then they tried loading an actual tank into the first Mammoth to be completed. The tank tilted over the sill of the glider's hold, there was an expensive crunch, and the tank fell through the floor. So they winched it back out and rebuilt the floor, much stronger and also much heavier—the Mammoth's useful payload now dropped from twenty-two tons to thirteen tons. This was hardly enough for a tank, but by this time nearly everyone was beyond caring.

They calculated that a Ju-90 four-engined transport aircraft would have just enough thrust to tow the first Mammoth off the ground before reaching the end of the Merseburg runway, but these calculations had a certain lack of conviction about them, so they cleared a three-mile-long path through the forest off the end of the runway, just in case.

The day for the first flight came, and the calculations were correct, and glider and tug did get airborne before the runway's end. The eight-ton launching dolly was duly released, and it didn't rebound and smash the glider, as some had suspected; no, it just thudded into the ground and disintegrated. But Ernst Udet's guess had been exactly right; the Mammoth proved wildly unstable, yawing like a pendulum. Its pilot fighting to control it, climbed above the Ju-90 tug, pulling its tail upwards and preventing it climbing. Soon the tug, still pulling full power, was actually *diving*. At the last moment the Mammoth pilot released the towline, and the Ju-90 just managed to recover a few feet above the ground. Freed of its tow, the Mammoth became suddenly stable, and glided down to a perfect landing.

They cordoned off the area, and built a ramp over a railway line, and in due course two of the tanks that the Mammoth was supposed to carry came along and towed *it* back to the airfield. They made some half-hearted attempts to fly it again, but soon the Air Ministry cancelled the project, and put them out of their anguish. What were they to do with the dozens of partly-built Mammoths littering the factory? Workmen with saws cut them into pieces, and then still smaller pieces, and the bits were used as fuel in wood-burning trains on the railways. The Mammoth programme had cost forty-five million Reichsmarks.

Meanwhile, over at the Messerschmitt company, things had been going rather better. They too had their original contract doubled, but were allowed to use a mixed structure with a welded steel tube skeleton—much easier to fabricate. They had designed a glider that was quite orthodox, except for its grotesque size, and this orthodoxy helped give them a fighting chance of producing a practical aeroplane. The Messerschmitt designers chose a basic square-section welded steel tube fuselage with fabric covering over a wood secondary structure; and a strongly tapered strut-braced wing with wooden ribs attached to a built-up steel tube spar, all covered with ply forward and fabric aft. The tail assembly was all wood. Unlike Junkers, the Messerschmitt people were quite familiar with woodworking; and furthermore, they got the local furniture factory to make most of the wooden bits for them.

That structure was good orthodox stuff. Novelties were the hingeing of the entire tail assembly for pitch trim purposes; and outward-opening clamshell nose doors, which are familiar enough on freighter aircraft now but were quite novel then. Like the Mammoth, the Messerschmitt Gigant glider was launched on a dolly, but this was a simple affair of two Ju-90 mainwheels and two Me-109 mainwheels, weighing under two tons.

They rolled out the first Gigant just fourteen weeks from the off. It was the second largest aircraft that had ever been built anywhere; and at that moment a further eleven Gigants were in final assembly; and sixty-two more not far behind. For the first trials they used a Ju-90 tug, as had Junkers with their Mammoth. The Gigant flew well, except that the enormously heavy control forces proved a bit much for a single pilot, and it was decided to build a co-pilot's seat into future Gigants so he could help push and shove on the controls. After all, the thing spanned 180 feet, and was designed to fly at weights of up to 40 tons.

The only real problem with the Gigant was a product of its unreal size: there wasn't a tow plane powerful enough for it. The Ju-90 was only good enough for test flights when the Gigant was lightly-loaded. General Udet had applied his practical aviator's mind to the problem, and suggested a Siamese-twin version of the Heinkel He-111 bomber, with two He-111 fuselages and outer wings joined by a new centre-section with an extra engine in the middle, making five in all! This Heinkel-Zwilling was later built, and proved practical; but meanwhile something was needed *now*. The answer, it was decided, was to use three Me-110s flying in vic formation and attached to the Gigant by 10 mm steel cables. This was known as the *Troika-Schlepp*; further augmentation for take-off was provided by attaching clusters of hydrogen peroxide rockets to the strut-spar junction halfway out along the wing. There was also a 65-foot ribbon braking parachute that could be deployed from the rear fuselage for landing.

Thus schlepping a Gigant into the air was a hairy and cumbersome procedure. The rocket assist required special tank waggons, siphoning gear and skilled personnel. Take-off required a minimum 4,000 feet of paved runway, and, of course, three 110s all serviceable at that moment.

William Green in his *The Warplanes of the Third Reich* says:

'The preliminary preparations for take-off were so complicated that it was utterly impossible to send up several gliders simultaneously. The take-off sequence called for the Gigant to unstick first at around 55 mph, followed by the outboard towplanes and finally the lead towplane. After leaving the runway the 110s virtually hung on their airscrews, their pilots having to exercise a high degree of skill to maintain control, and during the climb-out at approximately 80 mph the strain on the steel cables increased and slackened in a series of violent jerks . . . In turbulent conditions the *Troika-Schlepp* was described by towplane pilots as "hair-raising".'

And there were prangs. One day they were practising with the *Troika-Schlepp* of three 110s just towing the wire ropes, unattached to anything: the starboard aircraft suddenly veered to port during take-off, became entangled in the centre aircraft's towline, and both crashed. They also practised by trying to tow a Ju-52 trimotor, with its outboard engines idling, just in case. One day, the left-hand 110 suddenly stalled and yawed sharply to port: the Ju-52 pilot pulled his towline disconnect levers with one hand and gave her full throttle with the other, but the port cable failed to disconnect and thrashed about below as he clawed for altitude. It cut a farm waggon in half, demolished farm buildings, trees, and finally wrapped around a telegraph pole, which it tore out by the roots. The trimotor pilot was able to keep airborne, and eventually to land safely, still towing the heavy pole!

The very first time a *Troika-Schlepp* was tried with an actual Gigant was almost a disaster. Just after breaking ground the main tow attachment snapped: the Gigant pilot fired off his remaining rockets, racked the thing round in a steep turn with the wing-tip

72. A Gigant glider being towed by a Siamese-twin combination of two He-111s.

just off the ground, streamed his landing parachute, and got safely down. On another test flight, on reaching the planned altitude, the Gigant pilot pulled his tow releases and turned away sharp right, as you do in gliders on dropping a tow to this day. But the *port* cable failed to release: the Gigant went right and one 110 left for a moment, then the 110's fuselage snapped in two. During a further flight, the rockets on one side of a Gigant failed to fire: it shot off to one side, its three tug aircraft all collided, and the whole assembly crashed down into the woods on the airfield boundary. That day the Gigant had been carrying real live troops, 120 of them, and all of them, plus the three 110 pilots, plus the six-man crew of the Gigant, died. It was very possibly, in terms of the number of dead, the worst aeroplane accident ever at that date (early 1941). Another Gigant spun in when its water ballast tank shifted.

Production continued regardless: by the end of the summer of 1941 the Messerschmitt company had finished the first 100 Gigants, and were well into the second 100, the two-pilot version. Since the Germans were no nearer being able to begin the invasion of England, for which the Gigants had been planned, the Luftwaffe decided to use them on the eastern front. They had the greatest trouble just getting them there: the *Troika-Schlepp* 110s, grinding away at full power and low airspeed, only had a range of 250 miles before they had to land and refuel. So they stopped often on their way to Russia, on already over-crowded airfields where the last things the exhausted, frozen ground crews wanted was 180-foot span gliders that landed on skids and had to be jacked up before you could even move them off the active runway. That is always assuming that the wheeled dollies for them had actually arrived. Plus the fact that they needed special long tie-down ropes; special service trucks and loading ramps; and tanks of peroxide, siphoning gear, and those specially-trained rocket motor servicing crews.

The Gigant glider was not the most *practical* weapon of war. Some of them did eventually get into action, but they were of no real use. So they pulled them back to Germany, and made plans to use them in the invasion of Malta, when their Siamese-twin He-11 tugs might be ready; and then they planned to use them against the Astrakhan and Baku oilfields; and subsequently to relieve the German forces besieged in Stalingrad; followed by service in the Crimea; and afterwards to ferry two paratroop divisions to Sicily. Then they gave up. Giant gliders, unpowered and without proper landing wheels, were just too unwieldy to be practical.

Meanwhile, of course, the Messerschmitt engineers were busy doing what they should have been asked to do at the start: produce a wheeled version of the Gigant that could take-off and cruise under its own power. The wonder that emerged had six engines mounted in a row down the leading edge of the wings, and sat on ten huge wheels that were mounted in rows down each side of the forward fuselage. Two flight engineers were added to the crew, and little offices were hollowed out for them in the wing leading edge, between the engines. Of course the pilots had over-riding throttle control of the engines, but the two engineers managed the synchronisation of the engines, and watched the oil pressures, and so on. Elsewhere, scattered about the aircraft's structure, were little nests for machine gunners to occupy: in the nose doors, and on top of the fuselage just aft of the wing, and in little blister bubbles on top of the wing itself. In addition, there were slits and slots and holes cut in the fuselage's fabric sides, so that the infantry seated within could take pot shots at any attacking fighters; they stood little chance of hitting anything, but at least it gave them something to do while under attack, and must have been a morale booster.

The Me-323, the powered Gigant, could lift twelve tons, and had some 500 miles of range. But it was much too slow. It was so slow that the engines constantly overheated, until they redesigned the engine cowls. Supposedly it cruised at 140 mph at low level, but I suspect 110 mph was more like it.

The 323 first went into service with the Luftwaffe late in 1942, ferrying anti-aircraft and anti-tank guns, bombs, ammunition and petrol across the Mediterranean to the Afrika Corps in Tunisia. They flew in stream with the main body of Ju-52 trimotor transports, and at first suffered few casualties, mainly because the Allies had few fighters in the area, while the German transport streams were strongly escorted. At first, the 323 crews had a good war.

'Airman Fred Rabe was proud, very proud. "We fly with a crew of five, seven, nine or eleven men," he told his fiancée one day, "and we can carry 130 fully-equipped soldiers, or a complete 8.8 cm anti-aircraft gun, or 52 barrels of fuel, or 8,700 loaves, or . . ." The girl interrupted him: "All those loaves? That would be enough to feed our part of town for two days," she said incredulously.

'For a moment the young airman appeared embarrassed; but soon his enthusiasm returned. "And when we make a specially sharp turn," he went on excitedly, "the flight engineer in one wing can see his mate in the other grinning his head off!" The reason for this particular phenomenon was a tendency of the aircraft to oscillate. The young girl did not share her fiancée's delight at flying such an oversized monster. After the war, if Fred landed himself a job at a filling station, he would be easier to handle, she thought hopefully.'*

Fred Rabe had other stories to tell of the 323s. Of the entire crew that took off in their Gigant one day to see if they could loop it over Mount Etna: their squadron commander in person had to get on the radio to order them to return. Eight days in the cooler for all of them. And there was the less light-hearted story of the 323 operating in Hungary, whose co-pilot one day failed to show up for a flight. They were at full gross weight, almost 100,000 lbs, and the load they were carrying was high octane petrol. The flight was urgent, so a Heinkel bomber pilot was assigned to fly as co-pilot in the Gigant. During the take-off run the aircraft captain kept calling for elevator trim, but discovered too late that his novice co-pilot was winding it on the wrong way, nose-down instead of nose-up. They never left the ground, but piled into the trees at the end of the runway

* From *Conquerors of the Air*, by Demand and Emde, Viking Press, New York.

73/4. Gigants loading horses (*above*) and a 15 cm howitzer (*below*).

and went up in a colossal fireball. There was one survivor: one of the flight engineers in his little between-the-engines cab had smelled a rat in time to jettison his cab cover and jump. Two broken legs, but at least he was alive. Like its glider ancestor, the 323 had enormously heavy controls; it was what pilots call a 'trim aeroplane'—you flew it on the trim tabs as much as on the controls. The pilot wrestled with the controls while the co-pilot wound the trim, and both were likely to be young men with little enough flying experience on anything, let alone something as cumbersome as the 323.

The German infantry flew when they had to, but they never liked the Gigants. 'Sticking plaster bombers', they called them, from the miles of doped tape and fabric that covered them. No doubt they'd heard all the Gigant horror stories as well. The infantry much preferred 'Auntie Ju', the trimotored Ju-52, which was made of metal like all real aeroplanes, and which had established a fine safety record as an airliner before the war.

As the Allied forces in North Africa grew in strength the Gigants became more and more vulnerable, with their very slow cruise speeds, ponderously slow controls, and fragile fabric skins. The Luftwaffe made the decision to abandon flights by individual 323s, but always to bunch them together in as large a formation as possible, so that they might benefit from the collective safety of their massed machine guns. (The same principle was adopted by the Americans later with their daylight B-17 formations, and were about as ineffective against determined fighter attack.)

Thus came about the ultimate disaster, the ultimate 323 horror story. Sixteen Gigants of the Luftwaffe's No. 5 Transport Squadron took off from Trapani in Sicily for Tunis, carrying a total of 140 men in their crews, and petrol for the Africa Corps as cargo. They must have already been 'twitched'; just four days earlier the Luftwaffe had lost twenty-four trimotors over the Mediterranean plus a further thirty-five that were so badly shot that they piled-up on landing.

Coming in on the African coast, the Gigants were met by a large force of British Spitfires and Marauders, who fell upon them like a pack of wolves. Though the 323s had self-sealing fuel tanks themselves, of course their cargo of fuel in drums was quite unprotected, and they were helpless. Fourteen of the sixteen were shot down and of the two that made it to Tunis, one was finished off in a raid two days later. Only one aircraft made it back to Trapani, loaded as full as anyone dared with wounded soldiers from Rommel's army. Among its crew was Fred Rabe, just twenty-two years old. Of his 140 comrades who had set off with him, 121 were dead.

The survivors of the 200 powered Gigants soldiered on for the rest of the war, but the spirit had gone out of the project. There were plans to use them to drop huge 18-ton bombs; but on the first test flight the Gigant came apart in the air, and all its crew died. There were plans to build an even bigger Super-Gigant, but only plans. I suppose that if they had been used in the type of lightning-quick campaign with an overwhelming first strike against a largely defenceless victim, over short ranges, the Gigants, powered or unpowered, would have served their purpose admirably. What they couldn't do was survive when there were enemy fighters about.

17

Komet or The Devil's Sled

Solid fuel rockets, fireworks, slow-burning explosives, in effect are all ancient devices, probably Chinese in origin. They have seen occasional use in wars as weapons more picturesque than deadly. In the 1920s and 30s advancing technology in chemistry, pumps, and metals that would keep their strength at high temperatures led to the possibilities of *liquid*-fuelled rockets. Research on these was begun in the United States, the Soviet Union and in Germany, and has since taken man to the moon, and unmanned research craft to distant planets; but the first applications of liquid-fuelled rocket motors were for aircraft propulsion. For this purpose these motors had both advantages and disadvantages: tremendous thrust which (unlike any other type of engine) did not fall off as the air got thinner at altitude, thus enabling a rocket aircraft to go faster the higher it went; the necessity to carry oxidant as well as fuel, thus reducing the useful load left for weapons or extra fuel; the necessity to use fuels that were peculiarly unstable, corrosive, and difficult and dangerous to handle; and since early liquid-fuel motors were virtually unthrottleable, and ran only at full power, had very short endurance under power.

One man working on rocket engines in Germany was one Hellmuth Walter of Kiel, who began trying to develop an underwater power unit for the German Navy, using potassium permanganate fuel and hydrogen peroxide as an oxidant. Then the German aviation research establishment wanted him to make little rockets to be used in stability investigations; you'd fire one up or down on an aircraft's wing tip and see how long it took to roll back to level. (Such devices, known as 'bonkers', are used to this day.) Herr Walter's rocket had a handsome thrust, 90 pounds, and they even tried it as a propulsion unit for a light aircraft. It worked. At this point, no doubt, a simultaneous gleam must have come into other eyes. You can imagine them standing around on the airfield, all trying to speak at once: 'Why don't we build a big rocket engine and power a fighter aircraft with it?' Why didn't they? They did.

It was obvious it would have to be a pretty odd aeroplane, since the engine would need to be not at the front but in the tail. Why not, they all thought, make it a tail-*less* aircraft—a flying wing? Now, who was there who knew about designing tail-less aircraft?

The answer was Alexander Lippisch, technical director of the Rhön glider company.

From all-wing gliders Lippisch had progressed to powered aircraft with no tails whose wings had sharply swept-back leading edges, a triangular shape which Lippisch called 'delta'. Lippisch was having an up-and-down career: so many of his delta designs crashed that at one stage a special commission investigating the crashes passed a resolution forbidding further work with deltas since they had 'neither practical value nor development potential'. (If you knew nothing of supersonic aerodynamics, as nobody then did, this was a reasonable conclusion.)

But Lippisch was fanatical about his deltas, and in Hitler's Germany you couldn't keep a good fanatic down for long. Furthermore, he had long been interested in rocket propulsion, so they gave him the job of designing a delta fighter with a lengthened fuselage to accommodate a 'special power plant'. They didn't tell him quite what this was at first, the whole venture, named 'Projekt X', being swathed in typically lunatic secrecy. Projekt X is probably where that old joke about all documents being stamped

75. This early delta-wing design by Lippisch would do 87 mph on a 28 hp piston engine.

DESTROY BEFORE READING began. But soon they had to tell Lippisch the truth: he was developing a fighter with a liquid rocket motor. 'My God' is supposed to have been all he said. And meanwhile, Hellmuth Walter was working away under a contract for a rocket with ten times the power of his bonker.

Professor Lippisch had begun his rocket fighter work with the German Government Research Institute for Sailplanes, but by 1939 he and they were not getting along. 'Continual harassment by security regulations' and 'the political situation becoming increasingly difficult' are given as the explanations; I suspect that Lippisch was not the easiest of scientists to employ.

In January 1939 he and a dozen of his colleagues transferred themselves to the Messerschmitt factory at Augsburg, with the Luftwaffe's development department as the customer. At Augsburg Willi Messerschmitt didn't exactly welcome him with open arms; his interceptor project 'languished for many months with one of the lowest priority grades'. Nevertheless Lippisch built, and got flown, a low-speed rocket research aircraft, the DFS 194, and moved on to an unpowered glider prototype of a possible fighter, which was known as the Messerschmitt Me-163 Experimental. This turned out to suffer from rudder flutter at one speed and aileron flutter at another, but they balanced the control surfaces to fix this, and found they had a clean and efficient machine, with a glide ratio of 1 in 20, almost in the high-performance sailplane class. It had nice handling, too.

Then one bright day the Luftwaffe's General Ernst Udet arrived at Augsburg to see what was happening. The Me-163 had been towed to altitude by a Messerschmitt fighter, and was gliding to and fro at 16,000 feet. Lippisch's test pilot Heini Dittmar pushed over into a steep dive and went whistling past the general at fully 400 mph, pulled up hard, came round again for another run, soared round and round the airfield to lose speed, and made a neat landing.

'What kind of engine has it?' asked Udet, fascinated. None, Herr General. 'No engine! Impossible!' He strode across to the machine. 'It's true, no engine. Let there be engines for the Me-163,' ordered Udet, and by the summer of 1941 a powered 163 prototype was flying from the German research establishment at Peenemunde on the Baltic.

Lippisch had calculated that the powered 163 would do 1,000 km/hr (well over 600 mph) at altitude, making it easily the fastest aircraft in the world. They used theodolites to measure the aircraft's speed (since fast runs were all done at about 13,000 feet) and had clocked 571.78 mph on one run when the old problem, rudder flutter, returned, and most of the rudder departed. Dittmar managed to get the rest of the aircraft down in one piece.

'Why not,' said Dittmar to Lippisch, while a new and better-balanced rudder was being made, 'tow the fueled-up 163 to altitude before lighting up the motor?' That way half the fuel wouldn't be used up on the climb, and the full burn could be used for level acceleration. Then they could *really* see how fast the 163 could go. On October 2nd, 1941, they tried it. Now you must realise that 1,000 km/hr in level flight was something of a magical figure in those days, a nice round one but an almost unimaginable speed; no aircraft had ever reached it, and some said none ever would. That day Dittmar did, and here's his own account of it:

'My airspeed indicator was soon reading 910 km/hr and kept on increasing, soon topping the 1,000 km/hr mark. Then the needle began to waver, there was sudden vibration in the elevons and the next moment the aircraft went into an uncontrollable dive, causing strong negative g. I immediately cut the rocket and, for a few moments, thought that I had really had it at last! Then, just as suddenly, the controls reacted again, and I eased the aircraft out of its dive. The phenomena I had just encountered were the first knock on the door of the sound barrier, which the 163 had not been built to penetrate.'

This is a clear description of 'compressibility', which is caused by shock waves developing around it as the aircraft approaches the speed of sound and the surrounding airflow reaches sonic speed in places. Dittmar was by no means the first pilot to encounter compressibility, which had puzzled pilots of Me-109s and Spitfires in the Battle of Britain, who discovered that their aircraft went temporarily out of control in steep dives, only to recover their ordinary tractability when they reached lower altitudes. The simple explanation was that the speed of sound (and the associated compressibility effects) is higher in warm air, and therefore at lower altitudes; as their aircraft dived, though its airspeed remained high, it retreated from the sound barrier.

They calculated that Dittmar in the 163 had reached Mach 0.84—84 per cent of the speed of sound. The German Air Ministry were highly sceptical; after all, their most advanced wind tunnel only went up to Mach 0.8! But Ernst Udet was 'virtually bursting with eagerness and demanding that weapons be fitted to the 163 as it was, there and then!' Lippisch calmed him down and explained that the 163A was in no way an operational aircraft, but needed redesign to take more fuel, as well as guns and other equipment. What are you waiting for, then? asked Udet, and in December 1941 they began construction of a prototype of the B model Me-163, named the Komet and a real interceptor at last. It was ready in April 1942.

Meanwhile, the Luftwaffe had begun pilot training using several of the unarmed A model 163s. One rocket pilot, Mano Ziegler, later wrote a book about his experiences, in which he described how he first saw an Me-163A in flight. He was alighting from an 'antiquated little train' at Bad Zwischenahn, where the 163s were based, when 'a tiny black speck appeared, growing with phenomenal speed into a boomerang-shaped object which turned, dived, levelled-off, and swept past as soundless as a phantom, and then, confound it, disappeared behind the trees.' Arriving at the airfield he found the 163 unit so secret that officially it did not even exist! While his posting papers were being examined a 163 took off.

'Suddenly I was startled by an ear-splitting roar. It sounded as though an immense red hot iron had been plunged into a huge bathtub—a veritable hiss of Siegfried's dragon! My head spun around and my surprised eyes saw a violet-black cloud driving a leaping,

76. The Me-163A was the first aircraft in the world to exceed 1,000 km/hr and 600 mph.

skipping "something" ahead of it, faster and faster until the object leaped from the ground, jettisoned a pair of wheels, and shot up into the sky. By the time I had closed my mouth, which had opened in astonishment, the thing had disappeared. There was nothing left to indicate that I had not suffered a hallucination apart from a dissolving violet-grey smoke trail. A little while later the strange craft reappeared and, like the other I had seen when standing on the station platform, glided soundlessly through the air, circled, and dropped on to the ground. I could not restrain my curiosity, and ran towards the spot where the thing now lay like a tired butterfly.'

His new colleagues showed him over the Me-163A, and opened a hatch in the fuselage to reveal 'a maze of pipes which resemble nothing more than the innards of a refrigerator'. His next discovery was made,

'of all places, in the mess. Items that had long since been promoted to precious festive menus were to be had here as a matter of course at every meal, every day! Creamed rice with fruit preserves, delicious omelettes with kidneys, blossom-white macaroni with goulash, and countless other dishes that had long ago disappeared from German tables. And for breakfast? Poached or scrambled eggs on toast; toast made with real *white* bread! . . . accompanied by *real* tea and coffee.' [This was the 'altitude diet'] '. . . a preventitive measure designed to avoid indigestible or flatulence-causing foods which we would have regretted having eaten when we attained the higher altitudes. I sadly bade farewell, therefore, to my favourite dish—pea soup with bacon!'

Mano Ziegler very quickly learned that there was more to being a rocket pilot than living like a king: the discomforts of the low-pressure chamber, for a start. Pilots were trained on the ground in a low-pressure chamber that was a 'steel colossus, half the size of a railway carriage' that had been captured from the Russians. 'A few men had already died in this chamber . . . and others froze to death.' For one of the 163's many defects was that although it could climb to 40,000 feet, the pilot's cabin was unpressurised.

The 163B's Walther rocket motor burned 'C-stoff' (a solution of 30 per cent hydrazine hydrate in methanol) with 'T-stoff' (a concentrated 80 per cent hydrogen peroxide solution mixed with various hydrocarbon stabilizers). No ignition was necessary; as soon as these two dangerous liquids were mixed they decomposed into hot gas. The liquids were pumped from their respective tanks into the motor's combustion chamber by a turbine pump, which was itself driven by a small flow of T-stoff through a steam generator where it was decomposed by a calcium permanganate catalyst. The ratio of T- to C-stoff was maintained at three to one by a regulator unit, and there were also pressure-reducing valves. The rocket was started by the pilot activating an electric motor that drove a small turbine pump to get the steam generator going. The combustion chamber was a double-walled device with C-stoff circulating between the walls to cool it. Besides the starter switch the pilot had but one engine control: a lever with five positions, off, idle, and first, second and third thrust stages—so engine thrust was far from being infinitely variable. Despite the complicated plumbing the motor was almost as simple as it sounds; it weighed only 365 pounds, yet developed a thrust of ten times that. It was attached to the airframe by just four bolts, and could be removed and replaced in two hours. The turbine was 'smaller than a margarine packet' and the regulator valve 'could easily be slipped into a trouser pocket'.

Modern rocket motors, such as those that took Apollo to the moon and back, are hardly very different, except that they are thoroughly developed and reliable. The 163's engine was the first production liquid-fuelled rocket in the world, and monstrously dangerous. Its fuels were a nightmare: 'some time earlier an unfortunate mechanic had poured a few litres of C-stoff into a bucket containing some dregs of T-stoff. He didn't live long enough to realise what he had done . . . T-stoff could only be kept in aluminium containers, as steel or iron tanks rapidly disintegrated while rubberized containers, like anything else made of organic matter, burst into flame immediately . . . the smallest dust particles or insects could set off a reaction which would blow the tank to smithereens. C-stoff, on the other hand, could only be kept in glass, enamel or anodically-treated containers, this fluid corroding anything made of aluminium.'

In the low-pressure chamber altitude changes for the new recruits were made progressively more violent, until they were being shot up to 8,000 metres in just one minute and back down to sea level in half that. 'Our bowels felt as though they were expanding like balloons, forcing us to scream with agony, while if we happened to be suffering with a slight head cold and a blocked sinus, these sudden pressure changes resulted in such searing head pains that the agony was indescribable.' It was also unnecessary, for it's highly unlikely this 'training' did the least good.

Flying training for the rocket pilots at Zwischenahn began innocuously enough in conventional gliders, Grunau Babies and Kranichs, and then on to gliders with progressively shorter wing spans and higher landing speed. Then they made unpowered flights in a 163A, towed aloft by a piston-engined Bf 110; early powered flights with half-full tanks; and finally full-fuel powered flights. The glider training was apposite; despite its fantastic speed and climb rate, the 163 was essentially just a powered glider. Every flight ended with a glide approach and landing—no chance to go around again if you screwed up. Thus every landing a forced landing.

Though the fuselage was constructed of metal, the entire wing was wooden, with fabric-covered control surfaces, like a light aircraft. Cockpit instrumentation was minimal. You took off on a wheeled dolly that you had to jettison at just the right moment after take-off, and you landed on a simple skid, just like a glider, except that you touched down at a horrendous speed—100 mph in a 163A and 140 mph in the 163B Komet, which was a ton heavier. You had to remember to extend this flexible skid before touch-down, for if you forgot, the jolting and shock of landing was enough to crush your vertebrae.

If dolly-and-skid take-off and landing gears were adequate and suitable for slow-soaring gliders, they were a disaster for the world's fastest combat aircraft. The wheeled dolly was unsprung (except for the 'give' in the tyres) and had no provision for steering: you could only take-off directly into the wind, from the smoothest surface. Nor could you steer once you ran out of rudder power on landing. You did have landing flaps, but no variable speed brake such as gliders have. The extreme short length of the Komet made it very prone to overturning in a rough landing, when even if the engine's turbine pump had done its best, there was always a residue of fuels left in the tanks, waiting to do their worst if you *did* overturn.

Those wretched fuels were absolutely the nastiest thing about the 163. A standard demonstration to new pilots was to pour a little of one into a saucer on the hangar floor and then add a drop or two of the other: 'The results were instantaneous—a hiss, a bang, and a jet of flame all in one!' Then they'd invite you to dip a finger tip into a cup of T-stoff: 'In a few seconds it turned white and began to burn!'

The rocket motor itself was 'highly temperamental: a take-off or a landing might provoke it into exploding, or it might explode without provocation at any time . . . no means had been found to ensure that we would not be blown to kingdom come without so much as a second's warning. Apart from this endearing characteristic, our instructors explained that it was virtually an everyday occurrence for the Komet's cockpit to fill with steam, almost completely obscuring the pilot's view, while fire was a serious hazard.'

Recommended action following almost every emergency was to bale out if you had the altitude: fire, bale out; take-off dolly would not release, bale out; engine cut before fuel was exhausted, bale out; if you couldn't reach the airfield for landing, bale out. And try not to hit the vertical fin on the way.

Perhaps as a result of the jolting it got during the run, the rocket motor in the 163 was inclined to cut at the end of the take-off run. If you were lucky you might have the impetus to get it around and back on the airfield for a landing. More likely the 163 went cartwheeling across the fields until it blew up in a flash of white fire; even reasonable crash-landings were inclined to finish with the Komet going over on its back, trapping you inside while T-stoff leaking from the ruptured tanks behind and on either side of your seat dissolved—literally *dissolved*—you alive.

Ziegler's book is full of awful descriptions of how Komet pilots died:

'Anxiously we watched the Komet touch down far outside the airfield perimeter, rebound into the air, drop back again like a brick and then skid into some rough ground and turn over on its back. A split second later a blinding white flame shot up, followed by a mushroom of smoke.'

'The burning Me-163 had banked around and was now diving straight at us! We ran for a few yards, looking over our shoulders in horror . . . as though piloted by some invisible hand, the burning wreck pulled out of its dive, banked steeply to starboard, and hit the ground . . . outside the perimeter of the airfield. A thick, whitish-grey pyre

77. An operational Komet fighter on its launching dolly.

of smoke ascended behind the young fir trees, its edges flushed with the glow from hungry red flames . . .'

'. . . like a stone, rebounding into the air, and then hitting the ground again. The port wing dug in and the Komet spun wildly like a top. A body flew out of the aircraft and, almost simultaneously, there was a vivid red splash of flame followed by a cloud of white steam.'

'A fantastic hiss followed immediately by the whiplash of an explosion interrupted our conversation, and seemed to tear the air in pieces around us . . . A Komet had exploded on the flight line! A frightful sight met our eyes. Where only a minute or so earlier a Komet had stood ready for take-off there was now nothing but a dark, smoking stain on the ground! Scattered in a rough circle hundreds of metres in diameter were scraps of twisted tubing, distorted pieces of metal—all that was left of a brand-new fighter. The bile rose in our throats as we saw a few traces of bloody sinews and a snow-white piece of bone stuck to a piece of jagged metal that may have come from the cockpit. Then one of the mechanics called us to a spot about eighty metres away from the centre of the explosion—he had discovered a naked leg ripped off just below the knee! . . . We just stood around in silence, feeling anger, nausea and fear, and the most appalling helplessness. Medical personnel came along and placed Walter's leg and that solitary fragment of bone on a stretcher. They searched the area carefully for another fifteen minutes, but there was nothing more to find.'

'. . . Franz stood there screaming and groaning alternately, and kept shouting for somebody to pour water over his body. But his face . . . Oh God! I was never to forget his face! There was no skin, no eyebrows, no hair, only a ragged stubble of what had been his proud moustache! I was nearly overcome by nausea, swallowed hard and clenched my teeth. Two of us took his arms and led him gently . . .'

Lucky were the rocket pilots to whom death came quickly:

'The Komet touched the ground, leaped back into the air and skated towards us for a couple of seconds, then half-rolled on its back and touched the ground with its starboard wing tip. In a flash the Komet became a fantastic catherine wheel which flew straight at us, turning over and over, showering burning debris in every direction . . . we found Eisemann dead but still strapped in his seat alongside the remains of the fuselage.'

The high spirits with which the rocket pilots had arrived at Zwischenahn tended to evaporate with exposure to the grisly spectacle of endless frightful crashes.

'I was afraid, that I could not deny,' remembers Mano Ziegler of his first 'sharp start'—powered take-off. 'I felt beads of perspiration forming on my forehead, my mouth was dry and the palms of my hands were sticky.' But once he was safely airborne, panic was replaced by the wild exhilaration of the rocket ride: 'Away I climbed like an express elevator, and I was reclining on my back with nothing around me but the infinite blue of the sky and a few strands of cirrus far above. Superb! No other word can express the pleasurable sensation as I shot ever upwards into the sky. My mind had been washed clean of all thoughts of danger and I could think of nothing but the beauty of flying and the joy of living.'

Less gloriously brave pilots—and there were many such—tended to seek urgent posting elsewhere before they had been at Zwischenahn long. These requests were granted, for serving on a 163 squadron was entirely voluntary.

Those Komet pilots who did complete the training programme then found that as an interceptor the aircraft was nearly useless. Its armament was two 30 mm cannons, slow-firing and given to jamming. The Fortress squadrons the Komets were sent up to attack were slow-moving, cruising at well under 200 mph, and while in a Komet you *could* reduce power, you did not have real throttle control to enable you to match your target's speed. At first the Komets tended to close on the bomber formations with a wild excess of speed, several hundred mph, leaving them only a couple of seconds to get off a few cannon shells before either the guns jammed or they had sailed past the bombers.

Later they evolved a technique of making glide attacks, first climbing under power to an altitude of several thousand feet above the American bomber formations, then diving down, power-off, to attack the low squadron of a formation, or better still, any lone Fortress that was straggling behind. The Komets would then use their motors to zoom away, perhaps for another attack if sufficient fuel remained. Usually it didn't. The necessity to slow down to the bombers' speed (and run the gauntlet of their powerful defensive fire) before any meaningful attack could be made with those slow-firing cannons was a major weakness of the Komet. So was the exceedingly short power endurance.

When Lippisch had been first designing the Me-163, its engine manufacturer had told him he could expect a fuel consumption at full thrust of six pounds per second. Lippisch had calculated that climbing to 40,000 feet would take only three minutes, and that the remaining fuel he had allowed for would give a 600 mph cruise at reduced throttle for a further nine minutes. But the Walter motors turned out to burn not six but eleven pounds per second, leaving the Komet pilots only two-and-a-half minutes' remaining power once they were aloft. It was barely enough to do anything useful.

Once their fuel was gone, the powerless Komets were easy prey for American Mustangs lurking near their airfields. Even once down and safely landed, the Komets lay about their aerodromes as immobile as stranded whales (and vulnerable to Allied straffing) until the special tractors needed to shift them could be brought up.

The Americans first saw Komets attacking them in July 1944; they and the RAF had been awaiting the new interceptor with real trepidation, but they quickly discovered the Komets to be no serious threat. Komets did shoot down Allied bombers, but it seems their own losses through accidents were always cruelly worse than any damage they inflicted.

'Subconsciously we must all have known that, for Germany, the war was lost, [wrote

78. The prototype Me-263, with a pressurized cockpit and retractable landing gear.

Ziegler] but none of us would consciously admit it and, instead, we dreamed of a thousand or more Komets ready to take off the instant an intruding formation was sighted . . . We even talked of our plans for after the war, and one of the most popular was the idea of organizing flying shows with the Komet. Of course, it was nothing more than a roseate pipe-dream, for we knew that one of us would "buy it" every few days and we would soon run out of pilots for our show. It may sound strange, perhaps, but in our own way we loved the Komet. Perhaps it would be more truthful to say that we were fascinated by her in the way that one can be fascinated by a woman that takes all the money from your pockets every day and then deceives you every night.'

Furious attempts were made to develop suitable armament for the Komet—either by improving the cannon, or by installing air-to-air rockets, but the war ended before any real success was achieved. One novel plan was to install in the wings upward-firing shells connected to photo-electric cells: all you had to do was to fly under a bomber and the shadow of it would trigger the shells and shoot it down. One Fortress *was* thus destroyed but the system was never satisfactory: the shock of the shells going off tended to shatter the Komet's cockpit canopy, and a simple patch of cloud or mist proved sufficient to trigger the device.

Rather than 'a thousand or more', only a couple of hundred Komets were ever built. A handful were captured intact by the Allies, but so far as I know no attempt was ever made to persuade a British or American test pilot to fly one after the war, as *was* done with the German turbo jet designs. The captured Komets ended up in museums. Long before the war's end Professor Lippisch had grown tired of squabbling with Willi Messerschmitt and the Luftwaffe and had retired to an aeronautical research institute in Vienna, where he designed a supersonic ramjet delta fighter, and a delta-winged bomber. Prototypes of both these were destroyed, like so much of the thousand-year Reich, in a bombing raid before they could be completed.

Some further development of the Komet continued without him; Messerschmitt wasn't interested, so the Luftwaffe gave the project to the Junkers factory, who were developing a pressurised retractable-gear Komet when the Russians overran them. The prototype of this Me 263 was given to Artem Mikoyan and Mikhail Gurevich (of MiG fame) who didn't understand swept wings and tail-less deltas and fitted straight wings and a proper tail of their own making to the 263's fuselage and flew it like that. It climbed at 15,000 feet per minute and could reach 625 mph, but its chronic disadvantages of short range and endurance persuaded the Russians to concentrate on jet aircraft.

The Americans were more impressed with what Lippisch had achieved. They built a series of high speed rocket-powered research aircraft after the war, and what they learned thereby gave them a mastery of trans-sonic and supersonic flight that has endured to this day. The Convair company of Fort Worth in Texas took Lippisch's delta wing plansform and developed from it the F-102 Delta Dagger and F-106 Delta Dart fighters and the B-58 Hustler bomber. In Europe Concorde is a clear derivative of the basic Lippisch delta wing shape.

18

The Brabazon

By 1941 the RAF had discovered how effective four-engined bombers could be, and invited British aircraft companies to tender to build a long range one that could carry a five-ton bomb-load deep into Germany. They didn't bother telling the Bristol Aeroplane Company till a year later, by which time the really big bomber factories had all the work they could cope with. How about Bristol's doing a fifty-ton bomber with maybe six engines?

The range and speed that the Air Ministry were asking for, Bristol's decided, were so outrageous that something very specially light and streamlined was required, so they designed a truly radical monster, clean as a sailplane, with a V-tail like a Bonanza, a slender fuselage but a great thick wing with eight of Bristol's own radial engines entirely buried within and geared in pairs to drive four pusher propellers mounted on stalks behind the wing. This was not a fifty- but a hundred-ton bomber, with a range of almost half-way round the earth. Interesting, said the Air Staff, but maybe we'd better just order more Lancasters—so they did.

A year later the new Minister of Aircraft Production talked to the chap who had been his predecessor, Lord Brabazon, a splendid aristocrat who as a wealthy young man had been an aviation pioneer in Edwardian days, even daring one squally day to take a basket of squealing porkers aloft to disprove the age old rebuttal of wild ideas: 'pigs might fly'.

Lord Brabazon was invited to form a committee to recommend what sort of civil airliners might be needed if and when Britain and her allies won the war. With the wisdom of perfect hindsight we can now answer, *American ones*, but it didn't look that way in 1942. The Brabazon committee recommended several types: one, a small twin, became the de Havilland Dove; another, a sort of British Constellation or DC-6 with four radial engines which could have been vastly successful, was of course never built. The one that really got them interested was a giant airliner with a range of half-way round the earth, or at least capable of carrying passengers non-stop from London to New York—an ambitious range in 1942.

Later that year the Ministry invited all the leading British designers to a meeting to discuss 'the practicability of developing a civil transport of this size and performance'; once again they didn't invite Bristol's, who after all weren't big aeroplane people, were they? But Bristol's chief designer, Leslie Frise, learned of this meeting via the chief designers' grape-vine, and early the next year he went round to see BOAC to ask them what *they* felt (which the Brabazon committee seems hardly to have thought to do).

He then went to see the Ministry with a proposal that Bristol's abandoned giant bomber could easily be transmogrified into a giant *airliner*. Three weeks later the Brabazon committee recommended to the Cabinet that their five types be built, with the giant having priority. Bristol's were recommended for the job it seems, largely because everybody else was too busy with bombers. And with what seems today to have been astonishing candour, the Ministry emphasized that 'financial conditions must necessarily be secondary'. (The history of Concorde suggests that they still think like that, but now keep quieter about it.) The sole involvement of BOAC, presumably the prime customer, was to 'associate itself closely with the layout of the aircraft and its equipment'. (There is an impish thought in my mind that maybe BOAC decided there and then that they'd have no part of the Bristol giant, come what may.)

What arrogance, that a Ministry committee of men who had never had to fill an airliner's seats or find next Friday's wages should thus presume to decide what airliners the post-war world would need! Yet there was some logic in the choice of a super-long-range giant machine: the prestige, in a war-time era when prestige even without profit seemed worthwhile in itself; and not having to stop for fuel at Gander or Shannon or Reykjavik might much improve economics and reliability.

In March 1943 the decision to build two prototypes of the Bristol Brabazon Type 1 was announced in Parliament; and in May, instruction was given to Bristol's to proceed with two prototypes, with maybe ten production aircraft to follow, and mind the project didn't interfere with any war work.

Frise decided at the start that a 150,000 pound aeroplane was 'nonsense'; he preferred the 250,000 gross weight of his abandoned bomber project. This would allow the Brabazon to carry sixty or seventy passengers westbound, or one hundred eastbound, with the wind helping. BOAC are on record, believe it or not, as saying this was far too many, and twenty-five passengers would be plenty! For comparison, an early model 707 weighing about the same as the Brabazon, with the same number of crew but flying twice as fast (twice the productivity) carries typically 150 passengers—or *seats*, anyway. What can BOAC have thought they were doing? Either they were being mischievous, which is hard to accept, or else they were still living in some P & O dream of luxury travel for the few. Perhaps it was the latter, since Bristol's first layout showed a two-deck cabin with a separate dining room, promenade walk and bar, and also sleeping berths for the eighty passengers; or simple day accommodation for 150 day passengers; but Bristol's preferred the sleeper version: no need to feed or entertain sleeping people, and you could charge them extra for the bunks, like the railways do.

Money no object, the planners had said, and money no object it was. They built a vast and beautiful new hangar in which to assemble the Brabazons. To extend the runway at Filton aerodrome they demolished almost an entire village and a considerable length of brand-new dual carriageway. They built a full-scale wooden mock-up of the aeroplane. 'It was a magnificent piece of work and we were very proud of it,' wrote the Brabazon test pilot, Bill Pegg, of this mock-up. 'Fine and expert craftmanship is really not needed in a thing like this,' he admitted, 'but it is quite impossible to get craftsmen—in this case carpenters—to do a temporary cheap job. "Look here," says the Works Manager to the boss of the chippies, "this is just a temporary structure and we can't spend a lot on it, so just get 'em to knock it together with a few nails, none of this expensive jointing and curves around the thing, just something quick and cheap, do you see?" Well, of course, it never happens, because the craftsman only knows how to do a good job. He simply never has joined bits of wood with nails and he is damn well not going to start now.' The mock-up contained, 'for instance, a most magnificent ladies' powder room with wooden aluminium-painted mirrors and even receptacles for the various lotions and powders used by the modern young lady.' Well, it was taxpayers' money, so why not?

Nor were Bristol's in any great hurry to get the Brabazon project over with: it was six and a half long years from the Ministry go-ahead before the prototype was ready to fly. It was a supremely beautiful aeroplane, with a long slender fuselage of constantly-varying cross-section, and a most elegant curved and pointed fin. The wing was huge, and immensely thick, so thick you could walk upright inside it out from the fuselage to inspect the eight 2,500 hp Centaurus radial engines (also a Bristol product), which were coupled through gearboxes in pairs to drive four sets of double contra-rotating airscrews. It was the first aeroplane in the world to employ electric signalling for engine controls—the designers didn't trust mechanical runs over such long distances; and also the first to have fully powered controls, duplicated to be sure, but still with no manual reversion should the double hydraulics both fail.

Nobody was too happy about relying entirely on powered controls; the Ministry insisted on mass balances against flutter even though the controls were quite irreversible. They even built a special Lancaster bomber with similar fully-powered controls first to be sure they worked. They built a full-scale hydraulic test rig, which gave test pilot Bill Pegg some moments. 'It shook us on one occasion to see the elevators on this rig go fully down for no apparent reason,' he admits. 'If this sort of thing had happened in flight it would have certainly been the end of the Brabazon—and a very spectacular end, too.'

Pegg went to America and wangled some rides on test flights of the new giant USAF B-36 bombers, which were similar to the Brabazon in having engines buried in the wings. 'We had one or two scares during the testing, including engines on fire.'

The Brabazon was by a hair the biggest aeroplane in the world: the American B-36 had the same span—230 feet—but a shorter fuselage. The Brabazon was fully fifty feet high to the top of its fin. It weighed 145,000 pounds empty—seventy tons—and was intended to operate at an all-up-weight of almost 300,000 pounds. They went to extraordinary lengths to keep the structure as light as possible; even the rivets were individually trimmed in length. The skin was nowhere thicker than 0.185 inches. Its eight engines at full chat developed a total of 20,000 hp.

Bristol's took the bold step of inviting the world's press to Filton to witness the Brabazon's first flight; *very* bold, since another British transport aircraft prototype just a couple of years before had actually *crashed* on its first flight, killing all aboard. The world's press were at Filton for days, in droves. The maiden flight itself was quite uneventful. There'd been trouble with the nosewheel power steering during taxi runs, and they'd disconnected it, relying instead on steering by differential braking on the main wheels, and although Pegg was worried about this arrangement it worked adequately.

All the systems in the aircraft were at this point something of a lash-up: there was no automatically sequenced undercarriage retraction routine, and instead the flight engineer had first to signal to retract the wheels, then close the doors behind them. Nor were the flaps all interconnected, but instead arranged to move in paired sections. Pegg found the inboard sections gave too much of a trim change, and left them up for the landing, something which shows clearly in the innumerable newspaper front-page photographs, but which was missed by every air correspondent—and it was then the heyday of the newspaper air correspondent. Supposedly they had all been tidily confined in a 'press enclosure', but a small horde of them managed to evade the company herding and were ready at the foot of the steps to interview Pegg after the flight. At this point a weird event took place,

'an occurrence which but for a few feet might have turned a day of triumph into tragedy. An extraordinary sight met my eyes as I descended the steps from the aircraft; not two hundred yards away . . . was a helicopter—which I knew had some urgent tests to complete that day. As I watched, it rose a few feet in the air and immediately fell heavily back on the ground, fortunately the right way up. Simultaneously, I saw its main rotor disintegrate, and pieces of rotor blade started flying all over the place, as if a bomb had exploded. I resisted the temptation to duck down behind something solid and fervently hoped that at least none of the Press had seen it.

'The helicopter, with the jagged remains of the rotor blades still attached to the rotor hub, lay very nearly in my path between the Brabazon and the office. As I made my way to the office, followed by a retinue of VIPs and Press men, I tried to steer a course to leave the broken helicopter as far off our path as seemed reasonable. But I was not far enough away to miss catching a glimpse of a very white-faced test pilot slowly getting out of the machine.

'I managed to hold the attention of the Press, and as far as I know, not a single one of them noticed . . .'

There were special marquees for the press, well-stocked with booze and good things to eat, and direct phone lines for the agencies.

The Bristol Aeroplane Company's directors were insistent that Pegg should join them for lunch, but he'd had enough for the day—a Sunday—and went home, rather late for lunch, but in time to hear a breathless broadcast by a BBC commentator of the day's big event. Pegg was astonished at

'how he managed to work the commentary up to such a dramatic climax as the aircraft left the ground. On several occasions later, I watched it take off, and it was a most uninspiring sight, seeming to amble down the runway and leave the ground at what appeared to be an incredibly low speed.'

The Press began pestering him at home via the telephone, for this was also the heyday of the cult of the test pilot as popular hero. Pegg naively tried to refer them all to his company's PR department.

'They had, however, heard this one before and persisted with their enquiries . . . They would call on my wife while I was at work in search of some human angle to the affair, stories of the family, what did I eat and drink and so on.'

More wordly was his small son, whose weekly letters home from boarding school contained requests for daddy's autographs; he was selling these to his school mates 'starting at sixpence a time but gradually dropping until he could not give them away'. Ah, the fickleness of ephemeral newspaper fame!

79. The Brabazon taking off 'seemed to amble down the runway, and take off at an incredibly low speed.'

It had taken so long to build the Brabazon that it was by now thoroughly out-dated, and in particular, too slow. It had now been decided that this first aeroplane was 'just a test bed'; the second prototype and production aircraft would be the 'Brabazon Mark II' model with coupled Bristol Proteus turboprops of considerably more power, cruising at 330 instead of 250 mph, and at 35,000 feet instead of 25,000.

What did BOAC think of all this? Being the state long-haul airline, they dared not say what they really thought, and confined themselves to bland statements every now and then explaining how helpful they were being to the project, while at the same time making no attempt to prepare to ever put it into service, but holding out for the American Boeing and Douglas airliners which they really wanted, and could perhaps make money with.

BOAC were right to have doubts about the Brabazon. Like the later VC-10 jet airliner, it had been designed to operate from the short runways found in those lesser-developed countries along what were still called 'the Empire routes' through Africa and the East. Short runways meant a low landing speed, which the Brabazon certainly had: it took off at 85 knots and approached at well under 100—absurdly slow. Nobody at Bristol's seems to have foreseen that if the rival American airliners were going to need long runways, then every little airport around the world was dutifully going to extend its runways to accommodate them, without a murmur of complaint. That left the Brabazon stuck with that immensely thick wing, with a thickness-chord ratio of 21 per cent, fine for slow flight and completely submerging radial piston engines, but useless for fast cruise and slim turbines. That wing simply wouldn't go 330 mph, not on any reasonable amount of power, anyway.

Furthermore, the Brabazon had been designed and built with a very light structure (to get the load and range) on the premise that the upper atmosphere where it would fly was an ocean of calm. But post-war weather research showed that you got some pretty nasty sharp-edged gusts at 25 or 35,000 feet, even in clear air—more violent gusts than the Brabazon's wing might be able to absorb. In view of this, the British airworthiness authorities refused to certify the aeroplane for high-altitude flight. So they tried to develop a gust alleviation system employing a vane sensor on the pitot boom projecting from the aircraft's nose that would sense gusts and then signal to the ailerons to deflect very rapidly up or down to counteract the gust. Would this have worked? Well, there is a lovely story of a test system being installed in a Lancaster; it is said that the Lancaster pilot tried it out during the delivery flight to Bristol, and reported to Bill Pegg that it seemed really to do the trick, and give a smooth ride. Only later did they find the system was hooked up backwards, making gusts worse rather than lighter!

Another aspect of the Brabazon's design which surely would have caused problems was its very small wing-tip ground clearance relative to its span. No problem when landing into wind in calm weather with a test aeroplane, but in service, being flown by ordinary airline pilots of ordinary skills, required to put the thing down in some violent and gusty cross-winds, there would have been scraped wing-tips or worse. They should have stuck to the high-wing layout of the original bomber.

80. The Brabazon on an early test flight. Note the very thick wing.

Flight testing of the prototype Brabazon went smoothly, with no hairy moments except a hydraulic failure necessitating a flapless landing. In June 1950 it was even granted a 'restricted' airworthiness certificate. Thirty seats were installed in the rear fuselage and numerous big-wigs were taken for free rides, after which they dutifully said how quiet, how smooth, how marvellous. 'The most economical aircraft for stage lengths of between 2,350 and 3,920 miles,' said Peter Masefield, boss of BEA. 'The only type capable of making direct flights between London and New York non-stop while still showing a profit.' And if BOAC didn't want it, he could use it as a 180-seater on the busy London–Nice run.

But even though it had only done a couple of hundred hours' flying, persistent and nasty cracks had begun appearing, notably in the propeller mounting structures. Fatigue cracks: the Brabazon had been designed, like the ill-fated Comet, before the dire menace of metal fatigue had been appreciated. Analysis showed that at best the bulk of the Brabazon's structure was good for a 'fatigue life' of only 5,000 hours—nothing for an airliner, whose economic operation depended on high utilisation.

Furthermore, the Princess flying boat was revealing that the coupled Proteus engine had such gear and transmission problems that it might never be sorted out.

They flew the Brabazon Mark I at the Farnborough Air Show and everybody was impressed. They flew it at low level round the seaside resorts of southern England so that the holidaying masses could see what their tax money had built. Then in February 1952 the Minister of Supply, Duncan Sandys, 'in view of the poor economic state of the country', 'temporarily' suspended work on the Brabazon. Of course, he 'reaffirmed' his faith in large aircraft, insisting that work would resume 'when conditions became more favourable'. By September he was 'sure all possible technical information had been received from the Brabazon,' and convinced that 'neither civil airlines nor fighting services could foresee any economic use for it.' The Brabazon was finished: 'I have accordingly given instructions that it should be dismantled.' The prototype and the half-finished Mark II and their jigs were sold to a scrap yard for £10,000—all except for a spare nosewheel assembly, which is in a glass case in the London Science Museum to this day, hooked up to a hydraulic pump, obediently retracting and extending at the whim of every small boy who cares to push the red button outside the case.

That 8,000 foot runway at Filton remains, though it is hardly used—certainly not for Concorde flight testing—and so does the final assembly building, which *is* used for Concorde production. These, the £10,000 for the scrap, and the gratification of small boys in the Science Museum are all that remains of a £12.5 million programme. There was a furore at the time: it had cost five bob from every man, woman and child in Britain, noted one critic.

Concorde, for comparison, has cost *£10* for every man, woman and child in Britain and France. It, too, is built at Filton, by BAC, the successor to the Bristol Aeroplane Company.

19

Flying 'Queens'

The British have always been a nautical nation: a little island surrounded so *intimately* by the sea that the British have never had any choice in the matter. There is no spot in Britain that is more than 80 miles from the sea; the kids are taught to sing sea shanties while still in nursery school. From the shores have sailed all the most successfully rapacious pirates—Henry Morgan, Sir Francis Drake, Horatio Hornblower. The British even win their own around-the-world sailing races.

So you might expect the British to be in the forefront of water-borne aviation, too. Alas, no. The last native floatplane (a Tiger Moth—and even that was on American Edo floats) was crashed early in 1973. A sea or floatplane of any kind hasn't been built for twenty years.

Yet, it wasn't always so. G. R. Duval's *British Flying Boats and Amphibians 1909–52* (Putnam) is 268 pages long, and contains such rich delights as the 1929 Supermarine Air Yacht, design by R. J. Mitchell of Spitfire fame, built to the order of the Hon. A. E. Guinness: parasol wing, fabric-covered duralumin frame, three 490 hp Armstrong Siddeley Jaguar radials, two little open cockpits side-by-side for the two pilots, and the navigator, and luxurious cabins for the six passengers and the steward who ministered to their every whim, which no doubt inclined more to champagne than Guinness. Cruises were made up and down the English Channel, and to the Irish lakes. (A 100-mph cruise, seven hours or fourteen with the auxiliary tanks full.) Then Guinness sold her to a Mrs J. J. James, who re-engined her and rechristened her 'Windward III' and left Southampton in her for the Mediterranean late in 1932. There the story ends: the aircraft's 'subsequent history is unknown', says the book. Is she perhaps corroding quietly still in some Naples waterfront wharf? What a find for an antiquer she would be.

The RAF operated big biplane boats in those days, making 'cruises' to the Mediterranean and on out to the Far East via Suez, patrolling 'in protection of British interests in the Persian Gulf, also patrol action against the local industry of smuggling and gun-running'.

The British flag carrier in those days was Imperial Airways, who were big users of flying boats. They ran four-engined Short Kents on the Mediterranean sector of their

England to India route—sixteen passengers each with a folding table and a share in the well-equipped buffet and cuisine in charge of a steward. Between Brindisi and Alexandria they flew, till one was set on fire 'by an Italian with a grievance now lost to history'.

British commercial flying boat services really got going when the British government decided in 1934 to carry all mail to the Empire by air and without surcharge; this meant a letter could go by air to Australia for three halfpence per half ounce, which is one-nineteenth of what it costs today.

Imperial Airways felt inspired to order twenty-eight of a big boat that hadn't even flown: the Short Empire Boat. These C and the bigger G class boats roamed over most of the earth—down both sides of Africa, out through the Far East to Australia, over the Atlantic to North America, beginning 'an era of British leadership on the civil air routes of the world such as she had never known before'—or *since*, for that matter.

The military version of these big Short boats was the Sunderland, fleets of which patrolled the Eastern Atlantic in the Second World War hunting U-boats. One Sunderland, manned by Australians, battled with eight Ju-88s at once, and triumphed, though with one man dead and four wounded. Imperial Airways's successor, BOAC, operated Short flying boats throughout the war and for a while thereafter—different versions of the same basic twin-deck design, being variously named Hythe, Sandringham or Solent. BOAC bought pressurised Hermes landplanes in 1950, and at the end of that year abandoned boats, for ever. Too low and too slow, I suppose. A private British operator, Aquila Airways, operated Solents from Poole Harbour in England down to Madeira and the Canary Islands for a while; then in 1958 they too gave up, and commercial flying boats were almost dead.

But not quite—in the early 1970s the Australians were still operating two, a Sandringham and a Sunderland, on the world's last flying boat service: from Sydney to Lord Howe Island, 420 miles out in the Pacific. It was not through sentiment: the boats were the only aircraft that *could* operate the service. The island then had no airstrip; even the lagoon could only be used two hours either side of high tide, and in consequence the only possible 'diversion' was back to Sydney. Senior pilot of Ansett Flying Boat Services was Captain Lloyd Maundrell. Interviewed in *Pilot* magazine, he said:

'They are easy aeroplanes to operate, so long as you land with the right technique. We come in reasonably fast, flare at about 105 knots and knife them in. But if you try to hold off and hold off you hit and—*ptoing*!—you've gone and you start porpoising. These things don't like being stalled on to the water. You can get a terrible porpoise and you might not correct it too well. The tendency to porpoise is most marked if the aircraft is out of trim, at all-up-weight, and on a calm sea. That's when they're hardest to fly—when there's no wind.

'When there is a 15 or 20 knot wind blowing, they're a piece of cake. You just open the four taps, you've got immediate rudder control and that's it. But with no wind you open up the throttles and away you go—swinging to blazes. So, suppose you're swinging to port, you reef off a starboard engine to correct it. This causes a loss of lift on the star-

81. The Hon. A. E. Guinness' 1929 Supermarine Air Yacht: open cockpits for the three crew, and a luxurious cabin for six passengers and a steward.

board wing so you drop that float. Now if you put that float into the water you'll swing to the right. It's a case of shutting one throttle and correcting with aileron straight away. At all-up-weight with no wind I reckon they are a *very* difficult aeroplane to fly.

'I think there's a certain old-fashioned animal cunning needed to fly a boat to a place like Lord Howe Island. It's a small, funny, sub-standard airline operation. Let's face it, it's classified as sub-standard; it has to be because the facilities, performance and aids couldn't be related to what happens on the mainland. It's so much easier to fly a modern aircraft with all the aids and everything available. It's all set out for you in the check-list, and you just follow it, almost like a parrot.

'With this type of operation it's different . . . there are so many bits and pieces. You've departed, you've been delayed and now at the island it is just before last light. Do you take off at last light, knowing you are committed to a full flight to Sydney and you've nowhere else to go? No easy decision, with all the nonsense and pressure that goes with it—and a service out tomorrow. It takes a lot of experience to suddenly make the decision and know it's the right decision.'

The Short Brothers were the most successful, but by no means the only British builders of flying boats; there were Blackburns, Supermarine, and Saunders Roe. Sammy Saunders had a neatly-trimmed white beard and a powerful personality, and had inherited a boat-building business at Goring-on-Thames, later moved to Cowes in the Isle of Wight. Saunders had invented a system of cross-sewing laminated-strip planking for speedboat hulls with copper wire, which got him into building speedboats, for Tommy Sopwith of Pup and Camel fame among others. One of Sopwith's partners was A. V. Roe, who

82. The Saunders Roe Lerwick had a short career with the RAF. 83. The SRA/1 jet fighter flying boat was too slow for a fighter.

ended up buying a controlling interest in the boat-builders—hence, Saunders Roe. The company never had too much success in the seaplane business, and might have done well to stick to boats. They stuck with their patent wooden hulls long after the other companies had gone on to metal. The only prototype of their rival to the Sunderland porpoised so badly it broke up on a taxiing run. Their Lerwick twin-engined flying boat for the RAF was horrible to fly, and had 'a vicious stall power-off and a loss of control at the stall with flaps down and power on. This latter characteristic' says *British Flying Boats* drily, 'was the cause of most of the Lerwick accidents during its short career with the RAF.' A survivor of one of these described things as 'one moment flying, the next swimming!'

Undismayed, Saunders Roe next planned a twin-jet fighter flying-boat, and a gigantic airliner flying boat, the Princess. Their real achievement was also to get real taxpayer's money to *build* both of them. Three examples of the SRA/1 fighter were built, powered by Metropolitan Vickers Beryl jet engines, devices based on the engines in Goering's Me-262s, and since vanished into oblivion. Saunders Roe's test pilot was an old barn-stormer named Geoffrey Tyson, who once flew a Tiger Moth across the English Channel inverted the whole way; and I can still remember with admiration his ambitious display of the SRA/1 at the Farnborough Air Show in 1948. It is not every day you see a low inverted pass by a flying boat. But the SRA/1 would only do 500 mph, and even back in 1948 that was too slow for a fighter.

Three giant Princess flying boats were also begun. It was a truly giant aircraft, bigger even than the American Martin Mars flying boats, and ten tons heavier than the huge Brabazon. The Princess was the biggest seaplane ever, with the largest pressurised hull ever attempted. Like the Brabazon, she was intended for BOAC, to carry 105 passengers in twin-deck luxury and spaciousness. That 'intention' seems to have been mostly in the mind of George Strauss, Supply Minister in the 1946 Labour government, who said that giant flying boats were 'essential in the long run for BOAC'. BOAC themselves were more reticent, suspicious, perhaps, of an airliner project that was embarked on by politicians, and with no suitable engines existing or planned for it.

Progress with the Princess was low and slow, and largely conducted by press release. A handout dated January 1948 said, 'It is hoped that the first of the new flying boats will fly in 1949.' Another, in March 1949 stated: 'Progress is entirely satisfactory and continues in accordance with the programme . . . alteration to the wing-tip floats, it should be made clear, will occasion no delay in meeting the completion date of the first aircraft which remains set for the end of 1950.'

In the continuing absence of any engine truly big enough for the Princess, she was cobbled up to take ten Proteus turbo-prop engines—the same as those planned for the Brabazon II. Two of these were conventionally installed in the Princess, while the other eight were coupled in pairs to drive (through gearboxes) contra-rotating propellers on co-axial shafts. This complex power transmission gave endless trouble; the Princess's designer told me, years later, 'that coupled Proteus was a *nightmare*'. There were problems, too, with the Princess's controls, which were fully powered, dual, with electric signalling ('fly by wire' in the 1940s!) with one of the first-ever artificial feel systems, whereby the controls were arranged to grow heavier as airspeed increased.

In October 1949 it was announced that 'as a result of the revised delivery dates of the engines there will be a delay of a few months in beginning flight testing,' but that 'nevertheless we shall hope to make use of the summer weather in 1951'. They had the gall to add: 'It is anticipated that the first three Princesses will be delivered to the Corporation [BOAC] on the due date'—a daring exercise in Orwellian 'Newspeak' that blandly assumed that everyone, government, customer, press and public, had by now forgotten what the original schedule had ever been. By 1952, when the first Princess was actually complete, the cost of the whole programme had escalated to £11 million from the original £3 million. £5 million alone of this was for the engines. One journalist, Bill Gunston of *Flight*, spent a deal of time trying to discover what that £5 million was actually *for*, since the Proteus engines were the same as in the Brabazon II, and had already been funded in that programme. All he did discover was that the ten engines in the Princess only developed 25,000 hp, rather than the 35,000 hp the officials quoted, and which the aircraft truly needed.

The first Princess finally made her maiden flight in August 1952; a magnificent sight, running high and proud up the Solent for take-off, like an ocean liner with wings, spearheading a giant cloud of spray. Only a month later Geoffrey Tyson brought her past the stands at the Farnborough air show in a near-vertical bank, with one wing-tip float almost parting the daisies 110 feet below his cockpit. It was years later that I heard that this impressively sustained steep bank was because the Princess had reached such a high airspeed that the artificial feel units in the powered controls virtually prevented Tyson from rolling the thing back to level, and that he was perhaps only a quivering bootful of top rudder from the biggest and most spectacular disaster in the history of air show flying.

By now BOAC, who were supposedly going to operate the Princesses, had become convinced that the big flying boat had no future. Its principal virtue was that you did not need to lay down expensive runways for it; but by the 1950s it was becoming clear that every city on earth was eagerly prepared to pave its outskirts with concrete to attract the American landplane airliners, which were also faster, cheaper to operate, and burned less fuel than any flying boat. And collision with floating timber was a problem you didn't have with landplanes, either.

Saunders Roe then pinned their hopes on a man named Brackley who ran an airline named British South American Airways and said he wanted seven Princesses. But Brackley died in a boating accident in Rio, and BSAA was given to BOAC to run, and they most certainly didn't want ten Princesses.

By now there was a new Conservative government in power, and not at all happy with the great white hippopotamuses they had inherited from the previous socialists. They had already announced their decision to abandon the Brabazon II—the only other use planned for the coupled Proteus engine. What to do with the three Princesses? The answer, of course, was to compromise: they'd keep on flying the first Princess a little, but would cocoon the second and third, supposedly storing them against the day that suitable engines might appear. Up from the opposition benches in parliament rose George Strauss, the man who had initiated the project. 'It would be a terrible pity,' he said, 'if these great boats, on which the future of civil aviation might depend, were not used.' But civil aviation already had its eye on jets for *its* future, so a terrible pity was what it was. For years the Princesses sat alongside Southampton Water, figures of fun for the crews of the transatlantic liners that they were to have put out of business.

Then in 1958 there came a revival of interest in giant flying boats from an unexpected quarter: the US Navy. 'They were working on the idea of a nuclear-powered flying boat as an ultimate deterrent,' Maurice Brennan, Saunders Roe's chief designer, told me. 'It made a lot of sense,' he claimed. 'You could even have carried anti-missile missiles.

84. The Princess was the biggest seaplane ever, with the largest pressurized hull ever attempted.

They were interested in the Princess as a test vehicle. I went across to Washington and talked to them and came back with a contract to put a General Electric reactor in, and it went in quite nicely. It was partly shielded by kerosine. There were General Electric, Pratt and Whitney, Convair, Martin, ourselves and the US Navy involved.' Then there was a giant inter-service squabble over the project, and the nuclear Princess came to naught.

Then some entrepreneur wanted the hull of one of the Princesses, safely moored, to serve as a coffee bar. After that, nothing. The last Princess (the first one built) was finally broken up in 1967. The scrap metal merchants would have made some money out of the aircraft; *they* always do. Sometimes they manage to buy old aircraft for less than the fuel remaining in the tanks is worth.

Saunders Roe then sadly forgot their dreams of giant flying boats, and designed a fantastic rocket-powered interceptor that was to have reached three times the speed of sound at 100,000 feet. But the call of the sea was still in their blood, and when a chap called J. Dundas Heenan came to see them one day, they were ready. Heenan was, he explained, a consulting engineer to the P & O shipping line, who were, he claimed, seriously interested in an aircraft that could carry at least 1,000 passengers, and provide a standard of comfort 'analagous to that enjoyed in sea travel'. They would want to carry some mail and freight between England and Australia. The aircraft was to operate in stage lengths of 2,000 miles, making the round trip in one week.

'We found,' said chief designer Maurice Brennan, addressing the Royal Aeronautical Society not long ago, 'that the specification would be met by a flying boat of 670 tons all-up-weight powered by twenty-four Rolls Royce Conways of 18,500 lbs thrust each. The craft would have cruised at 389 knots at 30,000 to 40,000 feet, range 4.8 hours or 1,880 miles. It would have had a highly competitive direct cost of 1.4 pence per passenger mile.'

The fuselage was to have had no less than five decks. Throughout the ship seating was to have been divided into six-passenger compartments, as in old-fashioned sleeper trains, with the seats converting into sleeping berths at night. First-class passengers even had separate bars and dining rooms, lounges and dressing rooms. There was an elaborate galley from whence food was to be conveyed to the upper decks by elevator. There was sleeping accommodation for the crew in the lowest deck inside the keel. The flight crew of seven had their own private resting quarters and toilet. There was a separate office for the ship's purser, and even space for a crew lounge.

Construction techniques were to be suitably advanced: no cross-sewn laminated wooden planking here. The engine bays were to be titanium, and big enough so that you could work on the engines even in flight. Not that you would have to; cruise power of 86 per cent rpm could have been maintained with up to six engines (symmetrically disposed, one hoped) shut down at once. Thus any engine changes needed could wait till the craft returned to its London base at the end of the week. There were to have been split flaps below the engine exhausts. The engines themselves were to be mounted well outboard,

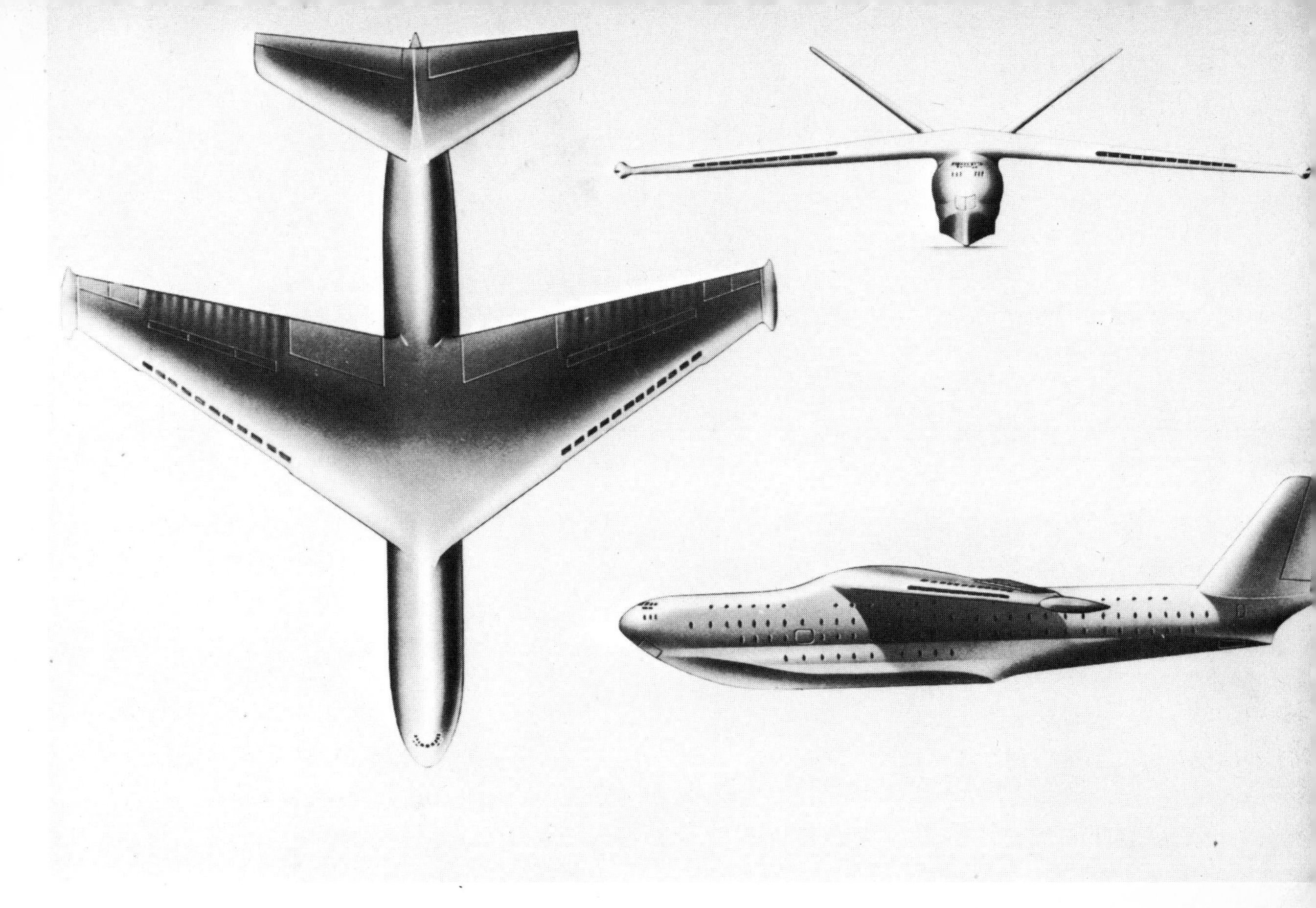

85. The Saunders Roe P.192 was to have had 24 jet engines and to take 1,000 passengers.

clear of hull spray, and breathing through extra intakes on top of the wing when the machine was on the water—the main intakes were opened only in flight. There were 'hydroflaps' in the rear fuselage for good water maneuvrability; and interconnected spoilers and ailerons for roll control, as on the Boeing 707. All controls were fully powered—the Princess had actually pioneered this, being one of the first big planes to fly with no manual control back-up system. It was 313 feet span, 318 feet long, 88 feet keel to fin tips.

Saunders Roe's performance figures showed a distance to unstick of between 1,565 and 2,630 yards, depending on temperature, at 129–135 knots. The rate of climb was 3,430 fpm with all twenty-four engines turning, and 2,085 with only sixteen. It was forty-five hours out from England to Australia, forty-eight back. The plan was for you to have boarded at Southampton after lunch, and to dine at the moorings in Egypt. You slept on the six-hour leg to Karachi, where you breakfasted. You arrived in Calcutta in the early afternoon, where you went ashore until the cocktail hour. You slept again between Singapore and Darwin, and arrived finally in Sydney in the early evening, sated with the luxury and ease of it all.

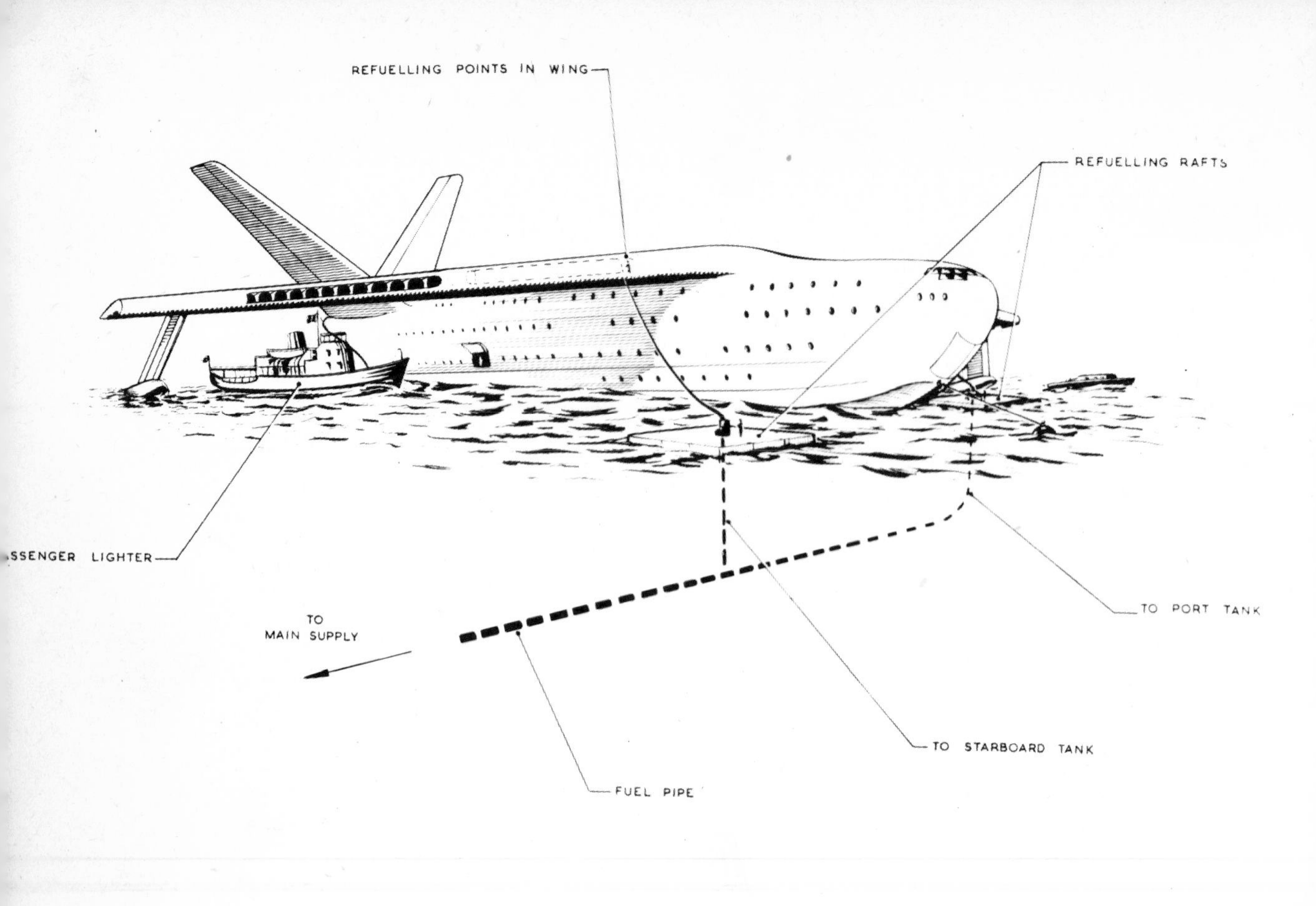

86. The 192 was to have been refuelled at the moorings while her passengers dined.

It was expected that three meal sittings might have been necessary. 'Take-off and landings could be made with the passengers in their beds, it being only necessary to fasten their seat belts.' Despite the forty cabin stewards carried, the total operating cost was expected to be around £1,000 per hour, and the direct operating cost per passenger, one way, £60. What the ship would have cost to build Saunders Roe never said; and there never looked like being a glimmer of a chance that P & O Lines or the British taxpayers or *anybody* else was about to fund it. The thing remains a glorious dream.

Saunders Roe no longer exists today; most of it was 'taken over' by Westland Helicopters for its modestly successful helicopter division. The rest of the company was put to building hovercraft—another great British invention for whose astounding success the world, and in particular the British, are still patiently waiting. The idea of the hovercraft was that it was to be intermediate in speed and cost between ships and aircraft. The trouble was, they gave it to the aircraft industry to develop and build, so it ended up as elaborately expensive as any aircraft, and as uncomfortable to ride in as anything since the stage-coach. There, at least, the 1,000-passenger P.192 might have excelled; it might have been very comfortable.

20

The Convair Jetliners

'Four hundred and twenty-five million dollars'—in 1962 dollars, which was 150 million 1962 pounds sterling. That is what *Fortune*, the American magazine of big business, in two superb investigative articles by Richard Austen Smith, estimated the Convair Division of the giant General Dynamics conglomerate to have lost on its jet airliner project, Convair models 880 and 990. To give this sum perspective, it was more than ten times the amount the British government wrote off on the Brabazon project (see chapter 18); four times what Lockheed had lost on the Electra airliner; or twice as much as Fords wrote off on the infamous Edsel car. It was the largest loss that had then ever been sustained on one single commercial manufacturing project. It was one-quarter of the net worth of the whole General Dynamics group. And all this despite the fact that it was a purely commercial business project, with no government control or taxpayers' funds involved, suggesting that when it comes to large aircraft projects, free-enterprise capitalism can run even wilder than governments.

Let me quickly add, since some Convair passenger jets are still in service, that there is nothing at all wrong with the aircraft that resulted from the programme, beyond that they almost bankrupted the firm that built them.

Richard Austen Smith placed the blame squarely on General Dynamics' top management, who, he says, 'failed to permit only programs in each unit which would not threaten the whole company, and failed to stop one enterprise when its failings became apparent', but instead, 'kept sending good money after bad in the hope that one lucky coup would square all accounts'. And, he explained, it was a story of '"fantastic" underestimating of costs, gross miscalculation of the market, entanglements with the capricious Howard Hughes, and the tragic death at the critical moment of the company's founder'.

General Dynamics was then a corporation of about 100,000 people split into nine divisions, of which the Convair division was easily the biggest: for example, Convair earned three-quarters of GD's $1,000 million earnings in 1956. Based in Texas and Southern California, Convair built mainly military aircraft and missiles for the USAF. It had been very successful with delta-wing aircraft that were based on the aerodynamic theories of Dr Alexander Lippisch (see chapter 17) including the Delta Dagger fighter and the B-58 supersonic bomber. It was Convair that had earlier built the giant ten-engined B-36 bombers. Convair had so far had one successful airliner project: the twin-piston-engined 240, 340 and 440 series, so good that many, mostly re-engined with turboprops, survive in service to this day.

But Convair were far from being a leading airliner manufacturer: these were Douglas and Boeing, in those days both working on their first jet transports, the DC-8 and 707. It was Howard Hughes, then still the controlling shareholder in TWA, who suggested to Convair that they too should design a jet transport, and for TWA.

'It might be said,' said Richard Austen Smith in his *Fortune* article, firmly saying it, 'that Convair should have been prepared for almost anything in any dealings with Hughes. The division had already gone through weird proceedings with Howard, trying to sell him some 340 transports back in 1950. To preserve the privacy Hughes habitually insisted on, negotiations for the aircraft had to be conducted by flashlight during the small hours of the night, out in the middle of the Palm Springs municipal dump.' You never called Hughes—he only called you, and very rarely, and then usually at four in the morning. You could never make an appointment to see him; but a chauffeur-driven car might pick you up at a certain street corner. He might break off to go to one of his studios to run a movie he decided you ought to see (still in the small hours of the night). He had no mercy for ordinary men (or girls) who slept ordinary hours—he just woke you up and kept you up if he wanted to. And he very rarely made up his mind on any business decision, and even when he did, he later changed it.

Howard Hughes, who had built aircraft himself, controlling their design and often being his own test pilot, insisted that if he was to buy a jet airliner from Convair, then he was to have a hand in its design too. The trouble was, said one Convair man, 'he kept us in a position where the plane was basically a TWA design, and he never could make up his mind what the design was to be'.

Yet Convair were still highly optimistic: they estimated they could sell something like 250 jet transports over ten years, earning $1,000 million of which a quarter could be pure profit. At the very worst, they estimated, they might lose $50 million if absolutely *everything* went wrong. Break-even in sales was at first estimated at only sixty-eight aircraft. Yet there were executives within Convair who were still against the programme: the vice-president who ran their military business thought a civil jet would eat uncomfortably into the resources in men and machines available for his own undoubtedly profitable work, and said that *he* knew as no one else did that engineers' cost estimates were not to be believed—double the figures they gave you and you were closer to the truth. Another executive thought that sales of a jet airliner could never be good enough to justify the effort and investment required. Another frankly doubted if they'd ever get Howard Hughes actually to pay for his aircraft. 'We were all worried about that, even before the contract was signed,' he said. 'But at that late date in jet development, he was our only prime customer.'

87. The prototype Convair 880 was 'rolled out' at Christmas, 1958.

Furthermore, the period when Convair were trying to decide whether or not to build a jet transport coincided with a splendid power struggle at the top of the whole General Dynamics group. This loose empire had been assembled by Jay Hopkins, a mogul out of the classic American business mould.

'Though trained as a lawyer,' says Richard Austen Smith, 'he was best known for his brilliance and audacity in finance. The grand design he brought to fulfilment was the creation of a diversified defense empire . . . capable of turning out weapons for all the armed services' . . . so that it might prosper 'whatever the budgetary vicissitudes of any individual service.'

Hopkins was also devoted to golf, and carousing: 'A man of almost oppressive energy, with a bottomless capacity for alcohol, who could stay up all night drinking, then in the morning lucidly present a complicated program to his board of directors.' A hard act to follow! Yet by 1953, in the words of a friend and fellow board-member, 'Jay was drinking too much and Washington had lost confidence in him. We had to get somebody in there who would restore confidence.'

The 'somebody' chosen was Frank Pace, another lawyer who had been Truman's

Director of the Budget and then Secretary of the Army during the rapid Korean War build-up. Jay Hopkins seems to have been contemptuously unimpressed with his new executive vice-president. 'Well, I just bought myself a show window,' was his comment on his board's new appointment, made to a friend during a round of golf in California. 'It cost me $75,000 complete with secretary. They give me hell because I'm never in the office, and I've got to have someone there to answer the phone.'

Yet Frank Pace was also a brilliant intellect, 'equally at home quoting Disraeli or some home-spun philosopher of his native Arkansas, and he also shot golf in the low seventies'. Yet in most ways he was Jay Hopkin's complete opposite; 'temperate in all things, oratorical, deliberate, anxious to be liked, a product of the federal staff system, prone to rely on his second-in-command in the making of decisions'. In many ways he was a typical government man. Jay Hopkins, on the other hand, was 'volatile, creative, earthy, intuitive, ingrowing, willing to listen but unwilling to share the making of decisions with anyone, a loner more likely to give the world the back of his hand than to extend the palm of it'. Perhaps typical of that kind of erratic genius who is, historically, and perhaps against the odds, the type who does succeed in building up a huge empire, be it business or any other kind. Also typically the kind of giant who makes no real plans for his succession. 'Jay Hopkins thought he was both omnipotent and omniscient,' said one of his colleagues. 'He just exuded confidence in the correctness of his opinions. He believed there was nothing he couldn't do.' In Frank Pace, Hopkins saw not a potential successor but 'an able assistant for a special assignment'.

Yet a successor was what there had to be, for Jay Hopkins was dying of cancer. He'd been operated on in 1955, and told everyone the surgeons had 'gotten it all', but in his heart he knew they hadn't. Thinking of the future, he did go so far as to tell Frank Pace that if he did want to become president he must find a good manager and a clever finance man as assistants to make up for his own lack of business and financial experience. Pace never did this, and Hopkins, unimpressed that his advice had been disdained, decided to look for some other person to succeed him. He never found one; and as he grew weaker and the need for a new chief executive grew ever more urgent, more and more of the General Dynamics board began to feel that Frank Pace was perhaps the only man available—even against Jay Hopkins' express wishes. The growing rebellion astonished Hopkins: 'Hell,' he said, 'that's *my* board. I picked every man on it.' But on April 29th, 1957, 'his' board voted Frank Pace to the top job. 'Well, after all, it's the board's responsibility,' said Hopkins. 'My usefulness is gone.'

The next day he went into hospital. 'A man has to have a lot of fight to live with cancer,' noted a friend of his, 'and that took all the fight out of Jay.' Four days later he died.

During all this time, with a growing power vacuum at the heart of the General Dynamics top management, the Convair division was taking the first hesitant steps towards the decision to build a jetliner, and eventual financial disaster. Convair had always been highly independent of 'head office', which was in any case situated thousands of miles away in New York City; with Hopkins gone it became even more so. Frank Pace's first management mistake was to give Convair not less but *more* autonomy. Jay Hopkins had allowed Convair three-fifths of his time; they earned that much of General Dynamics' income—but Pace didn't even give them so much attention. In later years he perhaps saw the hint there of a conspiracy by the Convair sub-management against him. 'Convair resisted all along any attempt by General Dynamics to do anything,' he said. 'There is not the slightest bit of doubt that the effort of General Dynamics to dominate Convair was completely resisted.' The number of times he 'personally sat down with' Convair's chief 'did not exceed seven or eight in a period of three years'. What a strange admission for a chief executive to make, that his subordinates ignored him!

Therefore, when the Convair jetliner project began to turn into the proverbial 'can of worms', the supposedly controlling General Dynamics management felt itself nearly powerless to intervene. From their point of view, their Convair division had got out of control.

The history of aviation has been defined as the history of aero engines. The jet engine offered great thrust and therefore a huge increase in speed; but early jet engines were inefficient, low on power and high on fuel consumption. At first it was a common opinion that a jet airliner would never be practical; that jets were so thirsty you'd never be able to carry the fuel for a reasonable range or enough people to make money. De Havillands saw a chance before anyone else, in the late 1940s, and built the Comet. They were premature; they only got a kind of performance out of the jet engines of the day by building a delicately light airframe; and this was in the days before the peril of metal fatigue was appreciated. The result was tragedy.

American airframe manufacturers waited longer, waiting for engines of higher thrust and lower specific fuel consumption, till strong airframes carrying plenty of fuel and paying passengers looked possible. Boeing were first, with a contract for a military tanker that would pay much of the development cost of a civil transport. Douglas dived in soon after, going for broke with the DC-8—never mind a military contract.

Convair saw themselves as on equal terms at first, a third contender in the great jet race. Perhaps this was their first and most overwhelming mistake, for, states R. E. G. Davies in *Airlines of the United States*, 'Boeing had set the pace with Douglas determined not to allow its traditional leadership [in building transports] to falter, and only a supreme blunder on the part of one of these companies could have given a third contestant a chance. And with the great industrial strength and integrity of these two formidable competitors, Convair never really had a chance, once their initial challenge had faded . . . airliner ventures are always colossal risks.'

Just quite how the decision to go ahead with the jet airliner was taken by General Dynamics and Convair was 'not too clear at the time, and certainly no clearer later when nobody wanted to be singled out for fathering a failure'.

Convair reported to GD's executive committee that they thought they could sell 250 jets, and that break-even would be after sixty-eight sales, and that TWA, Delta and KLM had all taken options. Fine fine, said GD: get letters of intent from the three airlines, a guarantee from the engine manufacturer (General Electric), and as soon as you have orders for sixty per cent of your break-even total, you can go ahead. But then Convair did some more figuring and found the first break-even number they'd thought of was too low. Then KLM dropped their option, but GD indulgently said, never mind, go ahead with the fifty per cent of break-even orders you've got; so they did. Already Howard Hughes was beginning to emerge as a major sales problem: he wouldn't let Convair sell the aircraft to any airlines that competed directly with his TWA; and he insisted on five-abreast seating in a narrow fuselage, whereas United Airlines, otherwise a prime customer, wanted, *insisted*, they would only buy if it had six-abreast seating.

It seems all those early cost estimates were hopelessly optimistic. One Convair man, working in the purchasing department, came early on to the astonishing conclusion that the bought-in bits of the aeroplane alone (engines, radios, airframe parts sub-contracted to other manufacturers and so on) added up in cost to more than the $\$4\frac{1}{4}$ million Convair were planning to sell the completed aircraft for! He went to his boss and said straight out that steadily-mounting losses were all the programme could bring, and that the $50 million it would cost to stop it, there and then, would be cheap by comparison. But recommendations that their fabulous jet airliner be abandoned were not welcome at that moment, so they fired him as a crank! (To do Convair justice, they did hire him back again two years later when everything he said had been proved only too bitterly true.)

After TWA and Delta, Convair's next best sales hope was United Airlines. It seems the Convair 880 still suited United well, even though it only offered five-abreast seating. United actually decided on the 880 in September 1957; it was the only jet airliner of just about the size and range they wanted. The Boeing 707 was too big, and had too long a range; but then Boeing decided to make a scaled-down version of it, the 720.

Convair's confidence that United would buy the 880 was shattered when a Convair vice-president happened to see a squad of United executives visiting Seattle, where Boeing is based. Still, Convair and United had actually agreed eighteen out of nineteen articles in a sales contract when word came that Boeing might still win. And win Boeing did: United decided that they really preferred to stick with Boeing's Pratt and Whitney engines rather than the General Electric engines in the Convair; and six-abreast seating would give them as many as twenty-five more seats in the Boeing aeroplane, so that its lower operating costs on a seat-mile basis would more than make up for its costing $200,000 more than Convair's 880 to purchase.

Boeing's decision to build the model 720 finished the Convair 880. Boeing and Douglas had both managed to develop true intercontinental range for their 707 and DC-8, something Convair had decided not to go after. This left the 880 as a smaller jet of only medium range, but when the 720 was announced it didn't even have this area of the market to itself any more.

Then Howard Hughes, still one of Convair's two real customers, turned difficult. One of Convair's executives would be summoned to meet Hughes in a Las Vegas night-club, only to spend all night sitting alone at Hughes' huge private table, with Hughes never appearing. One 'conference' went on until three in the morning, at which point Hughes insisted on showing the Convair men his awful movie *Jet Pilot*, whose star, Janet Leigh, he had woken up and brought to the projection room there and then. This sort of thing went on for months, until it slowly dawned on Convair that the horrifying reason for the delays and evasiveness was that Hughes didn't have the finance to pay for the aircraft! When the first two 880s were finished Hughes wouldn't let Convair test fly them in case they hid them from him; instead he impounded them, towed them out of the Convair hangar and put them in a locked and guarded hangar of his own.

But what of the remaining eighteen TWA 880s: should Convair finish them and then sue Hughes, or should they stop work on them till he found the money? They decided to do the latter, and it was a disastrous mistake, for when Hughes did find the financing, Convair could no longer remember in detail where they had got to with each of the aircraft, or which modifications had been made to them. 'It took a real expert,' said a Convair man, 'to diagnose the exact state of completion of each plane, plus what engineering changes should be made. For instance, he had to work with a stack of blueprints to decide whether the wiring was nearly finished, just begun, or had to be completely changed. Do you change the wiring? Do you rip it out? Additionally, there was some water damage from the months the eighteen planes had been sitting out on the field. Since the production line had been cut back some of the trained people had been let go, others had to be retrained, and all this was terribly expensive. Hughes did agree to pay for the excess completion costs on the four planes he impounded, but we had to pay for most of the others.'

The first 880 was ready at Christmas 1958, and they had the usual 'roll-out ceremony', at which Convair's executive vice-president made a fantastic speech in which he claimed: 'Today, the 880 is no gamble—I mean every facet of it—its structure, engines, reliability and comfort. We have the finest . . . If you look at the flexibility of the plane we will be selling it ten, fifteen and twenty years from now . . .' The 880 was indeed a gamble, and one where Convair kept calling double or quits, over and over, and losing every time.

Then American Airlines decided to pass up the 880 in favour of Boeing's 720. In desperation Convair offered to build a new model for America, the 990 with a new GE fan engine—the first fan engine to go in any airliner. The 990 was to be the fastest airliner in the world, cruising at 640 mph. OK, said American, we'll buy it, but you'll have to guarantee the speed and low noise and payload/range, and you'll have to take our twenty-five tired old DC-7s in part-exchange instead of a down payment, and credit us with twice what they're worth. Done, said Convair, though by now they were becoming panicky.

They didn't even tell the parent General Dynamics board they were committed to a new model. It would be, said Convair, simply a slight modification of the 880. Yet the 990 was almost entirely a new aeroplane. 'When the Boeing 720 took away our sale to United,' said Frank Pace years later, 'we found ourselves in competition with a plane just as good as ours. We had to go ahead with the 990 or get out of the jet business . . . It was absolutely vital for us to follow American's wishes—we had to have another major transcontinental carrier. I thought I was taking less of a gamble than I did entering into the 880 program.' But it was double or nothing again. And even the 990's proud claim to be the only jet with a fan engine didn't last a moment: Boeing put fans in the 720 and called it the 720B.

Meanwhile Convair had committed themselves to selling the 990 to American at a price of $4.7 million each; yet they had no real idea how much the 990 would cost to build, because they had yet to build one. Furthermore, they decided not to build even a prototype 990, but simply to build production aircraft. What if test flying showed changes were needed? Then all the 990s would have to be modified after they had already been built—at great expense. 'If the 990 didn't fly as stated we would be in terrific trouble,' said a Convair man. And if its performance didn't come up to the guarantees they'd given American Airlines, they were finished.

'In piston aircraft it is perfectly simple to predict the performance. You just plot the power available and the power required and where they intersect you get your maximum speed. But with jets, trying to guess the intersection of these curves is very difficult, and missing by 40 or 50 mph is easy and makes a fantastic difference. One way to avoid this is to have a lot more wind-tunnel testing. But when you've already underpriced the plane, you're not willing to spend too much money on wind tunnel testing. So you try to guess, and you make bad guesses.' Convair's guess was about 30 mph out. It only

88. The Convair 990, with fan engines and 'speed fairing' on the wings.

meant six minutes longer on a flight from New York to the West Coast, but it was enough for American Airlines to tear up the contract: they wouldn't be able to claim the 990 as the fastest airliner in the world. Double or quits, and Convair had lost again.

The first of American Airlines' 990s made its first flight four months late, in January 1961. There was a lot wrong with it. In the end Convair had to rework every 990, at their own expense, redesigning the wing leading-edge slats, moving the outer engine pods back, streamlining the engine pylons, altering the engine nozzles, fitting a new fillet where the wing joined the fuselage.

But the most bizarre modification of all was the addition to the back of the wings of four huge cigar-shaped bodies of grotesque ugliness. Convair called these 'speed fairings'; the world of aviation called them 'Kucheman carrots' after their inventor. They were the first application of the new aerodynamic discovery of the 'area rule'—that not only is the actual cross-sectional area of an aircraft important in determining its drag, but near the speed of sound, the rate at which that cross-sectional area changes from the aircraft's nose to its tail is also important. Kucheman's carrots filled an 'area gap' between the 990's wings and tail. The principal is the same one that makes it so hard to calculate the speed achieved by a high-subsonic jet: that as you approach the speed of sound, air-flow around the curves of an aeroplane achieves locally sonic speeds and high drag is generated even though the aeroplane as a whole is still subsonic.

They did get the 990's cruise speed up to within 10 or 15 mph of the target, but by now no one really wanted to know. No new orders came in; airlines that had ordered cancelled, or refused to accept delivery. American Airlines took twenty, and Swissair seven, of which they leased two to SAS, who promptly sub-leased one of those to Thai Airways. Three were taken by Varig and two by Garuda. It is not an illustrious sales record. Some Convair jetliners soldier on today: Swissair flew them until 1974, but others have now worked their way down to charter companies you would hardly have heard of. That five-abreast seating is still the problem: you can just make more money with a Boeing, that's all.

Yet though there undoubtedly was an appalling lack of effective management control within General Dynamics, we must accept the idea that airline ventures are always colossal risks. Douglas, though their jetliner programme was in general highly successful, still had to write off $300 million in development costs up to 1960; and later runaway costs saw them go under, to be taken over by McDonnell. The Tristar almost bankrupted Lockheed. Only Boeing seem to have avoided gigantic financial hazards, though they recently went for a whole year without getting a single new order, and they had to cut their payroll from 84,000 down to 21,000 just to survive. But perhaps the Convair débâcle was a peculiarly bad misjudgment, for even *had* the aeroplane programme been successful, it seems break-even sales figures would have been next-to-impossible to achieve.

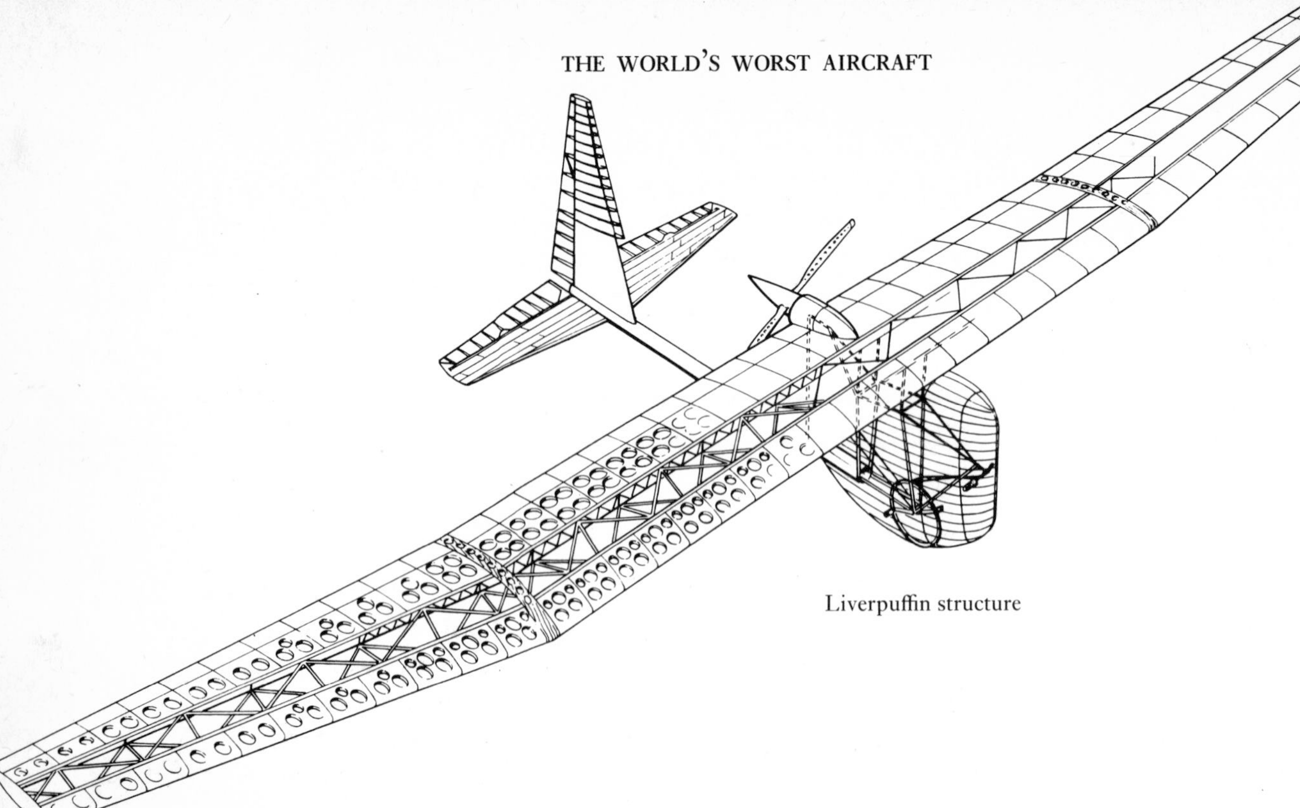

Liverpuffin structure

89/90. Liverpuffin was built by Liverpool University students, starting with the remains of the Hatfield group's crashed Puffin 2.

21

Man-powered Flight

'Everybody knows that Icarus fell in the sea and drowned; what is not so well-known is that his father Daedalus completed the flight successfully.' So wrote Dr D. R. Wilkie in the *New Scientist*. Daedalus was aviation's first mad scientist; father to a fine breed.

The giant prehistoric pterodactyls had a huge wing-span of up to eight metres, even though the metre had yet to be invented, but they were built extremely light and almost certainly weighed no more than 11 kilograms. The Great Bustard, today's heaviest flying bird, may weigh up to 14.5 kilograms.

One man-power is at best one-twentieth that of the Wright Brothers' engine. Say half a horse-power, sustained. Smaller animals have a larger output of energy per body weight than larger animals: mysteriously there is no obvious reason for this. It is the reason why humming-birds can hover, while eagles and albatrosses merely soar, and elephants cannot fly at all, except when being air-freighted from one zoo to another.

Birds only have flapping wings because 'freely rotating structures are a biological impossibility as there is no way of commutating the nerve and blood supply of a rotating part. Since our reciprocating limbs have to be stopped and reversed at the end of each stroke, they cost us a heavy price, for muscles use up energy not only when they do work, but also, though to a lesser extent, when they absorb it.'

Roger Bacon wrote 700 years ago: 'An inftrument may be made to fly if one fit in the midft of the inftrument and do turn an engine, by which the wingf, being artfully compofed, may beat the air.' I don't believe Roger Bacon can ever have tried it; I think he was merely theorising.

Powered flight had to await the invention of the light-but-powerful gasoline engine; and no successful man-carrying ornithopter has flown yet—certainly not a man-*powered* one.

Man-powered flight has lately become somewhat of a craze among the mad scientists of England. A glassfibre plastics millionaire named Henry Kremer, a 'small, alert figure, painfully shy with a single-minded concern for developing new materials', posted a prize in 1949 of £5,000 for the first man-powered take-off and flight around a figure-of-eight circuit. Only mad *British* scientists were eligible, but in 1969 Mr Kremer doubled his money to £10,000 and threw it open to *all* nations. He still has his money—such of it as inflation has left. No one has yet won the prize. The pedals have gone round and round, and much sweat has been perspired, though to little avail. Mr Kremer, 'a keep-fit enthusiast, particularly keen on swimming and skiing', is probably pleased enough at the mere thought of all that exertion. As *Life* magazine commented, 'Though so far no birdman has collected, no birdman has yet spent any tax money, polluted any air or made any discernible noise.'

Would you like to see a man-powered plane fly? It is extremely hard to arrange. Due to the extreme lightness and fragility of their structures they can only be wheeled out in that total calm stillness that follows dawn or precedes sunset; and the mad scientists never decide whether the calm is calm enough until the last moment.

I have seen a man-powered plane fly just once. I was sitting in the 'Chelsea Potter' public house in London's Kings Road, when along happened Charlie Fox, the great automotive and adventure writer. 'Yes,' said Charlie. 'Have a beer. No, we haven't time. We must be off to Benson, where they are going to attempt a world record this very evening with *Jupiter*, a man-powered aircraft built by the lads of the RAF's apprentice school at Halton.'

We drove through the gloaming, up downs and along dales and combes, till we arrived in a welter of tyre smoke at Benson, a green and pleasant RAF base. Here our credentials as journalists were closely examined, for RAF Benson is home to The Queen's Flight.

A modest score of pressmen had been assembled at Benson, and a makeshift bar opened, from which frothing pints of bitter beer were being freely dispensed.

We were 'fell in' in buses, and driven out to the runway, where there awaited the machine we had come to see, a vast floppy tadpole, loosely clad in iridescent Mylar, reclining sailplane-like on a wheel and a wing-tip. Here was the pilot, a small, gingerish Air Force schoolmaster in running kit; here were senior officers, all beaming smiles and medal ribbons; official observers of the Royal Aero Club, clad in sober Savile Row tailoring; and RAF policemen to keep us in order.

Jupiter, the plane, had a vast span, and resembled a glider of awesome fragility, with a pylon sprouting from its back bearing a gigantic propeller. The pilot, whose name was Potter, sat up front, astride the altered workings of a racing bicycle.

'Cycling is the most flexible means of man-power utilisation, hence its application in all man-powered aircraft to date. With cycling the full steady power production of the body can be developed. Under no-load conditions the maximum rate of pedalling is about 180 rpm, whereas the optimum for greatest efficiency is about 60 rpm.' (From *Man Powered Flight* by Keith Sherwin, published by Model & Allied Publications Ltd.)

But this *does* mean you can*not* have conventional airplane controls; instead, modified bicycle handlebars are twisted, tilted and rocked to move elevators, ailerons and rudder, all of which must have taken John Potter some while to get used to, since he was formerly a Hunter and Canberra pilot.

I would also tell you that there is schism among the mad scientists as to whether the pedals should drive both the wheel and propeller, or just the prop; Jupiter's power train connected both. As for pilot Potter's power output—a trained athlete can generate over one hp for under one second; his steady output then falls to around half a hp.

'Steady power output depends on an adequate supply of oxygen that can be absorbed at the lungs and transported by the bloodstream to the active muscles. The lungs and blood stream have a limited capacity so that a limit is set regarding the steady energy conversion,' said Dr Sherwin.

So a man—even a nice chap like John Potter—is a rotten engine. Half a horsepower at seventy-five percent, for an engine weight of 150 lbs at best. What kind of aerodyne can get airborne on that? A very insubstantially light, slow airplane. Typically only 120 lbs structural weight. (Do you count the pilot as 'useful load', or as 'engine weight plus fuel', or what?) It is amazingly slow, so that drag does not engulf all of that meagre 0.5 hp. Special airfoils must be used, fat sections giving good lift at absurdly low airspeeds, while holding profile drag to a minimum. Immensely long wings, like those of the highest-performance sailplanes, so that tip losses are minimised. (One British project had a span of 120 feet—as much as a jet transport—yet weighed only 125 lbs. So vast was the span that the wing, at rest, drooped like that of a dying gull. In flight, it straightened out to give the bird an impressive dihedral.)

Parasitic drag must also be minimised, so these slow dragonfly-airplanes are as streamlines as jets. Even the poor pilot must sweat away inside a curved canopy, lest his nose or ears or flying hair contribute so much as a mite of unnecessary drag. Constructional techniques are more like those of the aeromodelling world, with structures of spruce and balsa and fibreglass composites built-up over basic torsion boxes made from the thinnest aluminium tube. The finished structure is typically covered with a plastic film of unimaginable thinness, giving the whole airplane a vivid sheen like a soap bubble or a fly's wing. *Years* of mad-scientist hours go into building one. (Ten thousand man-hours went into the Weybridge *Dumbo*, the 120 foot span beauty I mentioned above.)

But back to Benson. Pilot Potter straddled his saddle, and was shut away by assistants behind the aircraft's removable nose, a transparent structure big as a man yet so light it would not strain your little finger to suspend it. We took up our positions alongside the runway, and waited. Potter made a test take-off, touching down again immediately. Then he taxied back, a helper lightly supporting each wing tip, turned towards us, and began his run, slow and majestic as a sailing ship. In a trice his spinning wheels had left the concrete, and he sailed past us ten feet up, in an eerie silence and at the speed of a modest sprint. Behind him, grinding in low gear, followed the over-numerous cars of the officials.

On and on he flew, his vast propeller seeming more to beat the air like a bird's wings than to rotate. He dipped and soared, from six to sixteen feet but never out of ground effect. When he finally tip-toed to a stop it was at the very farthest end of the long runway; a straight-line flight of 1,171 yards, and a new world record for man-powered airplanes.

91. *Above*: Jupiter setting a world record of 1,171 yards airborne.

92. *Below*: Southampton University's SUMPAC.

We cheered, and even the orange face of the setting sun seemed to smile. It's not often you see history made, and get to spend a lovely summer evening in the countryside too.

Of course, a straight-line flight, however long, wasn't enough to win pilot Potter any part of Mr Kremer's prize. For *that*, you must fly a figure-eight, making turns, and man-powered airplanes aren't quite up to prolonged turns yet. It's as much as they can do to keep going in a straight line. The trouble is that the aileron deflection required to initiate the turn tends to produce, with those immensely long wings, more yaw than the rudder can correct. (Some man-powered aircraft rotate *the whole wings* for roll control, which makes it worse still.) So long are the wings that once a yaw starts, momentum tends to keep it going, and of course, all this tends to happen just when the pilot is pedalling extra-hard anyway, his concentration goes all to pieces, and he gets things thoroughly crossed-up and stalls one wing in. The problems of turning an aircraft that can't get out of ground effect are *considerable*.

Now that we have cheered Potter's efforts and are back at RAF Benson's bar, it is a good time for me to give you a potted history of man-powered flight. *Ignoring* Daedalus, whose flight was at best not officially recorded, and innumerable other mad but amateur scientists down the ages who flapped or pedalled their way into nothing more conclusive than a lather of sweat and a tangle of broken carpentry; and *neglecting* Leonardo da Vinci, who was only a mere *theorist*, we arrive back to the same Alexander Lippisch we met in chapter 17. The year is 1929.

Lippisch built a bungee-launched glider with a flapping-wing mechanism by which the pilot might seek to prolong the glide. Man-*assisted* flight. In 1960 Lippisch claimed that wing-flapping still held promise of high efficiency, and was still worthy of investigation. One might laugh, were Lippisch not the undoubted inventor of the delta wing.

In 1935 two engineers with Junkers named Helmut Haessler and Franz Villinger built a machine which they called Mufli and which much resembled the most advanced modern concepts. Mufli's pilot lay down to fly, and the thing did need assistance to take off, but it did make a flight of 790 yards.

Two Italians named Enea Bossi and Vittorio Bonomi built a twin-propeller machine that flew 980 yards; but this Pedaliente also used a bungee cord for launch, and that 980 yards was mostly downhill. Both these two projects were inspired by cash prizes offered, and unclaimed. After them the dream of man-powered flight lay quiet until Mr Kremer's offer.

First of the present batch was the Southampton Man-Powered AirCraft, called, with a touch of that extravagant imaginative power for which mad scientists are renowned, SUMPAC. In 1961 it made the first undoubted man-powered take-off. Later it made flights of 650 yards and turns of almost 90 degrees. Finally, 'with a cyclist at the controls, a gust of wind took it to a height of 30 feet and it then stalled and hit the ground'.

Then there came along Puffin 1 and later Puffin 2 from a group of enthusiasts at the de Havilland company at Hatfield. Puffin 1 went *crunch* due to 'a change in the wind direction'; and Puffin 2 'hit a landing light when the pilot veered away from a region of turbulent air encountered at a height of six feet above the runway at dusk'.

Then came a whole spate of projects: by S. W. Vine in South Africa; by Professor Kimura and his students at Nihon University; by Professor Smolkowski and *his* students at the Southern Alberta Institute of Technology; by Josef Malliga in Austria; by a group of mad scientists at the Canadian Aeronautics and Space Institution at Ottawa; by other groups in Japan; by a group from the British Aircraft Corporation's drawing office who were bored with designing the MRCA, the pan-European equivalent of the F-111; and even one American one, from Mr McAvoy and some good old boys at Georgia Tech. Quite a few of these embodiments of a lifetime's dream went satisfyingly *crunch*, but none of them won Mr Kremer's prize.

The extent to which building one of these mechanical dragonflies can become an *obsession* must be seen to be comprehended. I have still an image of one of the leading mad scientists of this mad world of man-powered flight explaining to me that, it was true, his wife had left him; and of course he hadn't worked in a couple of years; he'd gone back to living with his mother—she kept him; but building a man-powered aircraft was well worthwhile because of the *self-confidence* it had given him.

Is there any point to it—beyond shy Mr Kremer's tantalising ten thousand? I'd say, *no*—except that I remember all those sage pundits who said the same of Wilbur and Orville's crazy experimenting. There are other disturbing parallels: the Wrights even had the same troubles in obtaining control in roll without losing it in yaw that plague the pedallers still. Dr Sherwin thinks that man-powered flight could well become a popular sport. The aircraft built so far, he suggests, are too extreme, too absurdly long in span, too light, in their insane pursuit of the Kremer prize. Dr Sherwin foresees more moderate machines of a mere 50-foot span, simply-built maybe along sailplane 'pod and boom' lines, which even an averagely-fit man could keep airborne (still in ground effect, true) for a hundred yards or so. Two machines like this, and you have got a race. Set up a standard class, like sailboats have, and we could see man-powered flight in the Olympics one day—distance, speed, high jump, long jump, what you will.

A little structural beefing-up of such a simple pedal plane, and you might have something fit to venture out of ground effect: a self-launching slope-soarer, for example. Make the wings fold, and you might be able to cycle down to your local Kitty Hawk or Kill Devil Hill, unfurl your pinions, then cycle off the top for an afternoon's sky sailing. Plastics, carbon fibres and so on give promise of great advances to come in very strong, very light structures. What other kind of aviation can you think of, besides hang gliding, that doesn't pollute the air, or make any noise, and which gives you astounding good exercise?

93. Puffin I, built by a group of de Havilland engineers at Hatfield.

Bibliography

1: Fore-runners

CHARLES H. GIBBS-SMITH *Aviation: an historical survey* H.M.S.O., London 1970

CLIVE HART *The Dream of Flight* Faber & Faber, London 1972

MARVIN W. MACFARLAND editor *The Papers of Wilbur and Orville Wright* McGraw-Hill, New York 1953

F. ALEXANDER MAGOUN and ERIC HODGINS *A History of Aircraft* McGraw-Hill, New York 1931

2: Balloonatics

C. V. GLINES *Lighter-Than-Air Flight* Franklin Watts, New York 1965

C. C. TURNER *The Old Flying Days* Sampson Low, London 1928

JOHN WISE *Through the Air* Today Printing, Philadelphia 1873

3: Lilian Bland

KENNETH MUNSON *Pioneer Aircraft 1903–14* Blandford, London 1969

JOHN W. R. TAYLOR *Aircraft 1973* Ian Allan, London 1973

4: Forssman's Folly

G. W. HADDOW and PETER M. GROSZ *The German Giants* Putnam, London 1962

5: Christmas Bullet

ROBERT CASARI Article in *Air Enthusiast* Fine Scroll, London, December 1973

PAUL R. MATT Article in *Historical Aviation Review* vol V Temple City, California 1967

6: Tarrant Tabor

J. M. BRUCE *British Aeroplanes 1914–18* Putnam, London 1957

Flight magazine Articles on May 8 and 15, 1919

7: Multiplanes

GIORGIO APOSTOLO *Caproni's Triple Triplane* Article in *Aeroplane Monthly*, February 1974

GIANNI CAPRONI *Gli Aeroplani Caproni* Edizione del Museo Caproni, Milan 1935
EVAN HADINGHAM *The Fighting Triplanes* Hamish Hamilton, London 1968
NOEL PEMBERTON-BILLING *Air War: How to Wage It* London 1916
C. R. ROSEBERRY *The Challenging Skies* Doubleday, New York 1966

8: Gee Bees
PETER BOWERS *The Gee Bee Racers* Profile Publications No 51, Windsor 1965
THOMAS GRANVILLE as told to BILL SWEET *The Gee Bee Story* Articles in *Sport Aviation* Experimental Aircraft Association, Hales Corners, Wisconsin March and April 1971
REID KINERT *Racing Planes and Air Races* vols II and III 1932–9 Aero Publishers, Fallbrook, California 1967
QUENTIN REYNOLDS *The Amazing Mr Doolittle* Appleton, New York 1953

9: Barling Bomber
GORDON SWANBOROUGH and PETER M. BOWERS *United States Military Aircraft Since 1908* Putnam, London 1963

10: R-101 Airship
HUGO ECKENER *My Zeppelins* Putnam, London 1958 (abridged from *Im Zeppelin Uber Länder und Meere* Christian Wolff, 1949)
DOUGLAS H. ROBINSON *Giants in the Sky* Foulis, Henley 1971
NEVIL SHUTE *Slide Rule* Heinemann, London 1954
JOHN TOLAND *The Great Dirigibles* Dover, New York 1972

11: Maxim Gorki
HEINZ J. NOWARRA and G. R. DUVAL *Russian Civil and Military Aircraft 1884–1969* Fountain, London 1970

12: Dornier DO-X
BILL GUNSTON Article in *Aeroplane Monthly* London IPC Transport Press, September 1973

13: Flying Flea
TERENCE BOUGHTON *The Story of the British Light Aeroplane* John Murray, London 1963
HENRI MIGNET *The Flying Flea* Sampson Low, London 1935
—*Le Sport de l'Air* Imprimerie Taffin-Lefort, France 1937
ARTHUR W. ORD-HUME Article in *Aeroplane Monthly* London IPC Transport Press, May 1973

14: Brewster Buffalo
EINO LUUKKANEN *The Brewster Buffalo* Profile Publications No 217, Windsor 1968
—*Fighter over Finland* Macdonald 1963

15: Fairey Battle
WILLIAM SIMPSON *One of Our Pilots is Safe* Hamish Hamilton, London 1942
PETER TOWNSEND *Duel of Eagles* Weidenfeld & Nicolson, London 1970
PHILIP J. R. MOYES *The Fairey Battle* Profile Publications No 34, Windsor 1965

16: Floundering Elephants
C. DEMAND and H. EMDE *Conquerors of the Air* Viking, New York 1968
WILLIAM GREEN *Warplanes of the Third Reich* Macdonald, London 1972

17: Devil's Sled
MANO ZIEGLER *Rocket Fighter* Macdonald, London 1963

18: Brabazon
BILL GUNSTON *Mighty Brabazon* Article in *Aeroplane Monthly* London IPC Transport Press, June 1974
BILL PEGG *Sent Flying* Macdonald, London 1959

19: Flying Queens
G. R. DUVAL *British Flying Boats and Amphibians 1909–52* Putnam, London 1966
BILL GUNSTON *Mighty Brabazon* Article in *Aeroplane Monthly* London IPC Transport Press, April 1974

20: Convair Jetliners
R. E. G. DAVIES *Airlines of the United States* Putnam, London 1914
RICHARD AUSTEN SMITH *How a Great Corporation Got out of Control* Article in *Fortune*, New York, January and February 1962

21: Man-powered Flight
PETER GARRISON *The Ultimate Engine* Article in *Flying* New York, July 1968
KEITH SHERWIN *Man Powered Flight* Model & Allied, Hemel Hempstead 1971

Index